Rethinking Cognitive Computation

# Rethinking Cognitive Computation

## Turing and the Science of the Mind

A.J. Wells

First published in 2006 by
PALGRAVE MACMILLAN
Houndmills, Basingstoke, Hampshire RG21 6XS and
175 Fifth Avenue, New York, N.Y. 10010
Companies and representatives throughout the world.

PALGRAVE MACMILLAN is the global academic imprint of the Palgrave Macmillan division of St. Martin's Press, LLC and of Palgrave Macmillan Ltd. Macmillan® is a registered trademark in the United States, United Kingdom and other countries. Palgrave is a registered trademark in the European Union and other countries.

ISBN-13: 978–1–4039–1161–2 hardback
ISBN-10: 1–4039–1161–4      hardback
ISBN-13: 978–1–4039–1162–9 paperback
ISBN-10: 1–4039–1162–2      paperback

This book is printed on paper suitable for recycling and made from fully managed and sustained forest sources.

A catalogue record for this book is available from the British Library.

Library of Congress Cataloging-in-Publication Data

Wells, Andrew, 1952–
    Rethinking cognitive computation : Turing and the science of the mind / Andrew Wells.
        p. cm.
    Includes bibliographical references and index.
    ISBN 1–4039–1161–4 (hardcover) – ISBN 1–4039–1162–2 (pbk.)
        1. Computational intelligence. 2. Turing, Alan Mathison, 1912–1954.
    3. Neural networks (Computer science) I. Title.

Q342.W46 2005
006.3—dc22                                                    2005051170

10  9  8  7  6  5  4  3  2  1
15  14  13  12  11  10  09  08  07  06

Printed in China

*For Mia*

'… if, as many of us now suppose,
minds are essentially symbol-manipulating devices,
it ought to be useful to think of minds
on the Turing machine model
since Turing machines are … as general
as any symbol-manipulating device can be.'

Jerry Fodor

'The modern human mind is not a simple medieval clock;
it is not a radio or telephone switchboard;
it is not a system of clever software;
and it is most definitely not
a general-purpose computing device
like a Turing machine.'

Merlin Donald

# Contents

# List of Figures

# List of Tables

# Acknowledgement

This book makes extensive use of Alan Turing's seminal paper 'On Computable Numbers with an Application to the Entscheidungsproblem' which first appeared in *Proceedings of the London Mathematical Society,* Series 2, 42 (1936–37). I am grateful to the London Mathematical Society for permission to quote from the paper.

# Preface

The principal theme of this book is that thinking depends as much on the environment of the thinker as it does on his or her brain. Thinking is, in short, an ecological activity. Most people accept that thinking depends intimately on the brain but its dependence on the environment is rather less clear. Does damage to the environment, for example, have mental effects analogous to those that flow from damage to the brain? It may be better to talk about environmental change rather than environmental damage, but either way I think the answer is clearly 'Yes', and the book is an attempt to spell out, in some detail, a framework for psychological investigation based on this ecological assumption.

Fundamental support for the ecological assumption is drawn from the theory of computation proposed by Alan Turing, the mathematician. Turing invented an abstract machine which has two principal components. One is a model of the individual mind, the other a model of part of the environment. The mind part of the model, when functioning in isolation, is provably less powerful than the combination of the mind part and the environment part. Turing took care to ensure that the parts of the model accurately reflected constraints on real minds in real environments and this justifies confidence in the correctness of the ecological assumption when it is applied in a broader range of contexts than the specific context of paper and pencil calculation with which Turing was primarily concerned.

The mainstream of thinking about computation in psychology has developed along rather different lines, and ecological psychology, as it is currently understood, is generally critical of computational models. There is, therefore, a double challenge for a book like this. It has to persuade the community of computational psychologists to think ecologically and it has to persuade the community of ecological psychologists to think computationally. That is what I have tried to do. The book is addressed primarily to psychologists but I hope it may be of interest to others, like philosophers of mind and of cognitive science, who are also concerned about the nature of the mind.

In the course of writing the book I have become more clearly aware than I was previously of the extent to which my thinking incorporates lessons learned over a period of many years from particular people. They are parts of my social ecology and it seems appropriate, as well as a pleasure, for me to acknowledge them here although they have not contributed directly to the present work. In approximately chronological order they are Ken Breen, Joe Winter, Michael Kyne, John Daniel, Mike Cohen, Robin Iwanek, Keith Sumner, Geoff Sanders, David Cairns, Tom Westerdale, Liz Valentine and Charles Crawford. Thank you all.

I first encountered Turing's work in a course on abstract machine theory taught by Trevor Fenner of the computer science department at Birkbeck College, University of London. I was fascinated by the concept of an abstract machine which seemed both important and oxymoronic, but found the material hard to grasp. I am afraid I was a poor student but something must have stuck.

The idea for a book was initially suggested to me by John Preston of the philosophy department at the University of Reading, who invited me to contribute to a series he was planning to edit. Unfortunately the project never got off the ground but without the stimulus from John the current work might never have been started.

I am grateful to Frances Arnold for inviting me to write for Palgrave in the first place, and even more, for continuing to support the project when it appeared to be neither fish nor fowl, not altogether a textbook but not clearly a research monograph either. Jaime Marshall and Stephen Wenham have seen the project through the later stages of the publication process and I thank them too for their support. Vidhya Jayaprakash headed the team that produced the book and I am grateful to her and her colleagues for their meticulous work. I would also like to thank the anonymous reviewer, commissioned by Palgrave, who read, and commented helpfully, on the first draft of the book.

Bradley Franks read, and made detailed comments on, the first draft. His input has been invaluable, as has been that of John Valentine who read the second draft and made comments on almost every page. Without their scholarly feedback the book would have been much the poorer. Their contributions are second to none and range from the smallest points of detail to the widest philosophical issues. They have both also provided significant moral support and friendship at difficult times.

Other friends and colleagues have helped in numerous ways. Roger Holmes read the opening chapters of the first draft in his eightieth year, while in hospital, recovering from a stroke. Roger is a scholar of the old school and a fine example of that endangered species, the independent thinker. Alex Kirlik drew my attention to the passage from James Gleick's biography of Richard Feynman which is quoted in Chapter 20. Alex is one of that select band whose work is both ecological and computational. Helena Cronin made a helpful suggestion about the title of the book.

I am engaged in an ongoing dialogue with members of CESPA, the Centre for the Ecological Study of Perception and Action, at the University of

Connecticut. They remain sceptical about the application of computational thinking to ecological psychology, but their intellectual generosity and willingness to debate have helped to clarify my thinking. Their warmth and hospitality have also made visiting CESPA a real pleasure. I would like, in particular, to thank Michael Turvey, Claudia Carello, Claire Michaels, Bob Shaw and Bill Mace.

The London School of Economics and Political Science granted me a period of sabbatical leave during which the second draft of the book was written. The opportunity to think and write, uninterrupted by the manifold cares of contemporary academic life in Britain, has been hugely important to me and I am grateful to the School for its support. Sabbatical leave does not, at present, have to be earned by the generation of research income or other dubious 'indicators of excellence'. The School wisely recognizes that leave is a universal need for hard pressed academics. I very much hope that will continue to be the case. The burden of teaching, administration and pastoral care that one sheds while on leave falls on those who remain behind and I am grateful to my colleagues in the Institute of Social Psychology.

Family and friends have been important sources of support. I was a late starter in psychology and my parents, Arthur and Joan Wells, both helped my return to study as a mature student. My sibs, Mary, Tom, Nick, John, Mike and Lucy and their partners and children form a substantial extended family. I think that being one of many is, on balance, a good thing. Thank you all.

I have been blessed with long-standing friendships, some of them going back to my childhood. I can't quantify the effects these old friends have had on the book but I know they are there. Thanks to Nick, Frank, Matthew, Cuthbert, Ian and Anne, Tony and Ulla, Norman and Sim, John and Bev, and Cuz.

My wife, Mia Rodriguez-Salgado, is distinguished in many ways, quite apart from her good sense in marrying me. We share a study, working back to back, and as I write these words, she is at her desk on the other side of the room. Her exemplary scholarship and meticulous attention to detail have inspired me as has her devotion to her subject. I very much doubt that the book would have been written had I not had the good fortune to meet her. It would certainly have been much less fun. When we met I was enthralled by her laughter and firm footsteps. We have since walked, both literally and metaphorically, many miles together. I owe her more than words can easily express and the book is dedicated to her with love and gratitude.

ANDY WELLS

# 1    Introduction

## Computable numbers

In the middle of April 1936, Alan Turing, a young British mathematician, presented his teacher and mentor M.H.A. Newman with the draft typescript of a paper called 'On Computable Numbers with an application to the Entscheidungsproblem'. This is an unlikely sounding title for a paper which has turned out to be of fundamental importance for psychology but such are the twists and turns of intellectual fortune. The paper studied the concept of computability. In the 1930s computation was done almost exclusively by human labour so the concept of computability referred to the activities of people rather than machines. This provides the link to psychology. Some aids, such as adding machines, were available to the human computer but the everyday connotation of the term 'computation' was arithmetic done with paper and pencil. Turing studied computability by analysing the processes that people carry out when calculating in this way. He wanted to know which numbers were computable and was able to prove that the set of computable numbers was a subset of the real numbers. According to his definition a number was computable if it could be written down by a machine. The fact that this no longer sounds surprising is a tribute to the pervasive influence of Turing's ideas. The 'Entscheidungsproblem' is about the provability of statements made in formal languages. The questions it raises are mainly of concern to mathematical logicians and have limited applicability to the principal issues discussed in this book, but it is considered briefly in Chapter 13.

One product of Turing's analysis was a design for what he called a 'universal machine'. The universal machine was unlike anything that most people in the 1930s would have recognized as a machine but it was the abstract ancestor of the stored program digital computer. It had a finite control unit, roughly analogous to the central processor of a modern digital computer and it had a 'tape' which does the same job as the memory of a computer. The finite control unit is often called a mini-mind in this book because it is an abstract model of a human mind engaged in a specific task.

Turing offered persuasive reasons for thinking that the precise concept 'computable by a Turing machine' captured the essence of the informal concept of computability in a satisfactory way. He was also able to show that Turing machine computability was equivalent to the concept of 'effective calculability' introduced by Alonzo Church in a paper published in 1936. Effective calculability and Turing machine computability were very differently defined but identified the same set of numbers. The fact that two different approaches converged on the same set of numbers suggested that something fundamental had been identified.

'On Computable Numbers' (OCN) was published at the end of 1936 in the Proceedings of the London Mathematical Society but Turing's biographer, Andrew Hodges, reports that it attracted little immediate attention.[1] This was partly due, it seems, to the relatively obscure place in which the paper was published, and partly to the fact that mathematical logic was seen as somewhat distant from the mainstream of mathematics. OCN was also not an easy read. As Turing's biographer puts it, 'The paper started attractively, but soon plunged (in typical Turing manner) into a thicket of obscure German Gothic type ... . *Computable Numbers* made no concession to practical design, not even for the limited range of logical problems to which the machines were applied in the paper itself' Hodges (1983, p. 124).

OCN is undoubtedly difficult but it was a brilliant achievement and has continuing relevance for cognitive science, even though it is now almost seventy years since it was published. It is widely recognized as the single most influential formulation of the fundamental theory on which computer science rests. The paper demonstrates both the scope and limits of mechanical computation.

## Turing's later work

Turing continued his work in logic until 1939, including a period in the United States working with Alonzo Church, and then spent most of the Second World War working for the British government at Bletchley Park where he played a pivotal role in breaking the German naval Enigma codes and gained some experience in electronics. Shortly after the war Turing was employed by the National Physical Laboratory (NPL) at Teddington, just outside London, to head a team working on the design of an electronic computer and in 1946 he wrote a document for NPL describing a computer which was to be called the ACE (Automatic Computing Engine). The ACE design was influenced by the ideas of OCN and showed how it was possible to build a practical version of the abstract universal machine. Parts of the Pilot ACE, a machine which was for a time the fastest computer in the world,

---

[1] There has been some uncertainty about the precise publication date of 'On Computable Numbers'. Sometimes its date is given as 1936, sometimes as 1937, and occasionally as 1936–37. Copeland (2004) states unambiguously that the paper was published in two parts of the Proceedings of the London Mathematical Society, both appearing in 1936.

can be seen in the Science Museum in London. A little more is said about the machine at the start of Chapter 2.

In 1950 Turing published a highly influential paper in the philosophical journal *Mind*. The title of the paper was 'Computing Machinery and Intelligence'. Turing argued that there were no reasons in principle why a digital computer should not exhibit intelligent behaviour and many reasons to suppose that within 50 years computers would customarily be described as capable of thinking. He proposed a behavioural criterion for intelligence which he called 'the imitation game'. The game was to be played by an interrogator and two hidden respondents one of which was to be a human, the other a computer. Turing argued that a machine which could fool the interrogator into thinking it was the human respondent during a short conversation should be considered intelligent.

## Computation in cognitive science

Turing died in 1954 before the idea that the mind could be studied and explained in computational terms had become part of the mainstream in psychology and philosophy of mind and long before the term 'cognitive science' had been coined. In the 50 years since his untimely death the technology of computers has been developed in spectacularly successful ways but computational theory in cognitive science has had rather more mixed fortunes. Cognitive science is divided in two important ways about the idea that the mind is a computer. To describe the fundamental divide simply and starkly, some theorists are of the view that the mind *must* be a computer, whereas others are of the view that it *cannot* be a computer. Among the proponents of computational theory, broadly construed, there is also a divide. Some are committed to the idea that the mind is a *physical symbol system* while others propose that it is a *connectionist* or *neural network*. Disagreements between proponents of these two views can be as sharp as those between the two fundamentally opposed positions although there are also those who propose hybrid systems with both symbolic and connectionist components. There is, therefore, within mainstream cognitive science, fundamental disagreement about whether the mind is a computational system at all and, if it is, about what kind of computational theory best describes and explains the mind and thought processes. The contrast between the onward drive of progress in computing technology and the sometimes bitter disputes about computation in cognitive science is striking. This book is about computation in cognitive science and psychology. It critically evaluates both the physical symbol system and connectionist approaches and proposes a new kind of computational framework called ecological functionalism which has its roots in the ideas of OCN.

## The reception and understanding of Turing's work

A detailed account of the reception of Turing's ideas in the disciplines that now constitute cognitive science has yet to be written but it is evident even from a partial survey of the literature that opinion is divided about the applicability of his work to the study of the mind in much the same way that opinion is divided about the merits of computational thinking more generally as a means of explaining mental functioning. Jerry Fodor, for example, has said 'I am an enormous admirer of Turing – I think he had the only serious idea, since Descartes anyway, in the history of the study of the mind' (Fodor 1995, p. 87) whereas Aaron Sloman has said 'Turing machines ... are irrelevant to the task of explaining, modeling, or replicating human or animal intelligence' (Sloman 2002, p. 102).

One regrettable feature of much of the writing about Turing in the cognitive science literature, both pro- and anti-, is that it is poorly informed about what Turing achieved and how his ideas might be relevant to current thinking about how the mind works. As an illustration of the problem consider the following descriptions of the Turing machine. Some are incomplete, some are simply wrong, others are misleading:

a. A Turing machine has:
   1. an unlimited number of *storage bins*;
   2. a finite number of *execution units*; and
   3. one *indicator unit.*
   
   The indicator unit always indicates one execution unit (the 'active' unit), and two storage bins (the 'in' and 'out' bins, respectively). Each storage bin can contain one formal token (any token, but only one at a time). Each execution unit has its own particular rule, which it obeys whenever it is the active unit (Haugeland 1981, p. 11).
   
   Comment: *The terminology is odd and unnecessary. A 'storage bin' corresponds to a square on the tape of a Turing machine. An 'execution unit' corresponds to a functional state of a Turing machine. There is no 'indicator unit' in Turing's definition. To be fair to Haugeland it should be noted that, in a footnote, he calls his description 'a slight generalization of Turing's original definition'.*

b. The basic idea [of the Turing machine] had five components:
   1. a *serial* process (events happening one at a time), in
   2. a severely restricted *workspace*, to which
   3. both *data* and *instructions* are brought
   4. from an inert but super-reliable *memory*
   5. there to be operated on by a finite set of *primitive operations*
   
   In Turing's original formulation, the workspace was imagined to be a scanner that looked at just one square of a paper tape at a time, to see if

a zero or one were written on it. Depending on what it 'saw' it either erased the zero or one and printed the other symbol, or left the square unchanged. It then moved the tape left or right one square and looked again, in each case being governed by a finite set of hard-wired instructions that formed its *machine table*. The tape was the memory (Dennett 1991, p. 212).

Comment: *Points (1) to (5) describe a simple stored program computer not a Turing machine. The reference to Turing's original formulation is incorrect. The machines in Turing's 1936 paper (the 'original formulation') never erase a zero or one once it has been printed.*

c. A Turing machine is very simple: it consists only of a read/write head and a memory tape – a paper tape of unlimited length (Copeland 1994, p. 126).

Comment: *The definition is incomplete. It does not mention the finite control automaton.*

d. Any specific Turing machine is essentially a very simple sort of computer program – one which can transform certain inputs into some desired output. (In spite of the label, a Turing machine is not so much a physical device as it is a way of thinking about functional relationships based on analogy with an [imagined] physical device.) (Guttenplan 1994, p. 101).

Comment: *The definition is misleading. It implies that a Turing machine needs some hardware to run on.*

e. A Turing machine is composed of a tape, a read-write head, and a finite-state machine. The *tape* is essentially its input-output device, corresponding to the keyboard/monitor of your PC or Mac. The *read-write head* can read a symbol from the tape and can write one on it. The head can also move itself – change its position on the tape by one square left or right. The read-write head is analogous to a combination keystroke-reader/cursor-control/print-to-the-monitor routine. The *finite-state machine* acts as the memory/central processor. It's called a finite-state machine because it can keep track of which of finitely many states it is currently in; it has some finite memory (Franklin 1995, p. 77).

Comment: *The tape of a Turing machine corresponds to the memory of a computer not to its input/output equipment for which there is no direct analogue in the Turing machine. The finite state machine corresponds roughly to the central processor of a computer, not to the processor plus memory.*

f. The [Turing] machine consists of a tape divided into squares, a read-write head that can print or read a symbol on a square and move the tape in either direction, a pointer that can point to a fixed number of tickmarks on the machine, and a set of mechanical reflexes. Each reflex is triggered by the symbol being read and the current position of the pointer, and it prints a symbol on the tape, moves the tape, and/or shifts the pointer. The machine is allowed as much tape as it needs (Pinker 1997, p. 67).

Comment: *There is neither a pointer nor any 'tickmarks' in Turing's definition.*

g. The [Turing] machine itself is separated into two different components: an infinitely long ticker tape which serves as a memory and a machine head which manipulates the contents of memory. The tape is divided into a series of cells, any one of which can only contain a single symbol. The head includes mechanisms for moving left or right along the tape (one cell at a time), for reading the symbol in the current cell, and for writing a symbol into the current cell. The head also includes a register to indicate its current physical configuration or machine state. Finally, the head includes a set of basic instructions, the machine table, which precisely defines the operations that the head will carry out (Dawson 1998, p. 15).

Comment: *There is no register to indicate the machine state in the head of Turing's machines. The machine table is not a component of the head in Turing's definition. It is a way of describing a Turing machine, not one of its parts.*

h. A Turing machine possesses a segmented tape with segments corresponding to a cognitive device's internal states or representations. The machine is designed to read from and write to segments of the tape according to rules that themselves are sensitive to how the tape may be antecedently marked (Maloney 1999, p. 333).

Comment: *The 'segments' of a Turing machine's tape do not correspond to the internal states of a cognitive device. They correspond to the squares on a piece of arithmetic paper.*

One general comment is also important. None of the eight definitions cited says explicitly that the Turing machine, as Turing defined it, was an abstract model of a person doing a paper and pencil calculation. Thus the crucial link between Turing's work and psychology is lost. The broader context of definition (b) makes reference to this point but does not indicate how the components of the model relate to the human example from which it was derived. There is an almost complete absence, in the cited definitions, of the human example from which the Turing machine was derived although it is entirely clear in Turing's own work and essential for understanding the applicability of his theory to the study of the mind.

The characterizations of the Turing machine cited above are, unfortunately, typical of the way that much of the literature in cognitive science has treated Turing's work. Turing the man is respectfully acknowledged as an important figure in the history of the discipline but there is a tendency to suppose, in accordance with Sloman's view cited earlier, that the details of Turing's work are of little or no relevance for the furtherance of computational thinking about the mind and can, therefore, be described sketchily or not at all. Steven Pinker, to take an influential example, has said that 'A lurching Turing machine is a poor advertisement for the theory that the mind is a computer' (Pinker 1997, p. 69).

## Summary and goals of the book

Turing's theory, properly understood, calls for a fundamental change in the use of computational ideas in cognitive science and psychology more generally. It offers a fresh perspective on the debate between proponents of the symbol systems and connectionist frameworks and it provides part of the foundation for a new computational framework which I have called ecological functionalism. Turing's work highlights the difficulties faced by both symbol systems and connectionism and points in the direction of their solutions. This book, therefore, has three principal purposes: first, to provide an accurate and detailed exposition of Turing's theory; second, to use Turing's theory as the foundation for a critical evaluation of the symbol systems and connectionist frameworks; and last but by no means least, to set out the basic ideas of ecological functionalism.

Chapter 2 is a scene-setting exercise. It provides a psychological context for the computational study of the mind. The setting of computational ideas in the broader context of a small part of the history of psychology since the middle of the nineteenth century will, I hope, make it easier for the reader to understand their impact and significance. Chapters 3 and 4 introduce functional states and the ways in which they can be connected to form what I call 'mini-minds'. The concept of a functional state is the principal abstraction that needs to be grasped in order to understand Turing's work. Recollection of my own struggles when I first encountered Turing machines and the reactions of students who have endured my attempts to teach them Turing machine theory have persuaded me that time spent working on the elementary ideas is time well spent. Chapter 5 shows how mini-minds are connected to environments. This chapter completes the introductory material.

The next eight chapters discuss the material of OCN. The paper itself is only 36 pages long but, like a jack-in-a-box or Dr Who's Tardis, there is a great deal compressed into a small space and a full exposition takes considerably more space than the original statement. Readers may be reassured to learn that six of the eight chapters, the more technical ones, are quite short. Chapter 6 deals with Turing's analysis of the informal concept of computability. It documents the way in which Turing set about dissecting the processes that are carried out when a number is computed by a human working with paper and pencil. The chapter shows how the components of the Turing machine were derived from and constrained by the human examples about which Turing was thinking.

A case can be made for the claim that it is more important for cognitive scientists to study Turing's ideas via the original text than it is for mathematicians and computer scientists. Both of the latter are primarily interested in the technical results which are nowadays expressed in simpler ways. The particular value of the original text for cognitive science lies in the way that it explains the close relationship between the Turing machine and the human activity which it models.

The Turing machine is an abstract description of the processes involved in calculation with paper and pencil. Turing began by considering what people do when they calculate with paper and pencil and ended with the Turing machine. The Turing machine is not an arbitrary mechanism devised for calculation. It has the characteristics it has because of the way it is related to the system of which it is a model. The clear and direct way in which the elements of the Turing machine are derived from the human example is generally missing from the introductory treatments of Turing machines in the sources that I have read. Steven Pinker is a good example of a pro-computational theorist who has missed this point. In response to a rhetorical question about whether the brain is a Turing machine he says

> Certainly not. There are no Turing machines in use anywhere, let alone in our heads. They are useless in practice: too clumsy, too hard to program, too big, and too slow. But it does not matter: Turing merely wanted to prove that *some* arrangement of gadgets could function as an intelligent symbol-processor. (Pinker 1997, p. 68)

In fact it matters a great deal. Turing was demonstrably concerned to show that his 'gadgets' were subject to the constraints under which humans do their calculations. That was the whole point of the Turing machine.

Chapter 7 describes two example machines that Turing used to illustrate the basic ideas of his theory. The simpler of the two machines is functionally equivalent to one of the examples in Chapter 5. Chapter 8 discusses the notation that Turing developed to describe complex machines. Turing's strategy was to define simple machine processes and to combine them to produce complex machines whenever it was possible to do so. A considerable part of the task of understanding the universal machine can, therefore, be achieved by a study of the functioning of the elementary processes on which its construction is based. Chapter 9 discusses Turing's format for standard descriptions. Standard descriptions are the software of the universal machine. Chapter 10 discusses the component processes of the universal machine and Chapter 11 discusses the cycle of processes that the universal machine uses to simulate the functioning of another Turing machine.

Chapter 12 describes the structures and processing of the universal machine in detail. The universal machine is the culmination of Turing's achievements in the 1936 paper. It is the theoretical ancestor of the stored program, digital computer although it carries out its computations in a way that is not feasible for a practical computer. It provides, however, a fascinating historical picture and a feel for the intricacy of a large Turing machine. The example machines that one finds in most of the literature tend to be rather small and structurally relatively simple (although their behaviour can be extremely difficult to understand). Turing's universal machine, by contrast, is large and structurally complex, but its processing, at least in outline, is straightforward. The design of the machine is influenced by Turing's notation in interesting ways.

Chapter 13 discusses and explains Turing's proofs of the limitations on mechanical computation. There are three proofs: the first is the proof of the unsolvability of the halting problem; the second is the proof of the unsolvability of the printing problem; the third proof, which uses the two other results, shows that Hilbert's Entscheidungsproblem is unsolvable. Turing's limitative proofs, along with the incompleteness theorems of Kurt Gödel, have been used to argue that the mind cannot be a computer. An argument to this effect by Roger Penrose is examined at the end of Chapter 13.

Chapter 14 discusses the relationship between abstract machines like the universal Turing machine and real, practical, high speed, electronic computers. The discussion is focused on what has become known as Von Neumann architecture but also discusses briefly an additional model from OCN. Understanding the principles of von Neumann architecture enables the reader to see the similarities and differences between modern computers and Turing machines. These differences are important for understanding and evaluating the computational theory of mind. Chapter 15 discusses the important concept of virtual architecture which is a way of thinking about the relationship between the software and hardware of computers.

Chapter 16 uses the material of the earlier chapters to examine the theoretical commitments of the computational theory of mind and Chapter 17 critically evaluates the theory. It is argued on both theoretical and empirical grounds that the commitments discussed in Chapter 16 are implausible. The mechanisms described by the computational theory of mind are too powerful because they attempt to model the entire cognitive world in the head of the agent.

Chapter 18 describes and evaluates the commitments of connectionist theorising. Connectionism suggests that the brain is a neural network that computes by non-symbolic means, principally by the summation of multiple inputs and the adjustment of connection strengths. The mechanisms described in standard connectionist models are insufficiently powerful because they do not take into account reliable structure in the environment.

Chapter 19 introduces ecological functionalism, a new approach to cognitive computation which draws its inspiration from Turing's analysis in OCN. The new approach is ecological because it argues that structure in the environment and in the organism are equally important for cognition and treats cognitive computation in terms of interactions between these two sources of structure. A new approach is needed because the shortcomings of both the symbol systems and connectionist frameworks are fundamental. Each concentrates on one source of structure and neglects the other. Once one adopts the ecological perspective it becomes apparent that Turing's theory, which was designed for the study of serial processes of rule-governed calculation, needs to be extended. A formal system called the $\pi$-calculus is introduced. The $\pi$-calculus was designed to study systems of processes which run concurrently and communicate with each other. It is suggested that the $\pi$-calculus can provide a formal vehicle for developing ecological functionalism.

Chapter 20 takes a more psychological view of ecological functionalism and discusses the ways in which it might satisfy a list of constraints on theories of the mind, developed and discussed by Allen Newell, one of the pioneers of artificial intelligence and computational psychology.

Some of the technical chapters contain exercises which are intended to help the reader to acquire some familiarity with the techniques used. The exercises are generally straightforward and answers are not provided except for the exercises in Chapter 5 for which answers are given in Appendix 5.1.

# 2  Making the Modern Mind

## Introduction

The Science Museum in London has a large gallery on the ground floor devoted to a permanent exhibition called 'Making the Modern World'. The exhibition spans two hundred and fifty years from 1750 to 2000 and includes a range of iconic exhibits such as Stephenson's railway locomotive, the Rocket; the V2, a rocket of a different kind; a Model T Ford; Crick and Watson's model of the helical structure of DNA and the command module from the Apollo 10 space flight. Many of the exhibits are visually striking and beautifully engineered. One can understand a good deal about them from their physical appearance. They have a presence and allure which helps to explain the large number of 'Do not Touch' notices.

The gallery is arranged chronologically. As one moves past the heroic engineering of the steam age and approaches 1950, a glass case becomes visible standing next to the towering V2 rocket and literally under the wing of a Lockheed Electra airliner. Inside the case is a polished wooden desk with a hooded oscilloscope screen, rows of switches and buttons, and a telephone dial. Alongside the desk is a large grey metal frame holding racks of thermionic valves and other components. At the back of the frame a maze of connections between the racks can be seen. These exhibits are the operator's desk and the control unit of a computer called the Pilot ACE which was one of the first electronic computers built in Britain. It was, for a time, the fastest computer in the world. The description on the glass case includes the following passage:

> The design for ACE embodied the original ideas of the mathematician Alan Turing. This reflected his pre-war theoretical work on computation and his conceptual discovery of the Universal Turing Machine – a computer that is not structured to carry out particular tasks, but can perform any task specified by programming instructions.

A few yards further down the gallery, when one gets to 1975, there is another glass case containing another computer, the Cray-1A supercomputer. The Cray is sleeker and more futuristic in its appearance than the Pilot ACE but there is a striking contrast between both computers and many of the other exhibits in the gallery. The computers are drab and really not very interesting to look at. Their appearance gives no clue to their remarkable capabilities. Whereas one might be tempted to climb into the Model T Ford and seize the steering wheel or clamber into the Apollo 10 command module and imagine oneself orbiting the moon and peering out at the lunar surface, there is little incentive to sit at the operator's desk of the ACE. Neither the ACE nor the Cray supercomputer grips the imagination immediately in the way many of the other machines in the exhibition do. And yet these computers are 'universal' machines. They embody ideas about machinery that are at least as far reaching as those that led to any of the other exhibits in the gallery. The contrast between the mundane appearances of the ACE and the Cray and their extraordinary capabilities is a forceful illustration of the primacy of theory for our understanding and appreciation of computers. It is not what they look like or what they are made of which is most important but what they do and how they do it.

The gallery in the Science Museum helps the visitor to understand where the computer fits in the era of technology that has characterized the modern world. The purpose of this chapter is to review a small number of ideas and issues, conceptual equivalents of the exhibits in the gallery, to help the reader understand roughly where computational ideas are located in the history of psychological study of the mind and how they bear on issues that have historically been of importance to the discipline.

The fundamental issue addressed by computational theorizing is the nature of the relationship between the mind and the brain. Questions about this relationship are, of course, not new. Plato, Aristotle and other theorists of classical antiquity had views about the matter and René Descartes is famous for his dualistic philosophy which was based on the postulation of distinct physical and mental substances. Specifically psychological work on the mind–brain relationship is more recent. When the foundations of modern psychology were laid in the second half of the nineteenth century with the development of systematic experimental methods, a good deal was already understood about the anatomy and physiology of the brain although the knowledge available was elementary by contemporary standards. There was, however, almost nothing known in detail about the relationship between the brain and mental functions.

## William James: mind, brain and consciousness

William James, whose classic work *The Principles of Psychology* was published in 1890, took as a fundamental postulate the idea that mind and brain were closely linked. He said 'the brain is the one immediate bodily condition of the mental operations' (James 1890, vol. 1, p. 4) and characterized the remainder of the book as 'more or less of a proof that the postulate was correct' (James op. cit., p. 4). Despite this clear linkage of mind and brain there are places in the book where the difficulties of characterizing the linkage are only too evident. James was too clear sighted to miss problems he could not resolve but unwilling to ignore them. There is a whole section in chapter VI of volume 1 entitled 'Difficulty of stating the connection between mind and brain', and there is a passage in a later chapter on the relations between the mind and other objects which ruefully accepts that 'The relations of a mind to its own brain are of a unique and utterly mysterious sort' (vol. 1, chapter 8, p. 216). A reader of the *Principles of Psychology* quickly becomes aware of the confident characterization of mental processes on the one hand and the much more speculative and guarded characterization of neural processes on the other.

Computational ideas, as they have traditionally been deployed in psychology, offer a thought-provoking hypothesis about the possible relationship between mind and brain. The idea is that the relationship between mind and brain is like that between the software and the hardware of a computer. Putting it simply, the mind is the brain's program. If this is so, two important conclusions follow. First, a purely physical understanding of the mind–brain relationship can be achieved because both software and hardware in a computer are physical entities. This solves a longstanding problem about how thoughts could be causally efficacious. Second, the independence of psychology from neuroscience is established because there is a sense in which programs are independent of the computer hardware on which they run. This is an idea around which much debate has focused. To understand the issues and evaluate the idea, the way that a programmable computer works has to be understood. This is explained in later chapters of the book.

Although the relationship between mind and brain was fundamental for William James, he and others saw the principal task of psychology as the analysis of conscious mental states. The principal method used for this task was introspective self-awareness but, despite intense work on the problems, techniques for introspection could not be standardized across different laboratories and the psychology of conscious mental states became mired in disputes about both phenomena and methodology.

## J.B. Watson: behaviourism

In 1913, John B. Watson published a short paper entitled *Psychology as the behaviorist views it* in the prestigious journal *Psychological Review*. Watson proposed that psychologists should abandon the study of consciousness and focus their attention on behaviour. He suggested that a psychology could be developed which would 'never use the terms consciousness, mental states, mind, content, introspectively verifiable, imagery, and the like'

(Watson 1913, p. 166). The goal of his psychology was the prediction and control of behaviour and Watson's claim that terms like mind and consciousness would never be required was based on the idea that 'In a system of psychology completely worked out, given the response the stimuli can be predicted; given the stimuli the response can be predicted' (Watson 1913, p. 167). Watson, in effect, substituted the study of the environment for the study of the mind. The various forms of behaviourism never completely eradicated psychological interest in the study of consciousness but behaviourism, particularly in the form developed by B.F. Skinner, was a prominent, perhaps dominant, approach in both American and British psychology for half a century. As late as 1974, Skinner was still propounding anti-mentalist doctrines.

> The present argument is this: mental life and the world in which it is lived are inventions. They have been invented on the analogy of external behavior occurring under external contingencies. Thinking is behaving. The mistake is in allocating the behavior to the mind. (Skinner 1974, p. 104)

The behaviourist critique of introspectionist psychology included the charge that it was inescapably subjective and consequently unscientific. Computational theorizing about the mind avoids the charge of inescapable subjectivism by framing hypotheses about mental processes in ways that can be shared and tested. The symbol processing and connectionist approaches do this in different ways which are based, to some extent, on different treatments of the environment. One of the positive effects of behaviorism was to draw to the attention of psychologists the importance of understanding both the inner and outer environments and there is a continuing debate in cognitive science about the nature of the links between organisms and their environments and the relative importance of inner and outer structure in the determination of behaviour. Inner and outer structure are of equal importance in determining the behaviour of Turing machines. There is a meshing of inner and outer structure in the configurations of Turing machines and the co-determination of behaviour by these two sources is at the root of ecological functionalism which is proposed in this book as an alternative to both the symbol systems and connectionist models of cognitive computation.

## F.C. Bartlett: the effort after meaning

In 1913, the year in which Watson's manifesto for behaviourism was published, a program of research leading to a very different kind of psychology was begun by F.C. Bartlett who later became the first professor of experimental psychology at the University of Cambridge. Bartlett studied memory from an experimental standpoint which tried to take account of the individual and social circumstances which influence what people remember. His book *Remembering* was published in 1932. Bartlett's thinking can be illustrated by comparing his view of psychological experimentation with that of a behaviorist such as Skinner. The behaviourists developed experiments using apparatus which was carefully designed to limit the possible associations that could be made between stimuli and responses. The Skinner box is representative of the genre. It is an apparatus which offers discrete response options such as levers to press or buttons to push. The actions of an experimental subject, most frequently a rat or a pigeon in Skinner's own work, can be linked to any schedule of reinforcement desired by the experimenter. Behaviourist methods are simple and elegant and much has been learned from them but they tend to conceal the contribution of the experimental subject and thus perpetuate the illusion that the principal or only contribution of internal states to the determination of behaviour is the learning of associations. Computational theories, by contrast, highlight the internal structures that contribute to the determination of behaviour and Bartlett's work provided important insights into the nature of those contributions.

Bartlett believed that attempting to simplify stimuli and responses in order to isolate invariant relationships between them was a procedure fraught with psychological difficulty. The difficulty was that 'Uniformity and simplicity of structure of stimuli are no guarantee whatever of uniformity and simplicity of structure in organic response, particularly at the human level … Uniformity of the external stimulating conditions is perfectly consistent with variability of determining conditions, and stability of determinants may be found together with variability of stimuli' (Bartlett 1932, p. 4). The fundamental reason for this, Bartlett said, was that people bring preformed biases, expectations and temperamental differences into experimental situations and try to find meaning in them. They differ, in other words in how they perceive what we now call the demand characteristics of an experimental situation. Bartlett called this the 'task factor'.

> Because this task factor is always present, it is fitting to speak of every human cognitive reaction – perceiving, imaging, remembering, thinking and reasoning – as an *effort after meaning*. Certain of the tendencies which the subject brings with him into the situation with which he is called upon to deal are utilised so as to make his reaction the 'easiest', or the least disagreeable, or the quickest and least obstructed that is at the time possible. When we try to discover how this is done we find that it is always by an effort to connect what is given with something else. Thus, the immediately present 'stands for' something not immediately present, and 'meaning' in a psychological sense, has its origin. (Bartlett 1932, pp. 44–5)

Accounting for the meaningfulness of experience is one of the major challenges computational psychology has to face. It ranks with, and is related to, the challenge of understanding consciousness. The difficulty is simply put. Computational psychology seeks explanations of mental processes in mechanistic terms but machines, as they are commonly understood, are neither conscious nor find meaning in their surroundings.

Bartlett is also important for his proposal that the experiences of the organism are structured in active patterns which he called 'schemata'. This proposal formed the basis for the idea of a 'frame' which has had considerable currency in artificial intelligence research.

## Kenneth Craik: mental models

In 1943, two publications appeared which have influenced computational thinking in psychology. One made specific reference to Turing's work on computable numbers; the other did not. There is a certain irony in the fact that the work which did not cite Turing was done at Cambridge where Turing was a Fellow of King's College, while that which did was done in the United States. In a short book called *The Nature of Explanation* Kenneth Craik, who had studied with Bartlett, proposed the hypothesis that one of the capacities of the brain is 'that it imitates or models external processes' (Craik 1943, p. 53). Craik suggested that the construction of a mental model involved three processes:

> the translation of external events into some kind of neural patterns by stimulation of the sense-organs, the interaction and stimulation of other neural patterns as in 'association', and the excitation by these of effectors or motor organs. (Craik 1943, p. 53)

Craik's book was one of the first, perhaps the first, to propose that external events are translated into neural patterns which represent them and that reasoning involves the manipulation of these neural representations. This idea is fundamental to the computational theory of mind. It has been attributed to Turing, for example by Fodor (1994, 2000) and by Pinker (1994) but in fact it was not Turing's idea. Craik's proposal emphasizes the role of the neural machinery in reasoning whereas Turing emphasizes the interaction between neural machinery and external symbols. There is a huge difference between these proposals. Craik did not argue that the neural patterns should be thought of as words or numbers, but he did suggest that the scope and limits of the modelling process could, to some extent, be explored by studying the scope and limits of symbolic processes that do use words and numbers. It is a short step from this relatively cautious position to the proposal that the neural patterns are internal symbols like words or numbers and later theorists readily took the step, encouraged by the existence of computers that process internal symbolic representations.

## McCulloch and Pitts: artificial neural networks

The other publication of 1943 which has had a significant impact on computational psychology was by Warren McCulloch and Walter Pitts. McCulloch was a neurophysiologist and Pitts a mathematician. Their paper, *A Logical Calculus of the Ideas Immanent in Nervous Activity*, set out a mathematical theory based on the operations of idealized neurons. The theory equated nervous system activity with logic processing. It was based on the idea that the output of a neuron, the presence or absence of an action potential, was its primary information processing activity. The output expressed a simple logical function of the neuron's inputs. If, for example, a neuron with two inputs A and B fired only when both inputs were present its activity was equivalent to the logical function A *and* B, whereas if a neuron with one input C fired only when the input was absent, its activity was equivalent to the logical function *not* C. More complex logical functions would be computed by neurons which took the output of simple functions as their inputs. The notation that McCulloch and Pitts used is difficult for non-logicians to understand. Minsky (1967) provides a more accessible introduction to neural networks of this kind. The idea that the brain can be thought of as a complex logical network provides an immediate link between nervous system activity and thinking. McCulloch and Pitts can, therefore, be counted among the ancestors of the connectionist approach to cognitive computation although their networks were not capable of learning. There is a direct link between the work of McCulloch and Pitts and that of Turing. Towards the end of their paper McCulloch and Pitts asserted that their networks, if equipped with tape and scanners, were formally equivalent to Turing machines and they argued that this equivalence provided a psychological justification for Turing's definition of computability. This seems to me a rather odd thing to say since, as we shall see, Turing's definition was clearly psychologically grounded from the outset and McCulloch and Pitts used model neurons which are physically unrealistic in some respects. It would, I think, be more correct to argue the converse, namely that the formal equivalence of McCulloch–Pitts networks and Turing machines provides a psychological justification for the networks.

## John von Neumann: computer architecture

In 1945 John von Neumann, a brilliant mathematician and computer pioneer, wrote a document with the prosaic title *First Draft of a Report on the EDVAC*. The EDVAC was one of the first digital computers and embodied the design principles that have since become known as 'Von Neumann computer architecture'. Among the important concepts set out in the *First Draft* was the idea that the program which directs a computer's operations could be stored in the same memory as the numerical data and accessed at electronic speeds. This is the 'stored program' principle. There was also a strong case made for serial rather than parallel operation. Von Neumann used the notation that McCulloch and Pitts had used in their neural networks paper and this has led some commentators to suggest that von Neumann architecture was derived from thinking about how the brain worked. In fact there is rather little to justify this suggestion although in later years von Neumann began to develop a single theory of what he called 'complex automata' which he intended to apply to both brains and computers. It is important for psychologists to know about von Neumann architecture because the computational theory of mind is related to it. Chapter 14 discusses it, but I shall argue that von Neumann architecture does not provide the basis for a satisfactory computational theory of mind and that we need to return to ideas based on Turing's 1936 paper which provide the different foundation on which ecological functionalism is based.

## Donald Hebb: the neuropsychology of learning

In 1949 Donald Hebb published *The Organization of Behavior: A Neuropsychological Theory*. Hebb was opposed to the more radical forms of behaviourism which argued that behaviour could be understood solely in terms of stimuli and responses. He proposed that the best way to understand human and animal thought and behaviour was by studying the brain which produced them. He suggested that connections between neurons become strengthened when their firing is positively correlated. This principle underlies the way in which modern connectionist networks learn associations between inputs and outputs. Hebb also proposed that memories are formed by the creation of cell assemblies which are cyclical and self-stimulating to a degree, and he suggested that thinking consists in the sequential activation of cell assemblies. Hebb is widely credited as the most important precursor of the connectionist approach to cognitive computation.

## Miller, Galanter and Pribram: plans

In 1960 George Miller, Eugene Galanter and Karl Pribram published *Plans and the Structure of Behavior*. The title of the book was well chosen. The reference to the structuring of behaviour reflects the dominance of behaviourist thinking in American psychology at the time the book was written.

> The ancient subject matter of psychology – the mind and its various manifestations – is distressingly invisible, and a science with invisible content is likely to become an invisible science. We are therefore led to

underline the fundamental importance of behavior and, in particular, to try to discover recurrent patterns of stimulation and response. (Miller, Galanter and Pribram 1960, p. 6)

Despite the emphasis on behaviour, the reference to plans in the title indicates that the authors were unhappy with the idea that organisms were simply passive recipients of whatever the environment might throw at them. Organisms, they said, build up internal representations of their environments and the fundamental problem for psychologists is to describe how actions are controlled by these internal representations. The problem is complicated by the fact that behaviour is hierarchically organized. Linguistic behaviour, for example, is clearly hierarchical with phonemes being organized into words, words into sentences and sentences into larger structures. Other kinds of behaviour are also clearly hierarchical. A visit to a supermarket can be described and analysed at various levels of complexity. Miller, Galanter and Pribram argued that plans provided the link between internal representations and behaviour. 'A Plan is any hierarchical process in the organism that can control the order in which a sequence of operations is to be performed' (op. cit., p. 16). The link to computers was explicit. 'A Plan is, for an organism, essentially the same as a program for a computer, especially if the program has the sort of hierarchical character described above' (op. cit., p. 16). In the final chapter of the book, the authors discussed the possibility of identifying parts of the brain that functioned like the memory and processor of a computer but stopped short of arguing that the brain actually was a biological computer.

## Newell and Simon: physical symbol systems

That step was taken explicitly by Allen Newell and Herbert Simon in a paper published in 1976 called *Computer Science as Empirical Inquiry: Symbols and Search*. Newell and Simon defined what they called a physical symbol system and advanced a hypothesis about it:

> *The Physical Symbol System Hypothesis.* A physical symbol system has the necessary and sufficient means for general intelligent action. (Newell and Simon 1976, p. 41)

Newell and Simon deliberately offered a strong and provocative hypothesis. By using the terms 'necessary' and 'sufficient' they implied both that an intelligent system had to be a physical symbol system and also that any system which was a physical symbol system could be made to exhibit intelligence. Naturally one wants to know what the distinguishing marks of a physical symbol system are, and it is here that the link with computers is made explicit.

> A physical symbol system is an instance of a universal machine. Thus the symbol system hypothesis implies that intelligence will be realized by a universal computer. However, the hypothesis goes far beyond the argument, often made on general grounds of physical determinism … it asserts specifically that the intelligent machine is a symbol system, thus making a specific architectural assertion about the nature of intelligent systems. (Newell and Simon 1976, p. 45)

Every intelligent system, they claimed, is a universal computer and every universal computer is, in principle, capable of intelligent behaviour. Newell and Simon traced the roots of the physical symbol system hypothesis back to Turing, but added to his work the concepts of the stored program computer and list processing. The latter is a way of thinking about data structures and processes which makes it clear that computers process symbols rather than just numbers and which allows for the generation of dynamic memory structures that change to meet changing task demands. The physical symbol system hypothesis is the clearest statement in the psychological literature of the thinking that underpins the computational theory of the mind.

### Rumelhart and McClelland: PDP

In 1986, David Rumelhart, James McClelland and their colleagues in the PDP Research Group published an eagerly awaited two-volume work called *Parallel Distributed Processing*. This work effectively rehabilitated the neural network tradition which had, for a variety of reasons, become something of a minority interest among psychologists during the 1970s. Enthusiasts for 'the new connectionism', as it became known, rejected the physical symbol systems hypothesis as profoundly unbiological and sought to establish a framework for studying cognitive computation which took more account of the structures and processing of the nervous system.

### The current situation

Since the mid-1980s proponents of symbol systems and connectionist networks have been ploughing their respective furrows. In some cases they have battled to establish the superiority of their framework, in others they have simply got on with the task of trying to explain and understand psychological processes from their respective standpoints. There have also been hybrid proposals involving elements from both frameworks. Proponents of symbol systems point to the power of stored program computers and to the depth of the mathematical theory that underpins them. They also argue that connectionist networks are insufficiently powerful to do various things that minds clearly manage to do. Connectionists, by contrast, argue that both the theoretical strengths and practical achievements of the symbol systems framework have been overplayed and that a framework which pays attention to the structuring of the nervous system is needed. By and large, Turing's work has been taken to underpin the symbol systems framework and to have little relevance for connectionism.

I hope it is clear from this brief and manifestly incomplete story that computational ideas address issues of fundamental significance for psychology. They provide clues about the possible ways in which minds may be physically realized, they offer hypotheses about how these physically realized minds might be organized and they address complex issues about how purely physical systems can experience the world as imbued with meaning. It is my contention that Turing's work offers insights that have not yet been appreciated by most psychologists, even those who are enthusiastic about computational thinking. In the rest of the book, I try to explain Turing's work in a sufficiently clear way that his insights can be understood. Turing's work does not underpin the symbol systems framework in the way its advocates believe and it remains relevant to connectionism despite the lack of recognition of this fact from the majority of connectionists. Properly understood, Turing's work shows the strengths and weaknesses of both frameworks. It also provides the grounding for the approach to cognitive computation which I have called ecological functionalism.

Chapter 6 begins the examination of Turing's famous 1936 paper *On Computable Numbers with an Application to the Entscheidungsproblem*. By the end of Chapter 13 it will be clear what a computable number is, and how many of them there are. The structure of a universal Turing machine and how it works will have been described in detail. The nature of various unsolvable problems, including the Entscheidungsproblem, the proofs of their unsolvability and possible implications of these proofs for psychology will have been discussed. The material is not mind-stretchingly difficult in the way, for example, that some ideas in physics are, but it can be intricate and it takes time to digest. Chapters 3 to 5 provide introductions to the notation the book uses to describe Turing machines and indicate some of the power of Turing's approach to the problems he addressed.

# 3   Functional States and Mini-minds

## Introduction

The concept of a functional state is one of the primary concepts with which this book deals. It establishes a fundamental link between psychology and computer science and provides a way of thinking about many of the issues with which the book is concerned. A Turing machine consists of a set of functional states, called a finite automaton, which is connected to a special kind of environment. The functional states control the way the combined system of finite automaton and environment operates. The finite automaton and the environment are equally important. This chapter introduces functional states: Chapter 4 explores further ideas about them, and Chapter 5 discusses Turing machine environments. The basic ideas are familiar but using them in precise and systematic ways requires some less familiar thinking.

## Functional states and processes

Functional states are best thought about in the context of processes. *The Chambers Dictionary* defines a process as 'a series of actions or events; a sequence of operations or changes undergone'. All sorts of everyday activities can be described as processes. Writing a shopping list, going shopping, going on a journey, taking part in a meeting, playing a musical instrument, reading a book and thinking about how to write a chapter of a book can all be thought of as processes. Some processes may be easily interruptible whereas others may have to be continuous. Writing a shopping list is an interruptible process. Items are written down as the need for them occurs, perhaps over a period of days. A rally in a game of tennis, by contrast, is a continuous process which begins with a service and ends when the ball goes out of play. The strokes that the players make are individually identifiable but are also parts of a continuous flow of movement. Some processes may be both interruptible and continuous. A rehearsal of a symphony orchestra or any other sort of musical ensemble is both interruptible and continuous. The music, as it is being played, is a continuous flow but the playing may frequently be stopped to discuss points of interpretation or to repeat difficult passages.

Functional states are used to describe and explain the contributions that the mental states of a person make to the processes in which they engage. They explain why on one occasion the word 'eggs' appears on a shopping list while on another it does not. They explain why someone decides to drink coffee on one occasion and water on another. They explain why the same stimulus produces different responses on different occasions. If someone hears a joke when they are happy it may produce a different response from that to the same joke heard when they are sad.

## Computing numbers

In his 1936 paper Turing was specifically concerned with the processes that are involved in computing numbers. He observed that the process of computing a number with paper and pencil involves two sorts of activities; visible actions like writing down a digit and moving a pencil from one location to another and invisible mental operations which link the visible actions and shape the whole process. To appreciate what is involved in linking actions and shaping a process consider the simple calculation 123 + 123. One way of doing the sum is to add the digits in the ones place, then those in the tens place and finally those in the hundreds place. Suppose you watch someone correctly calculating the sum in this way. First you will observe that they write down 6, then a 4 to its left giving 46 and finally a 2 to give the answer 246. You can infer from their performance that they have gone through a sequence of mental operations which might be described as follows:

> The two digits in the ones place are 3, so the first task is to add 3 and 3. That makes 6, so 6 goes in the ones place of the answer. The digits in the tens place are 2 so the next task is to add 2 and 2. That makes 4, which goes in the tens place of the answer. The digits in the hundreds place are 1 so the task is to add 1 and 1 which makes 2, which goes in the hundreds place of the answer. There are no digits in the thousands place so the task is finished.

Let us focus attention on the first step. The two digits to be added are threes; therefore the state of mind of the person adding must be such that they write the answer six. This state of mind is an instance of a functional state. Lots of time and effort is spent in schools helping children to acquire the functional states that enable them to do addition and other arithmetical tasks correctly. From the point of view of teachers of arithmetic it doesn't matter how the brain acquires these states or how they are realized in neural tissue. All that matters is that the child should respond 'six' when asked 'What is three plus three?' If the child does this in all and only the appropriate circumstances we say that they have learned that three plus three equals six. For multi-digit addition, a sequence of functional states each leading to a correct response is required.

## Functional states and everyday processes

The idea of a functional state can be generalized beyond the case of arithmetic and this is obviously important if functional states are to be widely used in psychological theory, because psychology involves much more than the mental states involved in arithmetic. Lots of examples will be considered in due course but let us briefly consider shopping lists again. If a parent says to a child, 'We need some onions' and the child goes and writes 'onions' on the shopping list we can conclude that the appropriate functional state has been acquired and used. Or if a violin teacher says to a pupil, 'Please play a scale of C minor in the second position' and the child responds appropriately we can infer that a sequence of functional states has been acquired and used. Games, like chess, which are played according to clearly specified rules are also instances of processes where the states of mind of the players can be given unequivocal functional explanations.

A definition of a functional state can be derived from these examples. A functional state is a mental entity that contributes to the sequencing of the observable actions and events of a process. In the heyday of behaviourism it was proposed that the functional states of an organism were formed from learned associations between stimuli and responses and that the sequencing of behaviour was largely determined exogenously, that is, by factors external to the organism. It is now accepted that the organism contributes much more to the sequencing of behaviour than simple associations between stimuli and responses and that behaviour is determined in part by endogenous states, that is, ones that are internal to the organism. These states have significant relations among themselves and are not driven solely by external inputs. People have goals and seek out particular stimuli in furtherance of these goals. The alcoholic who looks for a bar has different functional states from one who looks for a clinic. Functional states play essentially the part in the determination of behaviour attributed to schemata by Bartlett (1932) and to plans by Miller, Galanter and Pribram (1960). The goals and motivational structures of individuals can be explained in terms of the relations between their functional states and between those functional states and their inputs and outputs. The concept of a functional state is, therefore, very broad. It includes thoughts and feelings and anything else that makes a contribution, from inside the organism, to the control of ongoing sequences of actions and events. It does not follow from this that the notion is unconstrained. Each postulated functional state has to be defined precisely in terms of its connections to inputs, outputs and to other functional states. A notation for representing the structure of relationships between functional states is the principal topic of the rest of this chapter.

A good way to introduce the notation is to consider some of the ways in which we describe mental states, both our own and those of other people. We talk about states of happiness and sadness, for example. We use the terms 'happy' and 'sad' and related terms like 'cheerful' and 'miserable' to describe both momentary states of mind and also more enduring dispositions or aspects of character. 'He's sad today because he has just learned that his grandmother is ill' or 'She's a happy person. Always smiling.' A little thought about the use of these terms suggest that they relate both to feeling and to action. Being happy feels different from being sad and is typically associated with different kinds of actions. When we're happy we tend to laugh and smile, whereas when we're sad we're more inclined to cry. When we see someone else who is sad we tend to want to try and cheer them up. We also act strategically with respect to our perceptions of the mental states of others. If we want someone to do us a favour we try to ask them at a time when we judge them to be feeling well disposed towards us.

Another basic point is that we find ourselves in different states of mind at different times. The state of mind in which you find yourself first thing in the morning may depend on how well you slept or on what you were doing the previous night. 'How are you this morning?' is a familiar question which may elicit very different answers according to circumstances. States of mind are also changed by the receipt of information. Learning that you have passed an examination with distinction promotes a very different state of mind from that which follows from learning that you have failed the exam.

## Functional and physical analysis

One important feature of the functional approach is that it allows us to describe mental states and the relations between them without having to make any commitments about the nature of their physical realization. This, of course, is something we do every day. If I say to my wife 'I'm determined to finish chapter five today', I am saying something which tells her about my current state of mind and how I'm intending to spend the day. Such a description allows her to make predictions about my likely behaviour. It suggests that I'm more likely to remain at my desk than to go out for lunch with friends, that I probably won't welcome interruptions, and so on. What I say doesn't make any reference to how my brain works to produce my mental states and is not intended to. Functional descriptions and analyses of mental states are independent of descriptions and analyses of brain states. Suppose one's goal were a psychological analysis of happiness and sadness, it would be perfectly legitimate to base the analysis solely on the common sense understandings of these terms and the relationships between them and their external causes. People are often happy when their work goes well, when they make new friends and when they go on holiday. They are often sad when their personal relationships encounter problems and when they hear bad news. In some cases good news can make a sad person happy but it is not guaranteed to do so. The subtleties of interaction between mental states and factors that affect them can be explored without delving into their physical underpinnings. However, the fact that we can explore functional states without thinking about how they are instantiated in the brain should not be taken to mean that their physical foundations are unimportant. Ultimately we do wish to know how the mental is related to the physical and the link between them is worth considering briefly.

There is a broad scientific consensus that mental phenomena have physical foundations and that the mind depends, in ways not yet fully understood, on the brain. If the brain is damaged there are often recognizable mental consequences which may be observed as changes in behaviour or personality. A complete understanding of mental phenomena would include not just an account of the functional relations between mental states and the factors that affect them but also an account of how particular mental states are instantiated in the brain. One of the deep problems is to explain how it is that the functions carried out by neurons, the basic information processing components of the brain, produce or support the functions carried out by minds. How, in other words, do we get mind from brain? Chapter 2 showed that this question has a long history in psychology. The activities that neurons carry out don't, at first sight, appear to be the sorts of activities that can easily explain mental states. A shorthand way of exemplifying the difficulty is to say that neurons are not happy or sad but people are. One explanatory strategy that may provide part of the answer is functional decomposition. It may be possible to explain a functional mental state in terms of sub-functions, to explain the sub-functions in terms of sub-sub-functions and so on. The hope is that one might conclude the process with low-level functionality that maps onto or coincides with the functions of neurons thus providing a complete picture of the range of functionality from mental to neural. A great deal of time, money, effort, clever experiments and expensive items of laboratory equipment like MRI scanners have been invested in research that assumes functional decomposition to be broadly the right strategy for getting from mind to brain or vice versa. For the purposes of this book, the focus is on how to give precise descriptions of the patterns of connection between functional states and the ways in which a system responds to inputs. The essential points that need to be captured are the ways in which different functional states are connected to each other and to the events and actions which cause or are caused by them. We need to catalogue mental states and the relations between them in order to give the neuroscientists some targets to aim at.

## Representing happiness and sadness

Turing invented a notation to describe functional states and their connections to each other. His notation is interesting but quite difficult to understand and work with and for a first approach it is much better to use a graphical technique. The focus for the present is on the relations between functional states and inputs. Outputs are considered later. As a simple example consider again the psychological states of sadness and happiness and their relationships to good and bad news. We'll assume that people are either happy or sad but not both at the same time and that the receipt of good and bad news affects the state one is in. Normally we expect good news to make people happy and bad news to make them sad. The notation represents these relationships pictorially.

The first step is to represent the states themselves. Figure 3.1 shows a representation of the states 'happy' and 'sad'. The circles represent the different states and each is identified by its name which is written inside the circle. For convenience the names will generally be abbreviated to 'H' and 'S' rather than being written out in full. It's as simple as that. Other states can be represented in exactly the same way by drawing circles and writing names inside them. The technique works equally well for more complex states such as 'Miserable because it's Monday morning' (MBIMM) in the sense that one can write down any name inside a circle and think of it as a functional state but the challenge then is to understand how such states relate to inputs and to other states. The circle round its name indicates that a state is distinct from other states. It doesn't matter how large or small the circles are; they all have exactly the same status.

A point to note is that the names of functional states need not be descriptions of familiar states like sadness and happiness. A state can be given any name we please. We might have a series of states called 'X1', 'X2' and so on. One reason for this is that we may wish to describe functional states which do not correspond exactly to the mental states with which we are familiar. Much of the functional life of the mind probably happens below the level of conscious awareness and there may well be states of mind which are functional in the sense that they are connected to inputs and to other states in significant ways but which cannot be clearly identified in the terms that we customarily use to describe the mental states of which we are aware. There

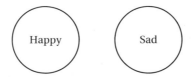

**Figure 3.1**    Two functional states.

will be more about this in due course but it is worth pointing out here for anyone who is familiar with connectionist networks that functional states as they are conceptualized in this chapter are not equivalent to the nodes in connectionist networks although both are represented pictorially by circles and connected by arrows. Functional states such as happiness and sadness are states of the whole person whereas the nodes in connectionist networks are typically thought of as 'sub-personal'. They are better thought of as abstract representations of neurons or groups of neurons.

The next step is to represent the connections between states. This is done in terms of 'transitions' which are represented by arrows. Figure 3.2 shows a transition from 'happy' to 'sad'. The arrow points to the state to which the transition is made. Transitions represent changes of state. Figure 3.2 represents a change of state of mind from happiness to sadness. We call figures of this kind state transition diagrams or just state diagrams. How do state changes happen? It is possible, as we all know, for changes to our mental states to happen for no apparent reason. It's just the way things are. Sometimes we're up, sometimes we're down, sometimes we feel wonderful and sometimes wretched, without an apparent reason. The fact that we can't identify a cause for a change in our psychological state does not mean that there isn't a cause. It may simply be that we aren't able to identify it. The notation described does not deal with uncaused state changes at all. Every change of state will have a clearly defined cause. The causes of state changes are external entities called 'inputs' which are not themselves states. Inputs are given names. To avoid confusion with states different names are generally used for inputs. The input that causes a transition is written by the tail of the arrow representing the transition. It is placed outside the circle representing the state. The inputs we are concerned with at present are named 'bad news' and 'good news'. The names are abbreviated to 'B' and 'G'.

Figure 3.3 represents a situation in which an input of bad news causes a happy person to become sad. The representation is intended to be very general. The bad news could be a phone call, a letter, a caller at the door with an unwelcome message, a broadcast or any other means of transmitting information. The state to which the arrow leads comes after the state at the tail of the arrow but no time scale is specified.

It is, of course, also possible for someone who is sad to become happy. There is, in other words, a possible transition from the sad state to the happy

**Figure 3.2**   Two functional states with a transition from happy to sad.

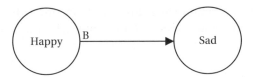

**Figure 3.3**  Two functional states with a transition from happy to sad caused by bad news.

**Figure 3.4**  Two functional states with transitions from happy to sad and from sad to happy.

**Figure 3.5**  Happy and sad functional states with transitions defined for inputs of good and bad news.

state. We could represent the fact that transitions can go both ways between happy and sad by using a double headed arrow but the convention is to use a separate arrow. Figure 3.4 shows the happy and sad states connected by two transitions, one in each direction. It represents the common sense understanding that bad news makes you sad and good news makes you happy.

Figure 3.4 is incomplete. We sometimes hear good news when we are happy and bad news when we are sad. In general, if we hear good news when we're happy we remain happy and if we hear bad news when we're sad we remain sad. Neither of these situations, in other words, causes a change of state of mind. To deal with them, we specify transitions from a functional state to itself. We represent such transitions using arrows which start and finish on the same functional state. The reason for this slightly counterintuitive approach is to provide a uniform treatment for all situations. Adopting the convention that situations where there is no state change are represented by transitions from a state to itself allows us to treat the relations between states and inputs in a single way. This simplifies the more sophisticated uses of the diagrams that we will look at in due course. Figure 3.5 is like Figure 3.4 but with two transitions added to represent what happens when a happy person hears good news and a sad person hears bad news.

A little further reflection on Figure 3.5 is in order. It is based on the assumption that the states described are mutually exclusive and that the person, of whose mental life it is a partial description, is either happy or sad but not both at the same time. It does not allow the possibility of someone's being sad in a happy sort of way or vice versa, both of which are mental states that we may well think possible. There is nothing to stop us from naming states of that kind, if we wish, but to use the graphical form of representation we have to think of them as distinct from both happy and sad. They would be represented by different circles in the state diagram. Another point to note is that state diagrams, by themselves, tell us nothing about what state a person might be in at a particular time. They are best thought of as providing conditional information. Thus we can understand Figure 3.5 as representing the following set of conditional statements: 'If a happy person hears good news they remain happy'; 'If a happy person hears bad news they become sad'; 'If a sad person hears good news they become happy'; 'If a sad person hears bad news they remain sad.'

## Mini-minds

Figure 3.5 describes a system which is called a 'finite automaton'. Finite automata can have many more than two states, any finite number in fact, but they all share in common with Figure 3.5 the fact that they can be in just one of their functional states at a given time and that transitions between functional states depend on the current state and the input. The states must also all be specified when the finite automaton is constructed. 'Finite automaton' sounds somewhat forbidding and robot-like, so I am going to use the term 'mini-mind' instead to emphasize the fact that the states of finite automata can describe human states of mind. Mini-minds can be thought of as complete descriptions of very simple minds or as partial descriptions of more complicated minds. In fact it's helpful to think of them as the minds of simple-minded creatures. The kind of imaginative engagement one needs is similar to that which we see when we watch children playing with toys and imputing mental states to them. If Teddy is feeling unwell he may be put to bed or taken to hospital but if he is feeling well he may want something to eat. Alan Turing, whose work is central to this book, had a teddy bear in Cambridge at the time when he was working on his theory of computation. It was occasionally seen by his students at King's College.

If they came to his rooms hoping for a glimpse of Turing's eccentricity, they were sometimes rewarded, as when Alan sat Porgy the teddy bear by the fire, in front of a book supported by a ruler, and greeted them with 'Porgy is very *studious* this morning'. (Hodges 1983, p. 94)

The behaviour of a mini-mind is determined by its current functional state and the input it receives. We can track its behaviour if we know the sequence of inputs and the state the mini-mind is in when it receives the first of those inputs. Imagine that you want to track the behaviour of the mini-mind of Figure 3.5. The first thing you need to know is what its current functional state is. It's like trying to find out whether Teddy is well or unwell. Because a mini-mind is a hypothetical entity it is up to the observer to decide unless the starting state is stipulated. Suppose then that one decides that the starting state is 'happy'. Then a sequence of inputs GB, that is one input of good news followed by one of bad, causes two transitions, one from happy to happy and one from happy to sad. If the starting state had been 'sad' the first transition would have been from sad to happy, and the second from happy to sad. Provided the starting state of the mini-mind is known its behaviour can be tracked for input sequences of any length.

The mini-mind of Figure 3.5 makes intuitive sense but the notation does not require mini-minds to correspond with our intuitions. Consider, for example, the mini-mind described by Figure 3.6. All the transitions in this system are to the happy state. If the mini-mind starts in the sad state its first action is a transition to the happy state. If it starts in the happy state then it remains there and never makes a transition to the sad state. In what follows, when it is important to do so, the starting state for a sequence of behaviour will be specified.

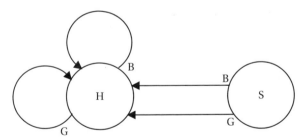

**Figure 3.6**   A mini-mind whose transitions are all to the happy state.

**Exercise 3.1**   It is well known that alcohol makes you drunk. Suppose for the sake of the argument that coffee makes you sober. Draw a mini-mind with two states, 'drunk' and 'sober' and transitions between them caused by alcohol and coffee.

**Exercise 3.2**   Can you calculate the number of different mini-minds that can be constructed with states H and S, and inputs G and B? (the answer is in Chapter 4)

This chapter has taken the first steps towards an understanding of the foundations of the theory of computation. The concepts of a functional state and of a transition between states have been introduced along with a graphical notation for representing them. In Chapter 4, the analysis is extended to larger mini-minds.

# 4 Exploring Sets of Mini-minds

## Configurations

An interesting question, posed at the end of Chapter 3, is how many different mini-minds can be specified for a given number of functional states and inputs. This question can be answered systematically and doing so provides some interesting insights about sets of mini-minds. To begin with it will be useful to introduce a new piece of terminology. The combination of a functional state and an input is called a 'configuration' and it can be represented by an expression such as (H,G) which is called an 'ordered pair'. As the name implies, the ordering of the elements is important in an ordered pair. In the ordered pairs which represent configurations, the functional state is always the first element and the input symbol the second. Thus the ordered pair (H,G) symbolises a configuration consisting of the functional state H and the input G. The mini-minds in Figures 3.5 and 3.6 have four configurations (H,G), (H,B), (S,G), (S,B). The term 'configuration' was introduced by Turing and plays an important part in his theory. The principal point to note is that configurations represent the co-occurrences of functional states and inputs that cause behaviour. Configuration (H,G), for example, represents the co-occurrence of the happy state and an input of good news.

## Instructions and machine tables

Configurations cause state transitions and a little more notation is used to represent this precisely and economically. (H,G) → H means 'The configuration (H,G) causes a transition to functional state H'. In Chapter 3 we noted that a transition from a functional state to itself describes the fact that the functional state does not change. This new notation provides a different way of describing mini-minds. The mini-mind of Figure 3.5, for example, can be described as follows: (H,G) → H; (H,B) → S; (S,G) → H; (S,B) → S. The two forms of notation provide exactly the same information but the pictorial form tends to be easier to understand when the number of states is large. An expression such as (H,G) → H is called an 'instruction' and the set of instructions defining a mini-mind is called a 'machine table'. Machine tables play a crucial role in the functioning of universal machines. Chapters 10–12 provide detailed discussions.

Each configuration of a mini-mind has a single transition associated with it, but there is usually more than one possible choice for the transition. Consider first the configuration (H,G). In both Figures 3.5 and 3.6 (H,G) → H, but there is no reason in principle why it should not have been (H,G) → S even though that would not make much psychological sense because good news does not make a happy person sad. Thus two different transitions for configuration (H,G) are logically possible even though only one is psychologically plausible. Similar arguments apply to each of the other configurations. The choice of transition for each configuration is independent of the choices made for the others. This means that there are $2 \times 2 \times 2 \times 2 = 16$ different, possible arrangements of transitions. Thus sixteen different mini-minds can be defined for systems consisting of the functional states H and S and the inputs G and B. Changing the names of functional states or inputs does not alter the combinatorial possibilities. So for any pair of functional states and pair of inputs, sixteen mini-minds can be defined.

An important point to discuss is the fact that each configuration has just one transition associated with it. Why, you might ask, do we not define systems in which a given configuration can cause a transition to more than one state? Surely, if we are to build plausible models of real mental lives, we need to allow for situations in which, for example, bad news does not always cause unhappiness. In terms of the notation this implies that although the configuration (H,B) might cause a transition to functional state S on some occasions, at other times it would leave the system in state H. Suppose I hear the good news that I have won a large sum of money. That makes me happy. Suppose I then hear the bad news that my car needs an expensive repair. That piece of bad news may not make me unhappy given that I know I can now easily afford to pay for the repair. Similarly, in times of great sadness, good news will not necessarily make us happy.

## Deterministic and non-deterministic models

The simple answer is that our mental lives are of course more complex and sophisticated than the mini-minds discussed here and appropriately sophisticated modelling techniques are needed to represent them adequately. However, the techniques used to define mini-minds form an important part of the foundations of these more complex models. Mini-minds are examples of what are called 'deterministic' systems whereas real minds appear to be 'non-deterministic' systems. The fundamental difference between them is that the immediate behaviour of a deterministic system is predictable given some specific pieces of information whereas the behaviour of a non-deterministic system is not. The mini-minds with which we have dealt so far have deterministic transitions because each configuration has a single transition associated with it. Thus if we know the configuration we know what the transition will be. If, however, a configuration could cause a transition to either H or S, the transition would be non-deterministic because knowing the configuration alone would not tell us the state to which the transition would be made.

The fact that minds appear to be non-deterministic systems does not imply that the study of deterministic systems is unimportant for psychology. It might, for example, be the case that minds are non-deterministic but brains are deterministic. If that turns out to be the case and, if it is also the case that minds are dependent on brains, then we will need to understand how a system which is deterministic at one level of operation can be, or appear to be, non-deterministic at another. One of the interesting discoveries in theoretical computer science is that under certain conditions deterministic and non-deterministic systems can be considered equivalent. There is more to be said about this topic but for the present we shall continue to explore mini-minds which are deterministic and have a single transition defined for each configuration. Systems of this kind are capable of representing complex relationships between functional states and inputs.

### Description numbers

The sixteen deterministic mini-minds for functional states H and S and inputs G and B can be listed systematically. Table 4.1 shows them all. The first column shows the four possible configurations and the remaining numbered columns show the transitions for each mini-mind. Column 0 shows the mini-mind displayed in Figure 3.6, and column 5 shows the mini-mind displayed in Figure 3.5. The mini-minds are numbered from 0 to 15 rather than from 1 to 16 because of a useful mapping from the names of states to binary digits which allows us to describe the mini-minds numerically. Take H = 0 and S = 1 and order the configurations in the sequence (H,G), (H,B), (S,G), (S,B). Then list the transitions in the same order. The mini-mind in column 0 has transitions HHHH = 0000 binary which is decimal 0, the mini-mind in column 15 has transitions SSSS = 1111 binary which is decimal 15, and each of the other mini-minds has a number which expresses its transitions. The mini-mind in column 10, for example, has transitions SHSH = 1010 binary or 10 decimal. The notation works the other way round as well. If you are given the decimal number of a mini-mind you can work out what its transitions are. The numbers are called 'description numbers' because each describes the associated mini-mind. Description numbers feature prominently in Turing's theory. His particular numbering system is introduced in Chapter 9.

**Table 4.1**   The 16 mini-minds definable for two states H and S and
two inputs G and B

|       | 0 | 1 | 2 | 3 | 4 | 5 | 6 | 7 | 8 | 9 | 10 | 11 | 12 | 13 | 14 | 15 |
|-------|---|---|---|---|---|---|---|---|---|---|----|----|----|----|----|----|
| **(H,G)** | H | H | H | H | H | H | H | H | S | S | S | S | S | S | S | S |
| **(H,B)** | H | H | H | H | S | S | S | S | H | H | H | H | S | S | S | S |
| **(S,G)** | H | H | S | S | H | H | S | S | H | H | S | S | H | H | S | S |
| **(S,B)** | H | S | H | S | H | S | H | S | H | S | H | S | H | S | H | S |

**Exercise 4.1**   Draw the state diagram for each of the 16 two-state,
two-symbol mini-minds and consider whether any of them apart from
number 5 has a plausible psychological interpretation.

**Exercise 4.2**   Mini-mind 3 has no transitions between its two states.
Can you give this phenomenon a psychological interpretation?

## Logical possibility and psychological plausibility

It becomes clear when one examines the 16 two-state, two-input mini-
minds that most of them do not make sense psychologically. There is, therefore, an important distinction to be made between logical possibility and
psychological plausibility. In mini-mind 10, for example, good news makes
the system sad and bad news makes it happy which is psychologically per-
verse. Mini-minds 3 and 12 are of some interest. News arguably has no effect
on either mini-mind but the dynamics of the systems are nevertheless different. Mini-mind 3 remains in whatever state it starts in regardless of the
input, whereas mini-mind 12 switches state from happy to sad and vice versa
whenever it has an input without regard to whether the input is good news or
bad. These differences suggest that the functional state technique is capable
of registering quite subtle distinctions of behaviour even in very simple
systems.

## Counting mini-minds

For any two functional states and any two inputs there are sixteen definable
mini-minds. Most systems of interest will have more than two states and two
inputs and it is valuable to know how to calculate the number of mini-minds
that can be defined for arbitrary numbers of states and inputs. In general for
$n$ functional states and $k$ inputs, there are $n^{nk}$ definable mini-minds. One
way of arriving at this value is as follows. Given $n$ functional states and
$k$ inputs, there are $n \times k$ definable configurations. Each of these $nk$ configurations has an associated transition which can be made to any one of the

$n$ functional states. This means that the total number of different possible arrangements is the number of possible destination states for a transition raised to the power of the number of configurations, that is $n$ multiplied by itself $nk$ times, which is written as $n^{nk}$. In the systems we have examined so far, $n = 2$, and $k = 2$. Thus $nk = 4$ so there are $2^4 = 16$ mini-minds definable with two functional states and two inputs as we have already seen. Suppose there are three functional states and two inputs. Then $n = 3$, and $k = 2$ so $n^{nk} = 3^6 = 729$. If, instead, there are two functional states and three inputs, $n = 2$, and $k = 3$ so $n^{nk} = 2^6 = 64$. If both $n$ and $k$ are increased to 3, $n^{nk} = 3^9$ so there are 19,683 mini-minds definable for systems with three functional states and three inputs.

> **Exercise 4.3**   $n^{nk}$ increases faster when $n$ is increased than when $k$ is increased. Can you derive a psychological moral from this numerical fact?

## Four-state mini-minds

Two state, two input mini-minds are obviously limited but as the number of states or inputs is increased it becomes possible to describe more interesting kinds of behaviour. We now consider mini-minds with four functional states rather than two. As before, the inputs consist of good news and bad news, 'G' and 'B', but two additional states are added, very happy (VH) and very sad (VS). The formula $n^{nk}$ shows that 65,536 different mini-minds can be defined with these resources. This relatively large number suggests that it would not be practical to list and examine all the mini-minds in the way that was perfectly feasible for the two state, two input set of Table 4.1. Moreover, such an exercise would be of limited psychological value because many, perhaps most, would be psychologically implausible. However, it is likely that the set contains at least some instances which are of psychological interest and a question therefore arises about how to identify them. Exploring the set and finding ways to answer this question are the main concerns of the rest of the chapter. The explorations are small scale by comparison with the numbers of functional states of real minds but the distinction between logical possibility and psychological plausibility is one that exists at any scale. What one hopes to achieve with a large set of logical possibilities is a broadening of the scope of one's psychological hypotheses and what the constraints of plausibility achieve is a narrowing of the search space to manageable proportions. It is possible to investigate sets of mini-minds systematically and doing so brings to the fore some of the real strengths of the functional state technique for forming and exploring psychological hypotheses. These investigations are based on reasoning with description numbers. This is a powerful technique and in Chapters 12 and 13 some of Turing's celebrated reasoning about description numbers is explored. The investigations here are much simpler

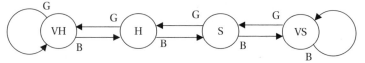

**Figure 4.1**   A four-state mini-mind showing how happy and sad states are related to each other.

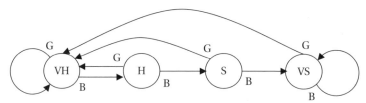

**Figure 4.2**   An optimistic mini-mind.

than his but provide a useful introduction. First, however, let us look at some examples of four-state mini-minds.

Figure 4.1 shows an obvious example. The happy and sad states are related to each other in the same way as in Figure 3.5 of Chapter 3. However, if the mini-mind of Figure 4.1 is happy and has an input of good news it becomes very happy and if it is sad and has an input of bad news it becomes very sad. In general, good news takes the mini-mind of Figure 4.1 to the next happier state unless it is already very happy and bad news takes it to the next sadder state unless it is already very sad. Now consider the mini-mind shown in Figure 4.2.

An input of good news, whatever the current functional state, causes a transition to the very happy state, whereas an input of bad news causes a transition to the next sadder state. As a result, if it is given a random sequence of inputs, the mini-mind spends most of its time in one of its happy states and may therefore be described as 'optimistic'.

**Exercise 4.4**   Draw the state diagram for a 'pessimistic' mini-mind.

It is clear from the examples of Figures 4.1 and 4.2 and Exercise 4.4 that the set of four-state mini-minds contains some instances that, though simple, are psychologically plausible. This raises two questions. First, can we be more precise about what 'psychologically plausible' means? Second, how many plausible instances does the set contain?

## Plausibility constraints: selecting subsets of mini-minds

In the absence of an explicit theory of the relationships between states of happiness and sadness and inputs of good and bad news, the sensible starting point is to consider our intuitions about them. Figures 4.1 and 4.2 both embody the plausible assumptions that good news makes you happier and that bad news makes you sadder although they do so in somewhat different ways. Mini-minds in which good news makes you sadder or bad news makes you happier are logically possible but psychologically implausible. As a first approximation, then, a psychologically plausible mini-mind is one in which good news does not make you sadder and bad news does not make you happier. Any other transitions are allowable.

To formulate these intuitions precisely we consider the possible transitions for each configuration. Because there are four functional states and two inputs there are eight configurations whose transitions have to be described. These are (VH,G), (VH,B), (H,G), (H,B), (S,G), (S,B), (VS,G), (VS,B). Each of these configurations can, in principle, cause a transition to any one of the four states VH, H, S, VS. However, psychological plausibility constrains these choices. If good news cannot plausibly cause a transition to a sadder state, there is only one choice for (VH,G). The transition has to be (VH,G) $\rightarrow$ VH. The choice for configuration (VH,B) is not limited in this way. Any of the four choices is compatible with the plausibility constraint. Considering (H,G) next there are two possibilities that are consistent with the constraint; (H,G) $\rightarrow$ VH, (H,G) $\rightarrow$ H. For (H,B) there are three possibilities because only (H,B) $\rightarrow$ VH is ruled out by the constraint. Similar considerations show that there are three plausible transitions for (S,G), two for (S,B), four for (VS,G) and one for (VS,B).

**Exercise 4.5** Write down the plausible transitions for configurations (S,G), (S,B), (VS,G) and (VS,B).

Bearing in mind that the total number of plausible mini-minds is a product of the number of transitions available for each configuration, we have $1 \times 4 \times 2 \times 3 \times 3 \times 2 \times 4 \times 1 = 576$ mini-minds with four states and two inputs which meet the constraints that good news should not make you sadder and that bad news should not make you happier. Though 576 is a much smaller number than 65536 it is still quite large. Description numbers can be used to identify the 576 plausible mini-minds and any of the others that we might wish to consider. To do this we have, first, to construct the description numbers. There is no hard and fast rule about how to do this. The only requirement is that the method must be systematic. One possibility is to extend the scheme used for the two state, two input mini-minds discussed earlier.

We start by putting the configurations in a specific order. The one used above, (VH,G), (VH,B), (H,G), (H,B), (S,G), (S,B), (VS,G), (VS,B), is sensible. Next a numerical code for the states is required. Since there are four of them they can be coded using two digit binary numbers such that VH = 00, H = 01, S = 10, VS = 11. Now we can construct the description number for a

**Table 4.2**  The elements of the description number for mini-mind 4731

| Configuration | (VH,G) | (VH,B) | (H,G) | (H,B) | (S,G) | (S,B) | (VS,G) | (VS,B) |
|---|---|---|---|---|---|---|---|---|
| Transition | VH | H | VH | S | H | VS | S | VS |
| Description number | 00 | 01 | 00 | 10 | 01 | 11 | 10 | 11 |

mini-mind by concatenating the values for each transition. Taking the mini-mind of Figure 4.1 as an example, (VH,G) → VH so we write down 00. (VH,B) → H so we write 01 next to it giving 0001. Similarly for the remaining configurations. Table 4.2 shows them all. The resulting 16-digit binary number is the description number of the mini-mind. The decimal equivalent of 0001001001111011 binary is 4731 so the decimal description number of the mini-mind of Figure 4.1 is 4731.

The coding scheme provides a unique description number for each of the 65536 four state, two input mini-minds. The numbers run from 0000000000000000 to 1111111111111111 so the first mini-mind in the series has number 0, the second number 1 and so forth. In general, the $k^{th}$ mini-mind has description number $k$-1. Description number 0 describes the machine whose transitions are all to the state VH and description number 65535 describes the machine whose transitions are all to the state VS. We have to exercise a modicum of care to make sure that we correctly identify the mini-mind we want to talk about. If we refer, for example, to the fifth mini-mind in the series, we are talking about the mini-mind whose description number is four. For clarity in this chapter, I shall always refer to the mini-mind whose description number is $k$ rather than to the $k^{th}$ mini-mind. With the coding scheme in place we can use decimal description numbers to encode and decode the four state, two symbol mini-minds. (See Appendix 4.1, for simple ways to convert 16-digit binary numerals to their decimal representations and vice versa.)

The most important point about description numbers is that they make it possible to reason systematically about how the constraints of psychological plausibility apply to the set of mini-minds. In particular they enable us to identify all the mini-minds which meet the constraints. We can do this in a straightforward way by considering how the description numbers can be broken down into factors that represent specific transitions. Table 4.3 shows the factors for the whole set of 65536 mini-minds. Configurations are shown in the first column of the table and the possible transitions in the first row. The remaining cells of the table show the decimal values for each transition. To understand how they are arrived at consider the transition (S,G) → VS. Because of the way the description numbers are constructed, the transition is found in the sixth and seventh digits of the binary description number, starting from the right and counting from zero. The code for VS is 11, so the

**Table 4.3**  The decimal values for each possible transition of the four-state, two-input, mini-minds

|        | VH | H     | S     | VS    |
|--------|----|-------|-------|-------|
| (VS,B) | 0  | 1     | 2     | 3     |
| (VS,G) | 0  | 4     | 8     | 12    |
| (S,B)  | 0  | 16    | 32    | 48    |
| (S,G)  | 0  | 64    | 128   | 192   |
| (H,B)  | 0  | 256   | 512   | 768   |
| (H,G)  | 0  | 1024  | 2048  | 3072  |
| (VH,B) | 0  | 4096  | 8192  | 12288 |
| (VH,G) | 0  | 16384 | 32768 | 49152 |

binary number which represents this transition is 11000000 which is $2^6 + 2^7 = 192$ decimal. Each mini-mind is specified by one value from each row. To find the description number for a given mini-mind we add the values of the cells indexed by its eight transitions. For the mini-mind of Figure 4.1 starting with (VH,G) → VH and ending with (VS,B) → VS we have $0 + 4096 + 0 + 512 + 64 + 48 + 8 + 3 = 4731$ which we have already arrived at by other means.

> **Exercise 4.6**  What is the description number of the optimistic mini-mind of Figure 4.2?

Table 4.3 contains lots of information although some things are more obvious than others. It is easy enough to see that mini-mind 0 has all its transitions to VH. Slightly less obvious is the information that mini-mind 65535 has all its transitions to VS. A little less obvious still is the information that the mini-mind whose states are completely unconnected to each other has description number 1455. However, the principal value of the tabular format for present purposes is that we can use it to make explicit the constraints discussed earlier. Table 4.4 shows the values of the transitions allowed by the constraints.

Table 4.4 makes it easy to calculate the lowest and highest description numbers for mini-minds which satisfy the constraints. To calculate the lowest number we take the lowest value in each row and sum them: $3 + 0 + 32 + 0 + 256 + 0 + 0 + 0 = 291$. To calculate the highest we take the largest values and sum them: $3 + 12 + 48 + 128 + 768 + 1024 + 12288 + 0 = 14271$. Clearly the remaining 574 mini-minds have description numbers which fall between these two extremes. The numbers can be calculated systematically by working through all the possible combinations. Table 4.5 shows the description numbers of all 576 mini-minds which satisfy the constraints.

**Table 4.4**  The values for the transitions of the constrained subset of four-state, two-input mini-minds

|        | VH  | H    | S    | VS    |
|--------|-----|------|------|-------|
| (VS,B) | —   | —    | —    | 3     |
| (VS,G) | 0   | 4    | 8    | 12    |
| (S,B)  | —   | —    | 32   | 48    |
| (S,G)  | 0   | 64   | 128  | —     |
| (H,B)  | —   | 256  | 512  | 768   |
| (H,G)  | 0   | 1024 | —    | —     |
| (VH,B) | 0   | 4096 | 8192 | 12288 |
| (VH,G) | 0   | —    | —    | —     |

**Exercise 4.7**  Draw the state diagrams for mini-minds 291 and 14271 and compare their characteristics.

Given the description numbers for the constrained mini-minds it is straightforward to draw any state diagram we might wish to look at because each description number has a unique decomposition into powers of two and these tell us which transitions the mini-mind contains.

**Exercise 4.8**  Construct the state diagrams for a sample of mini-minds from Table 4.5 and think about their psychological plausibility.

It is worth reflecting briefly on what has been achieved so far. It is sometimes said that computational approaches to psychology are implausible because they imply that people are robots or unfeeling machines. What we have seen in the investigation of the mini-minds is something very different. The functional approach deployed here, which lies at the heart of computational thinking, is a way of making a systematic study of the possible relationships between functional states and inputs and of making precise what might be meant by intuitive psychological plausibility. It does not try to reduce people to machines.

Exploration of the 576 mini-minds suggests that the constraints may be insufficient because there are instances that have rather peculiar dynamics. The extremes, mini-minds 291 and 14271 to take just two examples, seem implausible. Bad news has no effect on any of the states of 291 whereas good news sends it to the very happy state which is thereafter inescapable. Mini-mind 14271 has the same dynamics but with the pattern reversed. Good news has no effect, bad news sends the mini-mind inescapably to the very sad state. These examples suggest that allowing news to have no effect on the current state of the system could be problematic from the point of view of psychological plausibility. The problem may be tackled by adding the further constraint that news should lead to a change of state if there is a plausible

**Table 4.5** The description numbers for the 576 four-state, two-input mini-minds that meet the initial set of plausibility constraints

| | | | | | | | |
|---|---|---|---|---|---|---|---|
| 291 | 295 | 299 | 303 | 307 | 311 | 315 | 319 |
| 355 | 359 | 363 | 367 | 371 | 375 | 379 | 383 |
| 419 | 423 | 427 | 431 | 435 | 439 | 443 | 447 |
| 547 | 551 | 555 | 559 | 563 | 567 | 571 | 575 |
| 611 | 615 | 619 | 623 | 627 | 631 | 635 | 639 |
| 675 | 679 | 683 | 687 | 691 | 695 | 699 | 703 |
| 803 | 807 | 811 | 815 | 819 | 823 | 827 | 831 |
| 867 | 871 | 875 | 879 | 883 | 887 | 891 | 895 |
| 931 | 935 | 939 | 943 | 947 | 951 | 955 | 959 |
| 1315 | 1319 | 1323 | 1327 | 1331 | 1335 | 1339 | 1343 |
| 1379 | 1383 | 1387 | 1391 | 1395 | 1399 | 1403 | 1407 |
| 1443 | 1447 | 1451 | 1455 | 1459 | 1463 | 1467 | 1471 |
| 1571 | 1575 | 1579 | 1583 | 1587 | 1591 | 1595 | 1599 |
| 1635 | 1639 | 1643 | 1647 | 1651 | 1655 | 1659 | 1663 |
| 1699 | 1703 | 1707 | 1711 | 1715 | 1719 | 1723 | 1727 |
| 1827 | 1831 | 1835 | 1839 | 1843 | 1847 | 1851 | 1855 |
| 1891 | 1895 | 1899 | 1903 | 1907 | 1911 | 1915 | 1919 |
| 1955 | 1959 | 1963 | 1967 | 1971 | 1975 | 1979 | 1983 |
| 4387 | 4391 | 4395 | 4399 | 4403 | 4407 | 4411 | 4415 |
| 4451 | 4455 | 4459 | 4463 | 4467 | 4471 | 4475 | 4479 |
| 4515 | 4519 | 4523 | 4527 | 4531 | 4535 | 4539 | 4543 |
| 4643 | 4647 | 4651 | 4655 | 4659 | 4663 | 4667 | 4671 |
| 4707 | 4711 | 4715 | 4719 | 4723 | 4727 | 4731 | 4735 |
| 4771 | 4775 | 4779 | 4783 | 4787 | 4791 | 4795 | 4799 |
| 4899 | 4903 | 4907 | 4911 | 4915 | 4919 | 4923 | 4927 |
| 4963 | 4967 | 4971 | 4975 | 4979 | 4983 | 4987 | 4991 |
| 5027 | 5031 | 5035 | 5039 | 5043 | 5047 | 5051 | 5055 |
| 5411 | 5415 | 5419 | 5423 | 5427 | 5431 | 5435 | 5439 |
| 5475 | 5479 | 5483 | 5487 | 5491 | 5495 | 5499 | 5503 |
| 5539 | 5543 | 5547 | 5551 | 5555 | 5559 | 5563 | 5567 |
| 5667 | 5671 | 5675 | 5679 | 5683 | 5687 | 5691 | 5695 |
| 5731 | 5735 | 5739 | 5743 | 5747 | 5751 | 5755 | 5759 |
| 5795 | 5799 | 5803 | 5807 | 5811 | 5815 | 5819 | 5823 |
| 5923 | 5927 | 5931 | 5935 | 5939 | 5943 | 5947 | 5951 |
| 5987 | 5991 | 5995 | 5999 | 6003 | 6007 | 6011 | 6015 |
| 6051 | 6055 | 6059 | 6063 | 6067 | 6071 | 6075 | 6079 |
| 8483 | 8487 | 8491 | 8495 | 8499 | 8503 | 8507 | 8511 |
| 8547 | 8551 | 8555 | 8559 | 8563 | 8567 | 8571 | 8575 |
| 8611 | 8615 | 8619 | 8623 | 8627 | 8631 | 8635 | 8639 |
| 8739 | 8743 | 8747 | 8751 | 8755 | 8759 | 8763 | 8767 |
| 8803 | 8807 | 8811 | 8815 | 8819 | 8823 | 8827 | 8831 |
| 8867 | 8871 | 8875 | 8879 | 8883 | 8887 | 8891 | 8895 |
| 8995 | 8999 | 9003 | 9007 | 9011 | 9015 | 9019 | 9023 |
| 9059 | 9063 | 9067 | 9071 | 9075 | 9079 | 9083 | 9087 |

Continued

**Table 4.5**  Continued

| | | | | | | | |
|---|---|---|---|---|---|---|---|
| 9123 | 9127 | 9131 | 9135 | 9139 | 9143 | 9147 | 9151 |
| 9507 | 9511 | 9515 | 9519 | 9523 | 9527 | 9531 | 9535 |
| 9571 | 9575 | 9579 | 9583 | 9587 | 9591 | 9595 | 9599 |
| 9635 | 9639 | 9643 | 9647 | 9651 | 9655 | 9659 | 9663 |
| 9763 | 9767 | 9771 | 9775 | 9779 | 9783 | 9787 | 9791 |
| 9827 | 9831 | 9835 | 9839 | 9843 | 9847 | 9851 | 9855 |
| 9891 | 9895 | 9899 | 9903 | 9907 | 9911 | 9915 | 9919 |
| 10019 | 10023 | 10027 | 10031 | 10035 | 10039 | 10043 | 10047 |
| 10083 | 10087 | 10091 | 10095 | 10099 | 10103 | 10107 | 10111 |
| 10147 | 10151 | 10155 | 10159 | 10163 | 10167 | 10171 | 10175 |
| 12579 | 12583 | 12587 | 12591 | 12595 | 12599 | 12603 | 12607 |
| 12643 | 12647 | 12651 | 12655 | 12659 | 12663 | 12667 | 12671 |
| 12707 | 12711 | 12715 | 12719 | 12723 | 12727 | 12731 | 12735 |
| 12835 | 12839 | 12843 | 12847 | 12851 | 12855 | 12859 | 12863 |
| 12899 | 12903 | 12907 | 12911 | 12915 | 12919 | 12923 | 12927 |
| 12963 | 12967 | 12971 | 12975 | 12979 | 12983 | 12987 | 12991 |
| 13091 | 13095 | 13099 | 13103 | 13107 | 13111 | 13115 | 13119 |
| 13155 | 13159 | 13163 | 13167 | 13171 | 13175 | 13179 | 13183 |
| 13219 | 13223 | 13227 | 13231 | 13235 | 13239 | 13243 | 13247 |
| 13603 | 13607 | 13611 | 13615 | 13619 | 13623 | 13627 | 13631 |
| 13667 | 13671 | 13675 | 13679 | 13683 | 13687 | 13691 | 13695 |
| 13731 | 13735 | 13739 | 13743 | 13747 | 13751 | 13755 | 13759 |
| 13859 | 13863 | 13867 | 13871 | 13875 | 13879 | 13883 | 13887 |
| 13923 | 13927 | 13931 | 13935 | 13939 | 13943 | 13947 | 13951 |
| 13987 | 13991 | 13995 | 13999 | 14003 | 14007 | 14011 | 14015 |
| 14115 | 14119 | 14123 | 14127 | 14131 | 14135 | 14139 | 14143 |
| 14179 | 14183 | 14187 | 14191 | 14195 | 14199 | 14203 | 14207 |
| 14243 | 14247 | 14251 | 14255 | 14259 | 14263 | 14267 | 14271 |

transition available for a given configuration. This means that (VS,G) → VS, (S,B) → S, (S,G) → S, (H,B) → H, (H,G) → H and (VH,B) → VH are ruled out because there are other plausible options for these configurations. Table 4.6 shows the transitions that remain when the additional constraint is added. Table 4.6 allows us to calculate that the addition of the further constraint decreases the set of mini-minds from 576 to 36. The extremes of this new set are mini-minds 4659 and 13179. Mini-mind 4659 is the optimistic mini-mind of Figure 4.2 and 13179 is its pessimistic counterpart. The description numbers for the thirty-six mini-minds in the reduced set are shown in Table 4.7. The set of 36 mini-minds illustrates the way in which intuitions about psychological plausibility narrow down a search space of logical possibilities. The set is small enough for the task of generating the state diagrams to be manageable and it contains a number of instances which are of some psychological interest. The set of state diagrams is included in Appendix 4.2. Examination of the set shows that some of the mini-minds have peculiar dynamics and this suggests that even these constraints may not adequately

**Table 4.6**   The transitions available under the increased set of constraints

|         | VH   | H    | S    | VS    |
|---------|------|------|------|-------|
| (VS,B)  |      |      |      | 3     |
| (VS,G)  | 0    | 4    | 8    | —     |
| (S,B)   | —    | —    | —    | 48    |
| (S,G)   | 0    | 64   | —    | —     |
| (H,B)   | —    | —    | 512  | 768   |
| (H,G)   | 0    | —    | —    | —     |
| (VH,B)  | —    | 4096 | 8192 | 12288 |
| (VH,G)  | 0    | —    | —    | —     |

**Table 4.7**   The 36 mini-minds in the reduced set

| | | |
|---|---|---|
| 4659  | 4663  | 4667  |
| 4723  | 4727  | 4731  |
| 4915  | 4919  | 4923  |
| 4979  | 4983  | 4987  |
| 8755  | 8759  | 8763  |
| 8819  | 8823  | 8827  |
| 9011  | 9015  | 9019  |
| 9075  | 9079  | 9083  |
| 12851 | 12855 | 12859 |
| 12915 | 12919 | 12923 |
| 13107 | 13111 | 13115 |
| 13171 | 13175 | 13179 |

express our intuitions. However, the point at this stage is not to capture perfectly our intuitions about the relations explored but to illustrate the interaction between the space of logical possibilities and a formalized notion of psychological plausibility. Other sets of constraints are possible and may reflect differences of intuition between people.

**Exercise 4.9**   It is arguable that the constraints which form the set of mini-minds in Table 4.7 are both too broad and too narrow because they admit some implausible instances and prohibit some plausible ones. Can you find an improved set of constraints?

The mini-minds discussed so far have illustrated the relationships between functional states and their inputs but the organization of the inputs has not been considered and the question of outputs has not arisen at all. To understand how transitions between functional states can cause behaviour as well as be caused by inputs, it is necessary to consider these matters. They form the topic of Chapter 5.

## Appendix 4.1    Binary to decimal and decimal to binary conversion

The familiar decimal numbers are based on powers of ten. 123 decimal is $(1 \times 100) + (2 \times 10) + (3 \times 1)$. Binary numbers are based on powers of two. 101 binary is $(1 \times 4) + (0 \times 2) + (1 \times 1)$. To convert 16-digit binary numbers to decimal we need to know the relevant powers of two. They are:

1, 2, 4, 8, 16, 32, 64, 128, 256, 512, 1024, 2048, 4096, 8192, 16384, 32768.

To convert a given binary number to decimal, start with the least significant digit, the rightmost one. For each digit which is a one, write down the corresponding power of two. Add them up. The result is the decimal equivalent of the binary number. For example:

1011001010110001    is    $1 + 16 + 32 + 128 + 512 + 4096 + 8192 + 32768 = 45745$.

To convert a given decimal number less than 65536 to binary the number needs to be factored into its powers of two. For each of these the relevant digit of the binary representation is set to one. An easy way to achieve this is to consider each of the powers of two in succession, starting with 32768. If the power is larger than the decimal number, write a 0 and consider the next smaller power. If the power is smaller than the number, write a 1, subtract the power from the decimal number and use the remainder as the new decimal. If the power is equal to the decimal number write a 1 and follow it with 0s for all the lower powers. For example:

$17536 = 16384 + 1024 + 128 = 0100010010000000$

32768 is larger than 17536 so 0 is written in the most significant position and 16384 is considered. This is smaller than 17536 so 1 is written in the next position and the subtraction is done. $17536 - 16384 = 1152$. This becomes the new number. 8192, 4096 and 2048 are larger than 1152 so three 0s are written. 1024 is smaller than 1152 so 1 is written and the subtraction is done. $1152 - 1024 = 128$. 512 and 256 are larger than 128 so two 0s are written. $128 = 128$ so a final 1 is written followed by seven more 0s.

## Appendix 4.2   Thirty-six four-state, two-input mini-minds

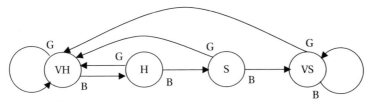

Mini-mind 4659

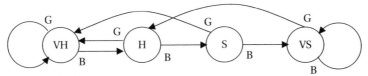

Mini-mind 4663

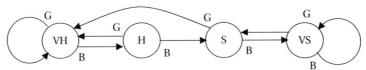

Mini-mind 4667

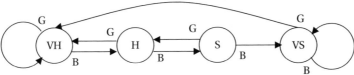

Mini-mind 4723

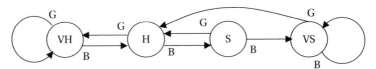

Mini-mind 4727

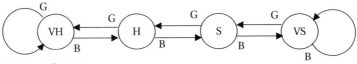

Mini-mind 4731

Continued

**Appendix 4.2** Continued

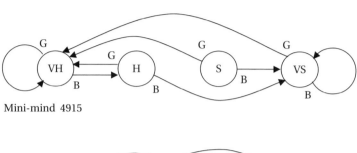

Mini-mind 4915

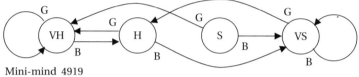

Mini-mind 4919

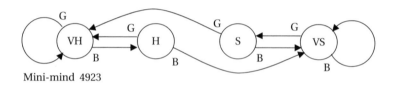

Mini-mind 4923

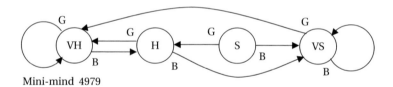

Mini-mind 4979

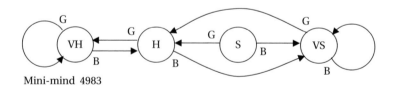

Mini-mind 4983

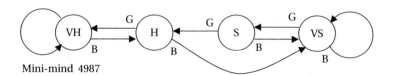

Mini-mind 4987

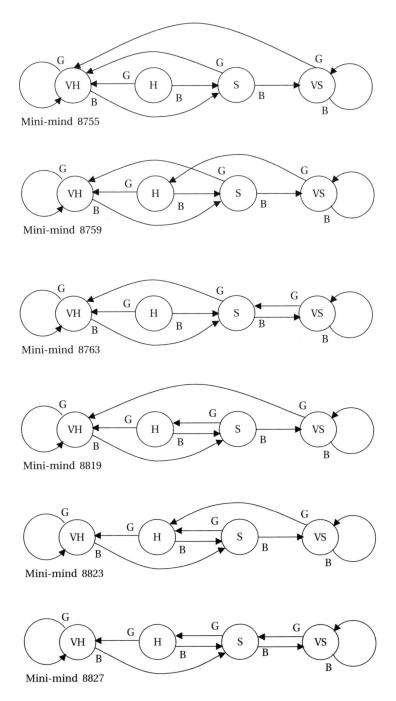

Mini-mind 8755

Mini-mind 8759

Mini-mind 8763

Mini-mind 8819

Mini-mind 8823

Mini-mind 8827

**Continued**

**Appendix 4.2**  Continued

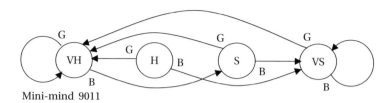

Mini-mind 9011

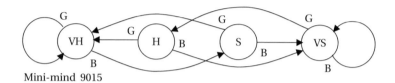

Mini-mind 9015

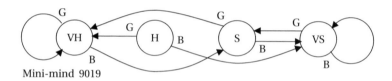

Mini-mind 9019

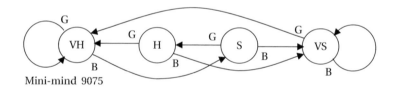

Mini-mind 9075

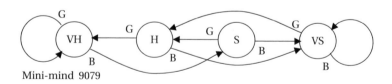

Mini-mind 9079

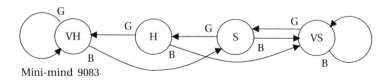

Mini-mind 9083

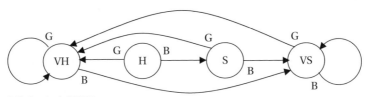

Mini-mind 12851

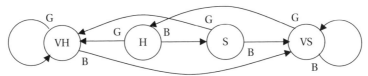

Mini-mind 12855

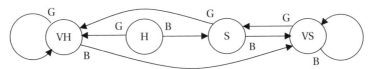

Mini-mind 12859

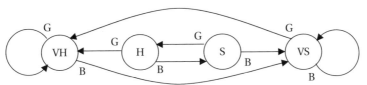

Mini-mind 12915

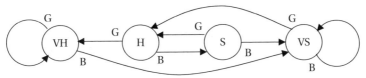

Mini-mind 12919

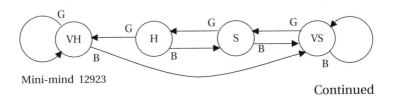

Mini-mind 12923

Continued

**Appendix 4.2**  Continued

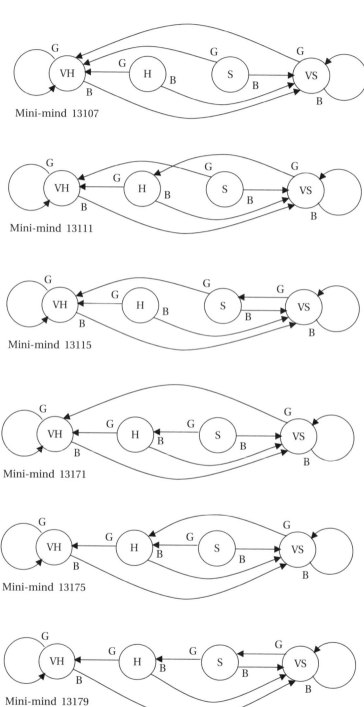

Mini-mind 13107

Mini-mind 13111

Mini-mind 13115

Mini-mind 13171

Mini-mind 13175

Mini-mind 13179

# 5 Environments and Actions

## Introduction

Chapters 3 and 4 introduced mini-minds. A mini-mind is a set of functional states related by transitions which are caused by inputs from an environment containing the mini-mind. The focus so far has been entirely on the state transitions of mini-minds. There has been no consideration of the structure of the environment which delivers inputs nor any consideration of responses by mini-minds which may have effects on the environment. These are the issues with which this chapter is concerned. The nature of the environment and the contribution it makes to the processing of Turing machines are crucial aspects of Turing's theory. Whereas Chapters 3 and 4 were concerned exclusively with the modelling of states of thinking and feeling, this chapter deals with thinking and feeling in the service of action. A Turing machine is a mini-mind connected to a specialized environment. The structure of the environment, the ways in which the mini-mind is connected to it and the resultant possibilities for behaviour are the principal topics of the chapter. Turing's theory of computation has a precise but very restricted model of the environment because he was concerned solely with the processes involved in computing numbers with paper and pencil. It remains a major challenge for psychology to develop functional models of real environments. This is a topic introduced here and discussed further in Chapters 19 and 20. The combination of a mini-mind and a suitably populated environment results in a functional model of processes of thought in action. The model abstracts from the physicality of the real environment just as the account of functional states abstracts from their physicality.

## Specifying places

An important aspect of a functional model of the environment is its concept of a location or place. Roughly speaking, a place is somewhere that can be identified and that has a boundary. Places exist at a variety of scales. London is a place that contains other places. England is a place that contains London. Systems for specifying places may be public or private. The maps of

Britain produced by the Ordnance Survey are a public system for locating and referring to places. 'Places I have been on holiday' is an example of a private system. The Ordnance Survey specifies places using a system called the National Grid which helps to contextualize the discussion of environments. The National Grid is an abstract system of squares of different sizes superimposed on the mapping of the country. The orientation of the grid is roughly North-South, East-West. Each part of the country is contained within one of the squares and places are identified by what are called 'grid references'. The largest scale has squares whose sides are one hundred kilometres long. These squares are identified by pairs of letters. The square TQ includes the part of London where I live. Each hundred kilometre square is divided into one hundred ten kilometre squares numbered from 00 to 99. The grid reference for the ten-kilometre square in which I live is TQ29. The ten-kilometre squares are divided into one kilometre squares by subdivisions of the numerical code. The one-kilometre square in which I live is TQ2986. Further subdivisions allow still more precise place identification. Six figures identify 100 metre squares, eight figures identify 10 metre squares, ten figures identify 1 metre squares and so on. A ten figure grid reference TQ29***86*** is sufficiently fine-grained to locate the desk at which I am writing these words. The theory of computation which Turing developed in 1936 dealt with highly specialized sets of places, namely squares on arithmetic paper. Their sides are at most about a centimetre long and would, therefore, require at least a 14-digit grid reference if they were to be located accurately within the National Grid framework. Grid references always identify squares. As the number of figures increases the sides of the squares get shorter but the reference is always to a square region never to a point. The National Grid is therefore properly thought of as an abstract system of square places and we can think of any plane environment as divided into squares. There are lots of examples of games that use environments composed of squares. Chess is one of the most well known.

## Places and objects

The places and objects that are psychologically salient in our everyday lives span a range of sizes. The smallest objects that can be handled easily are about the size of the squares on paper with which Turing was concerned. Smaller objects are hard to manipulate without tools and tend to be managed by specialists. When we write or calculate, the symbols we form are roughly centimetres in size as are the small everyday objects such as coins and keys that we carry around with us. The objects that we have in our immediate environments like pens, cups, mobile telephones, briefcases, pairs of scissors and so on are roughly tens of centimetres in size. Household appliances and furniture are of the order of metres, our living and work spaces are of the order of tens of metres. Neighbourhoods which are convenient for walking are hundreds of metres or perhaps one or two kilometres in extent. Neighbourhoods which are easily reachable by car are maybe tens of kilometres and a reasonable day's journey on good roads might involve places some hundreds of kilometres apart. Large scale air travel has made journeys of thousands of kilometres practical for various activities like holidays and business meetings. Politicians on the stump, travelling sales representatives, couriers and commuters all rely on rapid mobility from place to place. The ecological psychologist J.J. Gibson, whose work is discussed in greater detail in Chapter 20 wrote in very illuminating ways about environments and size scales, particularly in his final book Gibson (1979).

The National Grid provides a uniform way of describing places at a range of different size scales. Actions at different size scales can also be described in a uniform way in terms of objects and movements. One basic action is to put an object in a specific place. Such actions can have either temporary or permanent effects. When I put a coffee cup on my desk that is an action intended to have a temporary effect. When a builder places a brick and cements it in place while building a wall the effect is intended to be more long lasting. Another basic action is to move an object from one place to another. Moving an object empties one place and fills another. Small objects are relatively easy to move, large ones generally more difficult, but the principle remains the same. Objects as large as a house can be moved from one place to another given sufficient investment of time and effort. An important distinction can be made between objects which are self-propelled and those which are not. The objects in the environments of Turing machines have to be moved by the controlling mini-mind which is the only self-propelled object in its environment. The pieces in a game of chess are static and have to be moved by the players. A game of chess in which the pieces moved of their own accord would be a novel and interesting spectacle. A major challenge for psychology is to model the dynamics of everyday environments containing multiple self-propelled objects.

Although it may be unusual to do so, we can think of writing in terms of the placement of objects. The objects in this case, most often letters and numerals, are symbol objects and writing consists of placing these symbol objects on an appropriate medium. Writing with ink on paper has more or less permanent effects, writing with a pencil on paper has effects that may be modifiable and writing with chalk on a blackboard or with erasable markers on a whiteboard is intended to be temporary. One of the great advantages of the word processor is that it makes the movement of symbol objects from one place to another very easy. Cutting and pasting a paragraph, for example, is an instance in which a collection of symbol objects is moved from one set of places to another. It is valuable to stress the general applicability of the concepts of place, object and movement because they show that although the environment within which Turing defined his machines was highly specialized, his methods can be applied more broadly. Thinking of Turing's work in a wider frame of reference makes it possible to think about how it might be extended to deal with the wide-ranging subject matter of psychology.

## Linear environments

The functional environment of a Turing machine is a linear sequence of places. The houses arranged along one side of a street constitute a linear sequence of places. A series of squares such as a line on a sheet of arithmetic paper also constitutes a linear sequence. We shall need the concept of a sequence of places that has a definite, identifiable starting point but no definite end point. The places are to be squares. We need not be concerned about the size of the squares at the moment except for two provisos: they must be big enough to hold a single object from a specified set and they must be of a size that can be scanned at a glance by an observer. Squares of arithmetic paper meet these criteria as does an approximately square object like my desktop. The definite starting point for the sequence will be a square holding a unique marker.

It is theoretically important that there be no end point defined for the sequence of squares. The reason for this is to accommodate processes that have a fixed starting point but no clear endpoint. There are familiar instances that provide the sort of idea needed. Suppose I were to decide henceforth to adopt the life of a wanderer. I might pack my rucksack, put on my boots, leave the house and walk off down the road. If I stuck to my resolution I might end my life without ever returning home or visiting the same place twice. My journey would traverse a linear sequence of places which got longer and longer until I finally passed away. The longer I lived the longer the sequence of places would become. If I turned out to be immortal, the sequence of places would be endless, although on a finite planet I would eventually have to revisit places. Another example, drawn from the domain that was of concern to Turing is the calculation of numbers like $\pi$ which have endless decimal expressions. A calculation of all the digits of $\pi$ could not be finished in a finite amount of time because there are infinitely many of them. This means that the calculation is like an endless journey. If we were to write one digit of $\pi$ on each of the squares of a linear sequence of places we would need an indefinitely large number of them and an infinite amount of time to complete the task.

The sets of objects that can occupy squares have to be finite and specified in advance. There is no contradiction between this and the fact that a number like $\pi$ requires an infinite number of digits. We distinguish between types and tokens. When we write decimal numbers we use digits from the finite set $\{0, 1, 2, 3, 4, 5, 6, 7, 8, 9\}$ but a particular number may use any number of tokens of a given type. For example, 1223 has one token of 1, two of 2 and one of 3. The objects that computers deal with are symbols but, as already discussed, there is no reason in principle why the same methods should not be applied to familiar objects.

## Situated mini-minds

A mini-mind connected to a linear environment of squares is a system that perceives objects in its environment, that acts on the environment by changing the contents of squares and that moves around the environment from one square to another. Its functional states provide it with responses to its inputs. The connections between the mini-mind and the environment are abstractly specified in terms of what it can do rather than in terms of specific mechanisms. The mini-mind is located in one square of its environment at a time. This square is called the 'scanned' square. If there is an object in the square the mini-mind can perceive it and act upon it. Its configurations, therefore, consist of its scanned functional state and the contents of the current square. There is just one perceptual activity. An object can be recognized for what it is.

Suppose there were two kinds of objects in the environment, say china sheep and china dogs. The reason for this strange choice of objects is simply to make the point that computational ideas can be deployed with a wide range of objects, not just numbers. A mini-mind with suitable functional states connected to this environment can recognise an object as a sheep or a dog. It does not recognize individuals as individuals. All sheep are equal and treated in the same way. Likewise with the dogs. Four actions can be taken with respect to the scanned square. It can be left as it is; if it is empty, a sheep or dog can be put in it; if it is occupied, it can be emptied or the current object can be changed. There are three possible movements for the mini-mind. Stay put, move one square left, move one square right. The activity of the mini-mind consists of a sequence of perception-action cycles. Each cycle consists of an observation of the scanned square, an action, a movement and a state transition.

## Getting inside a mini-mind

Consider the following scenario. It is intended to describe what it might be like to be a Turing machine. Imagine that you wake from sleep and find yourself in a cube shaped room with nothing in it except a door marked 'R'. Your environment is the analogue, in three dimensions, of the two dimensional environment of a mini-mind. Your perception is bounded by the plain walls of the room. There is light to see by but no windows. Try to imagine that you have no memory of your life prior to this moment or any current emotion. It occurs to you that the room would benefit from a sheep. You find yourself, as it were, feeling 'sheepish'. We shall say that your functional state is 'sheepish'. Because of this you say 'Sheep' aloud and a china sheep materializes in the room. (The process of materialization may seem rather strange, but in some ways it is no more strange than the capacity we have, when we write, to make symbols materialize on a sheet of paper.) The presence of the sheep prompts you to move. Leaving the sheep where it is you go through the door marked 'R' into the next room closing the door behind you. The room is identical to the one you have just left except that it has two doors. The door you have just come through is marked 'L' and a door in the opposite wall is marked 'R'. It seems to you that this room should remain empty, (you feel 'emptyish') so you say nothing and go through its 'R' door into a room which is identical to the one you have just left. In this room you find yourself feeling 'doggish'. As a result you say 'Dog' and a china dog materializes in the room. You then move through the 'R' door into the next room, the fourth in the sequence. Here you feel emptyish and you move through the 'R' door into the fifth room. Here you once again feel sheepish. An observer, if there were one, would quickly discern a pattern of objects resulting from your behaviour. The pattern would have a four room cycle, sheep, empty, dog, empty, sheep, empty, dog, empty and so on. The pattern would repeat itself for as long as the observer chose to watch and would continue in that way whether you were observed or not. For you there is no sense of time, simply a process of movement from one room to the next accompanied by feelings and actions that produce the pattern the observer sees. You are not dreaming or sleep-walking; you have no sense of imprisonment or of lacking anything; your mental life has just become very simple. Functional states of the kind described do not involve goals or volition.

**The first sheep and dogs Turing machine**

The process described can be modelled by a mini-mind connected to an environment of squares. This model is our first Turing machine. Considering the mini-mind first, it has a state diagram which is very similar to those in Chapters 3 and 4. The only change is the addition of information to indicate its output and its movement. Figure 5.1 shows the state diagram. It has four functional states. The input to the mini-mind is, as before, indicated by a symbol near the tail of a transition arrow. The symbol '#' is used to represent no input. The lack of an input can be as significant as the presence of one. If someone says 'I'll call you back' and then doesn't, that is significant. Significantly irritating, usually. In the current example the # indicates the perception that a room is empty. The output of the mini-mind and its direc-tion of movement are indicated by symbols written near the middle of a

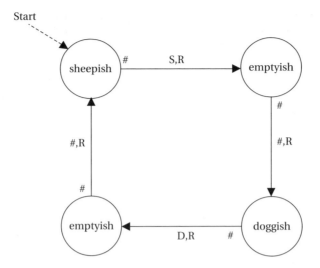

**Figure 5.1**   The first sheep and dogs mini-mind.

transition arrow. A # in this context indicates no output. The dashed arrow pointing to the sheepish state indicates the functional state in which the system starts. The configuration (sheepish, #) describes the mini-mind in the sheepish state in an empty room. A slight modification of the convention adopted in Chapters 3 and 4 allows us to describe the actions that are caused by this configuration. One is an output, (sheepish, #) → S; one is a movement, (sheepish, #) → R; and the third is a state transition, (sheepish, #) → emptyish. For convenience we can put them all together in the single expression (sheepish, #) → (S, R, emptyish).

As noted in Chapter 4, it is conventional to call expressions of this kind 'instructions' and the complete set of instructions defining the behaviour of a mini-mind is called a 'machine table'. It is crucial to note that there is a big difference between behaviour which can be described by instructions and behaviour which is governed by instructions. The distinction is discussed shortly. The current use of instructions is purely descriptive. The output expression (sheepish, #) → S represents both the utterance of the word 'sheep' and the appearance of a china sheep in the room. The utterance is, strictly speaking, unnecessary. Functional states can, as it were, produce results by the power of thought alone. We do not have to speak in order to act. The letter 'R' indicates the move to the next room through the door marked 'R' and the term 'emptyish' indicates a transition to the emptyish state. Three further points are worth making about the diagram. First, it has two functional states named 'emptyish'. Although they share a name they are distinct states and have different functional roles in the mini-mind. We could, if we wished, give them different names, for example 'emptyish 1' and 'emptyish 2' but it is not necessary to do so. Two emptyish states are needed because the configuration (emptyish, #), being deterministic, can have only one state transition associated with it but we need two transitions, one to the sheepish and one to the doggish states. In situations where the same configuration is required to have different actions it has to be assigned to different states. Second, it is obvious from the state diagram that if there is an endless supply of empty rooms, the mini-mind will never stop because its functional states are arranged in a repeating cycle. Finally, I hope it is clear that the choice of objects and actions is arbitrary. We might have chosen objects other than china sheep and dogs, or we might have chosen to equip the occupant of the room with a can of spray paint and have them write graffiti on the walls or floor. The important point is that when a mini-mind is connected to an environment and able to act on it, its behaviour has effects on the environment.

That brings us to a consideration of the environment. The environment to be modelled is a potentially endless sequence of connected rooms. It is portrayed as a series of adjacent squares, each of which represents a room. China sheep are represented by occurrences of the letter 'S' and dogs by occurrences of 'D'. An 'S' written in a square represents a room with a china sheep in it. The mini-mind, viewed from the outside, as it were, is represented as a thought bubble with the name of the current functional state written inside it. The thought bubble is shown emanating from the square representing the room in which the mini-mind is currently located. Figure 5.2 shows the first five steps of the endless process.

Figure 5.2(1) shows the starting configuration of the system (sheepish, #). The actions associated with this configuration are (sheepish, #) → (S, R, emptyish). Figure 5.2(2) shows the results of these actions which produce the next configuration (emptyish, #). And so it goes on. The dashed line at the end of the sequence of squares indicates that it may continue indefinitely.

## Complete configurations and traces of behaviour

The pictorial representation of the environment shows how the process evolves but is rather unwieldy for longer and more complex examples. I have adopted a simpler and more compact scheme. Figure 5.2(1) is represented as follows:

```
##############
|sheepish
```

The line of hashes represents a portion of the environment of empty rooms. Each # represents an empty room. When a room has something in it, it is identified solely by the symbol representing the content. The vertical bar '|' shows the current location of the mini-mind and the name of its current functional state is written next to the bar. A representation of the environment and the mini-mind with an indication of its position and functional

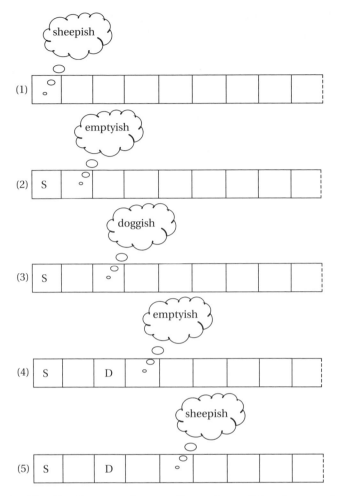

**Figure 5.2** The first five complete configurations of the sheep and dogs example.

state is called a 'complete configuration'. This is Turing's terminology and we shall encounter it frequently throughout the rest of this book. I shall call a sequence of complete configurations a 'trace' of the behaviour of the system. A trace of the next four complete configurations in the process appears as follows:

```
S############
 |emptyish

S############
 |doggish

S#D##########
  |emptyish
```

```
S#D###########
  |sheepish
```

The combination of a linear environment and a mini-mind which can perceive and act on that environment provides all the abstract machinery needed to discuss Turing's work. Turing machines, as we shall see, can be considerably more intricate than the examples considered so far, but the basic operations are always the same.

## Configuration-governed and rule-governed behaviour

It is essential to distinguish the process just modelled from another which has the same output but achieves it in a different way. Here's a description of the second process. You find yourself in an environment which is identical to the one of the first example apart from the following crucial difference. In the second environment you find a sheet of paper headed 'Rules' and a pencil. On the paper is the following set of instructions:

> Look in the box marked 'Current Rule'. Follow the rule whose number you find there. (When you look, you find that the number in the box is '1').
>
> Rule 1: Say 'Sheep'. Change the current rule to Rule 2. Go through the door marked 'R'. Look in the box marked 'Current Rule'. Apply the current rule.
>
> Rule 2: Say nothing. Change the current rule to Rule 3. Go through the door marked 'R'. Look in the box marked 'Current Rule'. Apply the current rule.
>
> Rule 3: Say 'Dog'. Change the current rule to Rule 4. Go through the door marked 'R'. Look in the box marked 'Current Rule'. Apply the current rule.
>
> Rule 4: Say nothing. Change the current rule to Rule 1. Go through the door marked 'R'. Look in the box marked 'Current Rule'. Apply the current rule.

You decide to follow the rules. Because Rule 1 is the current rule you say 'Sheep' and observe that a china sheep materializes in the room. Using the eraser conveniently placed on the end of the pencil you erase the '1' in the box marked 'Current Rule' and write '2' instead. You go through the door marked 'R' into the second room. In the second room you apply Rule 2; in the third, Rule 3; in the fourth Rule 4, and in the fifth you apply Rule 1 again.

An observer watching this process would see the same pattern of sheep and dogs appearing as in the first example but the way in which the pattern is achieved is very different. The first process is governed by configurations (functional states and inputs), the second is governed by the set of rules and there is a world of difference between the two. In the first example, the occupant of the room is caused to act by whatever their current functional state and input happens to be. In the second example, the occupant acts by following a rule. A functional state is not a rule although the behaviour it produces can be described by one. The difference can be illustrated by thinking again about happiness and sadness as functional states. It is not a rule that bad news makes you sad when you're happy, it's just what generally happens. You can of course make up rules such as 'If you hear bad news you should act as though you're sad' but this is a different way of producing behaviour.

Turing machines are governed by configurations, not by rules, although what they do can be described by rules and, as we shall see, in the special case of a universal machine, there is a sense in which its behaviour can be said to be rule-governed. But it is a derivative, secondary sense. Every Turing machine, universal or otherwise, is governed primarily by its configurations. Failure to appreciate the distinction between rule governance and configuration governance is rather common in cognitive science as can be seen from some of the definitions of Turing machines cited in Chapter 1. You will have noticed in the rule-governed example above, that it is necessary to specify the currently applicable rule. If that is not done, the system cannot act because it has no way to tell which rule applies. If you look again at the definitions in Chapter 1, you will find in (a) an indicator unit; in (f) a pointer and tickmarks; and in (g) a register and machine table. These are all ways of indicating an applicable rule and all indicate a failure to recognize that Turing machines are governed by their configurations, not by explicit rules. A system governed by its configurations is always in one of its functional states and acts according to the input it receives. It does not need any indication of what its configuration is. It experiences its configurations rather than perceiving them as parts of external instructions.

The distinction between configuration-governed and rule-governed behaviour is of great importance and more attention is given to it later in the book.

## A further example

For the present let us consider another example of a system governed by configurations in order to gain further familiarity with how such systems work. Imagine, if you will, that you again wake from sleep to find yourself in a room of the kind previously described with just one door in it marked 'R'. Alternatively, if you prefer, imagine that you are observing a creature in such a situation. The mini-mind of the system is shown in Figure 5.3.

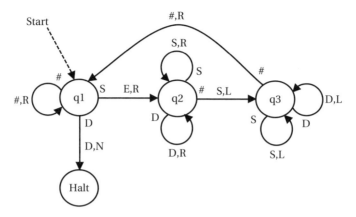

**Figure 5.3**   The state diagram for the second sheep and dogs machine.

Before thinking about what this mini-mind does when situated in a particular environment, there are a few points to notice about its state diagram. First there are some new elements of the notation. There is a state called 'Halt'. As its name implies, this state stops the mini-mind. It is clear from the diagram that there is just one configuration (q1, D) which leads to the halt state. The symbol 'N' indicates no movement and the symbol 'L' indicates a move to the room (or square) to the left. There is an instruction (q1, S) → (E, R, q2) which includes the action 'E'. This represents the utterance of the word 'Empty' in a room with a sheep or a dog in it. It causes the sheep or dog to disappear. Instructions such as (q2, D) → (D, R, q2) and other similar ones have no effect on the contents of the room. A third point to note is that the states other than Halt have names that give no indication of their functions. This has no effect on what the mini-mind does although it may make its activities slightly less easy to understand. It is useful to practice with mini-minds like this, because some of Turing's machines have functional states whose names are not indicative of their functions. Finally, the diagram indicates that the mini-mind is started in functional state q1.

With these points in mind please try the following exercises. Answers are in Appendix 5.1 but it's a good idea to work through them before looking at the appendix. The best way to do this is to write down the successive complete configurations of the process until it halts or you are confident it is not going to.

**Exercise 5.1**   Suppose the mini-mind is started in the situation shown by the complete configuration below; that is, in state q1 in the first room of an environment where there is a sheep in the third room and a dog in the fourth:

```
##SD######
|q1
```

   a. Does the mini-mind halt?
   b. If it does not halt, what does it do?
   c. If it does halt, which room is it in, how many sheep and dogs are
      there and which rooms are they in?

**Exercise 5.2**   Suppose the mini-mind is started in the situation shown
below:

```
#S########
|q1
```

   a. Does the mini-mind halt?
   b. If it does not halt, what does it do?
   c. If it does halt, which room is it in, how many sheep and dogs are
      there and which rooms are they in?

**Exercise 5.3**   Suppose the mini-mind is started in the situation shown
below:

```
SS##DD####
|q1
```

   a. Does the mini-mind halt?
   b. If it does not halt, what does it do?
   c. If it does halt, which room is it in, how many sheep and dogs are
      there and which rooms are they in?

Proceeding on the assumption (correct, I hope!) that you have worked
through the exercises, there are several points to note. The first is that the
behaviour of the mini-mind depends crucially on how the environment is
structured at the start of a process. The mini-mind of Figure 5.3 halts from
some starting configurations and not from others. There is an important,
albeit very general and no doubt widely appreciated moral for psychology
here. A behavioural process which halts after a finite number of steps is
clearly very different, categorically different one might think, from a process
which goes on for ever. The mini-mind exhibits behaviours of both kinds
depending on the starting environment. The moral is that explanations of
behaviour patterns must make reference to both internal and external
structure. This means that neither the environment alone nor the organism
alone can provide a complete basis for psychology. Radical behaviourism is
therefore untenable but so is neural reductionism which is more popular in
some quarters at present. The simple examples of Exercises 5.1–5.3 show
that even if everything possible were known about the structures and
processes of the brain a complete psychological theory would not thereby be
entailed. Psychology has to be based on the study of organism–environment

interactions. It is, in that sense, inescapably an ecological science. There is more about this in Chapters 19 and 20.

A second point of some interest concerns the detection of patterns of behaviour even in the absence of detailed knowledge of every step. The behaviour patterns of the mini-mind can be classified according to the presence or absence of dogs in the environment and the position of the mini-mind relative to the dogs at the start of a process. If there are no dogs in the environment or if the mini-mind is positioned to the right of any dogs at the start of a process, the process will never halt. If there is at least one dog to the right of the mini-mind at the start of a process it is guaranteed to halt regardless of whether there are any sheep in the environment or not. If there is at least one dog to the right of the mini-mind at the start of a process and some sheep between the mini-mind and the dog, the sheep will be gathered up and positioned to the right of the dog at which point the mini-mind will halt. Consider the following starting situation.

```
S##SSS####S#S##SS###D#########
|q1
```

This leads after a number of steps to the final complete configuration

```
###################DSSSSSSSS##
                   |Halt
```

Perhaps I have been playing with these simple machines for too long, but it seems to me that the mini-mind is reminiscent of a shepherd herding sheep with the help of a dog. Larger, more scattered herds take longer to collect together and where they end up depends on where the dog was to start with, but the broad pattern of behaviour is predictable as is the outcome of the process. Shepherds, of course, do not normally herd their flocks through a linear series of rooms, nor do they herd them by making them vanish and re-appear, nor do they herd china sheep with china dogs. However, regardless of the plausibility of this particular interpretation, the patterns exist and can be described.

## Memory in mini-minds

A third point, that will be of great importance later in the book, concerns the way in which the mini-mind can be said to remember things. Consider the following situation:

```
##SDDDDDDDDD##
  |q1
```

From this situation the mini-mind erases the S and moves right making a transition to functional state q2.

```
###DDDDDDDDDD##
   |q2
```

It then makes a further ten moves to the right in state q2 until it reaches the blank square after the sequence of Ds.

```
###DDDDDDDDDD##
             |q2
```

The configuration (q2, #) causes the machine to print S on the blank square, to move left and to make a transition to state q3.

```
###DDDDDDDDDDS#
            |q3
```

Functional state q2 can be said to remember that the mini-mind in state q1 encountered an S and that one has to be printed on the first available blank square. The memory for the S lasts as long as the mini-mind is in state q2. The way this kind of memory system works is seen fully when more than one input may need to be remembered. Suppose, in addition to sheep (S) there were also goats (G) in the environment and that sheep and goats had all to be moved to the right of any dogs in the environment. The mini-mind of Figure 5.4 shows the structure of functional states needed to run the process. The diagram looks complicated at first sight but is really quite straightforward. In order to remember two inputs S and G, an extra state has to be introduced. Configuration (q1,S) → q2, whereas configuration (q1,G) → q3: so the difference between S and G is 'remembered' simply by the path taken through the state diagram. q2 and q3 work in exactly the same fashion until a blank square is encountered. Then, (q2,#) outputs an S and (q3,#) outputs a G. q4 in Figure 5.4 has the same functional role as q3 in Figure 5.3. All the functional states in Figure 5.4 have four configurations defined rather than three because the extra symbol G has been added to the alphabet and has to be dealt with. The technique is quite general. If a third symbol had to be remembered another state would need to be added and additional transitions defined for existing states. The technique is cumbersome but Turing used it extensively in his universal machine design. A large scale example can be seen in Chapter 12, Figure 12.8.

**Exercise 5.4**  Take a simple instance, for example

```
#SGD##
|q1
```

and work through the processing of the mini-mind of Figure 5.4 to satisfy yourself that it functions as described.

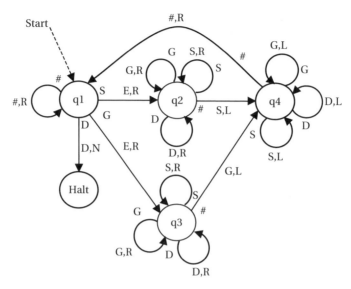

**Figure 5.4**   The state diagram for the sheep, goats and dogs machine.

## Counting situated mini-minds

One more topic which should be touched on briefly before moving to the discussion of Turing's work is the extension of the formula $n^{nk}$ for calculating the numbers of mini-minds which can be put together from $n$ states and $k$ inputs. The formula can be extended to calculate the number of ways in which a mini-mind can be connected to a linear environment with a given number of objects in it. The number of configurations $nk$ is still a crucial term, because configurations determine outputs and movements as well as state transitions. If we have $m$ possible movements and $r$ possible outputs, then each configuration has $n \times m \times r$ possible combinations of actions to choose from because a configuration determines the next state, the movement and the output. Thus the number of logically possible mini-minds situated in environments with $m$ movements and $r$ outputs is $nmr^{nk}$. This formula applies to mini-minds for which a halt state is not defined. If a halt state is defined, we need a slightly modified calculation because the halt state does not form part of any configuration although transitions can be made to it. The appropriate formula in such cases is $(n + 1)mr^{nk}$ for systems with $n$ non-halting states. This formula results in impressively large numbers of systems even when all the terms are small. For example, given the three non-halting states, three inputs, three outputs and three movements of the sheep and dogs example of Figure 5.3 we have $36^9$, which is more than 100,000 billion possible situated mini-minds.

A question which naturally arises given such large numbers is whether there is a way to reduce them by imposing constraints as was done in Chapter 4 for un-situated mini-minds. One possibility is to take the structure of relations between the states and inputs of a mini-mind as given and to think about how many ways there are for its interactions with a given environment to be specified. The extended formula shows that there are $mr^{nk}$ ways in which this can be done for an environment with $m$ directions of movement and $r$ outputs. Unfortunately $mr^{nk}$ is generally a large number of possibilities even when $m$ and $r$ are small. When devising Turing machines it is normally the case that one has a particular pattern of outputs in mind and the environment can be specified accordingly. However, humans generally are not able to choose the items with which their environment is furnished. It may be that people have the huge numbers of functional states that they do in order to be able to cope with the contingencies of environments which contain large numbers of objects.

Situated mini-minds can be given description numbers by a simple extension of the method described in Chapter 4. More digits are added to the numbers to specify the output and movement for each configuration as well as the state transition. The number of additional digits needed depends on the number of possible movements and outputs.

## Summary

The explanation of the basic structures and activities of Turing machines is now complete. Every Turing machine works in essentially the same way as the examples discussed in this chapter. Each Turing machine has a mini-mind with a finite number of functional states, and an environment consisting of a linear tape divided into squares. The squares may be empty or contain tokens chosen from a finite set of object types. The configurations of the Turing machine are formed from its functional states and the objects in its tape environment. The behaviour of the machine is determined by its current configuration, which causes an output, a movement and a state transition.

We now turn to the work that Turing did in On Computable Numbers. The description of Turing's work occupies the next eight chapters.

## Appendix 5.1    Answers to sheep and dog exercises

**Exercise 1**    Suppose the mini-mind to be started in the situation shown by the complete configuration below, that is in state q1 in the first room of an environment where there is a sheep in the third room and a dog in the fourth:

```
##SD######
|q1
```

a.  Does the mini-mind halt?
b.  If it does not halt, what does it do?
c.  If it does halt, which room is it in, how many sheep and dogs are there and which rooms are they in?

To answer the questions we start by tracing the activity of the mini-mind. At the start of the process the mini-mind is in the first room which is empty. This situation is represented by the complete configuration below.

```
##SD######
|q1
```

The relevant instruction is (q1, #) → (#, R, q1). This means that the mini-mind leaves the empty room unchanged and goes through the door marked 'R' into the second room without changing its functional state. The new situation is

```
##SD######
 |q1
```

This is a repeat of the previous situation so the same behaviour happens and leads to an encounter with a sheep in the third room.

```
##SD######
  |q1
```

The relevant instruction is (q1, S) → (E, R, q2). This means that the mini-mind says 'Empty' and the sheep vanishes. The mini-mind then goes through the door marked 'R' into the fourth room and changes state to q2.

```
###D######
   |q2
```

The appropriate instruction is (q2, D) → (D, R, q2). This means that the mini-mind leaves the dog where it is and goes through the 'R' door into the fifth room without changing state.

```
###D######
    |q2
```

The room is empty. Because the mini-mind is in state q2, the relevant instruction is (q2, #) → (S, L, q3). This causes the mini-mind to say 'Sheep', a sheep materializes in the room, the mini-mind goes through the door marked 'L' back into the fourth room and changes state to q3.

```
###DS#####
  |q3
```

The dog is still in the fourth room so the relevant instruction is (q3, D) → (D, L, q3) and the mini-mind goes through the 'L' door into the third room leaving the dog in place and without changing state.

```
###DS#####
  |q3
```

The relevant instruction is (q3, #) → (#, R, q1). The mini-mind leaves the third room empty, moves through the 'R' door into the fourth room and makes a transition to state q1, the first time it has been in this state since the fourth step of the process.

```
###DS#####
  |q1
```

The relevant instruction is (q1, D) → (D, N, Halt). The mini-mind leaves the dog undisturbed, stays where it is and halts. The process is finished. What it has done, in effect, is to move the sheep from the room on the left of the dog to the room on its right although it has achieved this by dematerialising the sheep in room 3 and materializing one in room 5.

```
###DS#####
  |Halt
```

The answers to the questions are (a) Yes, (b) Not applicable, (c) The mini-mind is in room 4, there is one dog also in room 4 and one sheep in room 5.

**Exercise 2**   Suppose the mini-mind to be started in the situation shown below:

```
#S########
 |q1
```

a.   Does the mini-mind halt?
b.   If it does not halt, what does it do?
c.   If it does halt, which room is it in, how many cats and dogs are there and which rooms are they in?

One path to the answers is to start as with Exercise 1 by tracing the complete configurations through which the situated mini-mind passes.

```
#S########
|q1
#S########
 |q1
##########
  |q2
##S#######
 |q3
##S#######
  |q1
```

At this point it is possible to see that the situation is the same as it was in the second complete configuration but with everything moved one room to the right. Since the mini-mind is deterministic, the sequence of transitions from q1 to q2 to q3 and back to q1 will repeat forever. The answers therefore are (a) No, (b) The mini-mind moves to the right forever, taking the sheep with it, (c) Not applicable.

The observant reader may have spotted that question (a) can be answered without tracing the behaviour of the mini-mind at all. The answer depends on noticing that the halt state can only be reached from q1 when there is a dog in the room. Since there are no dogs at the start of Exercise 2 and no action which puts a dog in a room which did not already have one, the mini-mind can never halt.

**Exercise 3**   Suppose the mini-mind to be started in the situation shown below:

```
SS##DD####
|q1
```

a.   Does the mini-mind halt?
b.   If it does not halt, what does it do?
c.   If it does halt, which room is it in, how many cats and dogs are there and which rooms are they in?

The process that takes place is, essentially, a combination of the actions of the processes in Exercises 1 and 2. The first part of the process removes the sheep from rooms 1 and 2 and puts sheep in rooms 3 and 4. Ten steps change the situation from

```
SS##DD####
|q1
```

to

```
##SSDD####
  |q1
```

A further nine steps remove the sheep from room three and install one in room seven. These changes lead to the complete configuration

```
###SDDS###
   |q1
```

Another nine steps remove the sheep from room four and install one in room eight leading to the complete configuration

```
####DDSS##
    |q1
```

The halting condition now obtains so the mini-mind stops. The answers to the questions are (a) Yes, (b) Not applicable, (c) The mini-mind is in room five; there are two dogs, one in room five and one in room six; there are two sheep, one in room seven and one in room eight.

# 6   Turing's Analysis of Computation

## Introduction

Chapters 3–5 have introduced the techniques needed for a study of Turing's work. A Turing machine is a mini-mind connected to an unlimited linear environment of squares. The purpose of this chapter is to explain why Turing developed such a machine, why it has strange characteristics like an infinite, one-dimensional tape and why, despite these strange characteristics, the Turing machine is important for psychological theory. The starting point for a proper appreciation of the Turing machine is an understanding of the analysis that led to it. Turing machines were the result of his thinking about the processes that a human, calculating with paper and pencil, could carry out. The underlying issue to which his work was directed, as mentioned in Chapter 1, was the concept of effective calculability. The relevant sense of 'effective' is the everyday notion of success in producing a result. The question of what constitutes an effective calculation arose when mathematicians with an interest in the foundations of their subject began, systematically, to examine how mathematics works and what it is about. Among their reasons for doing this were the discovery in the late nineteenth century of some deep-seated and disturbing paradoxes arising from ideas and practices that had previously seemed innocuous. Russell's paradox, which undermined Frege's attempt to found mathematics on logic, is a famous example. Russell's letter to Frege describing the paradox and Frege's reply have been reprinted by van Heijenoort (1967).

   In the 1930s three different formal approaches offering precise models of the intuitive notion of effective calculability appeared. They were lambda definability, Church (1936), general recursiveness, Kleene (1936) and Turing computability, Turing (1936). Background material and discussions of the three approaches can be found in Gandy (1988) and Sieg (1994). The three approaches turned out to be equivalent in the sense that they agreed about which numbers can be calculated by following definite sets of rules, but Turing's approach came to be seen as more convincing than either of the others. The main reason for this was that Turing investigated effective calculability by looking at the possible behaviours of a human working with paper and pencil. Turing did not ask 'What is a computable function?' or 'What is a computable number?' as Church and Kleene did. Instead he asked about what has to be done to compute a number or a function. 'The real question at issue is "What are the possible processes which can be carried out in computing a number?" ' (Turing 1936, p. 249). This question invites an answer which is striking in its directness and simplicity. The possible processes are exactly those that produce a sequence of symbols which represents the number to be computed. If the number to be computed is the positive square root of four, for example, the processes involved are those that produce the sequence consisting of the single symbol '2'. To answer the question about possible processes in a general way, Turing analysed the constraints that limit the capacities of a human computer and identified effective calculability with the capacities of a machine that reflected those limits.

Turing's focus on processes is significant for psychology because his method points beyond itself. The immediate subject matter is the computation of numbers but as Chapter 5 illustrates the investigation of processes is one which can be extended well beyond the concern with numbers. We might, for example, ask 'What are the possible processes that can be carried out in reaching a decision?' or 'What are the possible processes that can be carried out in perceiving that the person approaching is friendly or hostile?'

## Terminology

There is a terminological difficulty that affects everyone who writes about the early history of computing machines. The term 'computer' is ambiguous. To contemporary minds it refers primarily to machines but to Turing in 1936 it meant a human engaged in calculation. Considerable confusion can be engendered as a result and lexical separation of the two meanings is desirable. Robin Gandy, who studied with Turing and was his friend, suggested using 'computor' to refer to the human but the Oxford English Dictionary calls this a bad spelling of 'computer'. The dictionary offers 'computant', 'computator' and 'computist'. 'Computant' is rather pleasing. It has an echo of the skill of the executant and was used by the essayist Thomas Carlyle in 1827. 'Any man endowed with the arithmetical facility of a tapster, might have solved this problem without difficulty, yet, for an untaught computant, the gift of divination was essential.' Carlyle's suggestion that a little arithmetical skill is a great aid to problem solving is apt in the context of this book so I shall use 'computant' to refer to a human calculating with paper and pencil and use 'computer' to refer to a machine.

## The scope of Turing's analysis

Turing's analysis of computation is the subject of his famous paper *On Computable Numbers with an Application to the Entscheidungsproblem.*

The paper concerns both the scope and limits of mechanical computation and (eventually) established Turing's reputation as a major theorist. The paper begins with a sketch of what was to become known as a Turing machine and moves on rapidly via some simple examples to the design for a 'universal' machine. This was a single machine which could simulate the functioning of any of the countable infinity of Turing machines.

It is worth considering briefly what the term 'countable infinity' means. In Chapter 4 the number of possible mini-minds of a given size was calculated using the formula $n^{nk}$. The formula was modified in Chapter 5 to $nmr^{nk}$ to include outputs and movements and the concept of a description number was introduced. It was shown that the mini-minds of a given size could be put in a list ordered by their description numbers. A further list can be made consisting of all the lists of mini-minds of a given size. Because there is no limit to the number of functional states or inputs a Turing machine might have there is also no limit to the size of description numbers. However, because these numbers are integers they can be put in order. Thus there is no limit to the number of possible Turing machines but each has a definite place in the list. This is what it means to say that there is a countable infinity of Turing machines. The matter is discussed again, more precisely, in Chapter 9.

The universal machine, which is the theoretical ancestor of the stored program digital computer, demonstrates that the concept of mechanical calculation is very broad indeed but Turing went on to prove that there were clear limits to what could be done with a rigid, rule-following machine. These proofs are discussed in Chapter 13. 'On Computable Numbers' is a document of enormous significance for cognitive science and AI because it sets out both the scope and the limits of computing machines and does so in a way that relates them unambiguously to their human progenitors. Turing machines have been compared to various things including typewriters and factory assembly lines but in fact they stem from the careful consideration that Turing gave to the possible processes carried out by computants such as ourselves when we add up a restaurant bill or work out our income tax or compute the decimal expansion of $\pi$. There is no better starting point than his own description:

> We may compare a man in the process of computing a real number to a machine which is only capable of a finite number of conditions $q_1$, $q_2$, …, $q_R$ which will be called '$m$-configurations'. The machine is supplied with a 'tape' (the analogue of paper) running through it, and divided into sections (called 'squares') each capable of bearing a 'symbol'. At any moment there is just one square, say the $r$-th, bearing the symbol $\mathfrak{S}(r)$ which is 'in the machine'. We may call this square the 'scanned' square. The symbol on the scanned square may be called the 'scanned symbol'. The 'scanned symbol' is the only one of which the machine is, so to speak, 'directly aware'. However, by altering its $m$-configuration the machine can effectively

remember some of the symbols which it has 'seen' (scanned) previously. The possible behaviour of the machine at any moment is determined by the $m$-configuration $q_n$ and the scanned symbol $\mathfrak{S}(r)$. This pair $q_n$, $\mathfrak{S}(r)$ will be called the 'configuration': thus the configuration determines the possible behaviour of the machine. In some of the configurations in which the scanned square is blank (i.e. bears no symbol) the machine writes down a new symbol on the scanned square: in other configurations it erases the scanned symbol. The machine may also change the square which is being scanned, but only by shifting it one place to right or left. In addition to any of these operations the $m$-configuration may be changed. Some of the symbols written down will form the sequence of figures which is the decimal of the real number which is being computed. The others are just rough notes to 'assist the memory'. It will only be these rough notes which will be liable to erasure. (OCN pp. 231–2)

Turing went on to claim that the model was complete. 'It is my contention that these operations include all those which are used in the computation of a number' (OCN p. 232). It should be reasonably clear how Turing's terminology relates to the concepts introduced in earlier chapters. The 'machine which is only capable of a finite number of conditions $q_1, q_2, ..., q_R$' is a mini-mind and its 'conditions' are the functional states of the mini-mind. Turing calls them '$m$-configurations'. The tape with which a Turing machine is equipped is the linear environment discussed in Chapter 5. The machine is linked to the tape by the processes of scanning, printing and moving. Turing uses the term 'configuration' in exactly the way that it has been used in the earlier chapters of the book. It is a combination of a functional state and the contents of a square of the tape. Turing makes it completely clear from the start that the machine is based on a human model (see Figure 6.1).

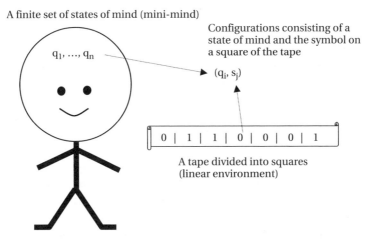

A finite set of states of mind (mini-mind)

$q_1, ..., q_n$

Configurations consisting of a state of mind and the symbol on a square of the tape

$(q_i, s_j)$

| 0 | 1 | 1 | 0 | 0 | 0 | 1 |

A tape divided into squares (linear environment)

**Figure 6.1**   The components of Turing's model of the human computant.

The analysis is concerned specifically with 'the process of computing a real number'. It is not a general analysis of human behaviour.

## Derivation of the machine model

The key part of OCN for those who wish to understand why Turing machines have the characteristics that they do, is section 9, particularly sub-section I, pp. 249–52. In that part of the paper, Turing justified his proposals for the machine design by analysing the processes involved in calculation by humans. The analysis starts with the simple observation, 'Computing is normally done by writing certain symbols on paper' (OCN p. 249). This observation makes it clear from the start that the subject of Turing's analysis was not mental arithmetic but paper and pencil calculation. The system he was studying was the mind of the computant using the external media of paper and pencil. The point is significant for cognitive science because it is generally assumed, wrongly, that the tape of the Turing machine is a model of the memory of the computant.

### The Turing machine tape

With regard to the characteristics of the medium, Turing noted that

> Computing is normally done by writing certain symbols on paper. We may suppose this paper is divided into squares like a child's arithmetic book. In elementary arithmetic the two-dimensional character of the paper is sometimes used. But such a use is always avoidable, and I think that it will be agreed that the two-dimensional character of paper is no essential of computation. I assume then that the computation is carried out on one-dimensional paper, *i.e.* on a tape divided into squares. (OCN p. 249)

This short statement is the origin of the famous Turing machine tape and is the reason why so much time was spent describing operations on linear environments in Chapter 5. The reason for the reduction of the medium to one dimension is that it makes the construction of computing machines easier without the loss of any functionality. Turing claims that any calculation which can be done on ordinary paper can also be done on a one-dimensional tape. It does not, of course, follow from this that the calculation can be done in the same way on a tape as it would on paper. From a psychological point of view, where the concern is often with *how* something is done as well as with *what* is done, the differences may be important. However, Turing's concern was with understanding the essentials of numerical calculation. The one-dimensional tape divided into squares includes the essential characteristic of distinct locations.

People who are familiar with Turing machines know that they have infinitely long tapes and this point has sometimes been used to argue that it is not possible to construct a 'real' Turing machine because the physical resources out of which it can be made are finite. The need for an infinite tape stems from the fact, discussed in Chapter 5 that the processes carried out by Turing machines may be endless. Each Turing machine, as Turing defined them, computes a single number with infinite precision. Turing never explicitly says in OCN that the tape has to be infinite but we infer this from the nature of the numbers to be computed. Turing machines which halt having used only a finite amount of space are real, practical possibilities; there would be no difficulty at all in building one. Turing, however, did not define a halt state for any of his machines but introduced a distinction between 'circular' and 'circle-free' machines which is relevant to questions about halting. The distinction is discussed in Chapter 7.

## The symbols needed for computation

After his brief discussion of the reduction of two-dimensional paper to a one-dimensional tape, Turing went on to consider the number of symbols needed for computation. His argument is brief and somewhat elliptical as well.

> I shall also suppose that the number of symbols which may be printed is finite. If we were to allow an infinity of symbols, then there would be symbols differing to an arbitrarily small extent. (OCN p. 249)

In this passage Turing is making a point about perceptual limitations. To understand the point, the distinction between symbol types and symbol tokens introduced in Chapter 5 is needed. The type of a symbol is what identifies it, that which makes it what it is. Symbols of type 0 are different from symbols of type 1. Tokens are instances of a particular symbol type. 1 and 1 are tokens of the same type; 0 and 1 are tokens of different types. If you find you have difficulty in reading someone's handwriting because you can't work out what the letters are, you are having trouble identifying the types of the letters. Turing's point is about types rather than tokens. Imagine a tape with squares whose sides are a centimeter long. How many distinguishable symbol types could you write on the square? Clearly the number would have to be relatively small because the more you tried to fit, the smaller the observable differences between them would be and the greater the potential for confusion. If there were infinitely many different symbol types of a size which would fit a tape square, the differences between them would be so small that there would be cases when a token would be misperceived and assigned to the wrong type and this would cause a mistake in the computation.

Turing appears to have had both human and machine limitations in mind although the explicit reference to printing suggests a focus on the action of machines at this point in the paper. He suggested that the restriction to a finite alphabet of symbols was not a serious limitation because sequences of symbols could be treated as single symbols. For the purposes of numerical computation it is clear that a finite alphabet of symbols does not put any limit on what can be calculated. We know that indefinitely large numbers can be represented in decimal or binary notation and, indeed, also in unary notation where we might, for example, have $1 = 1, 11 = 2, 111 = 3$ and so on. A collection of symbols like '111' is called a compound symbol. Turing's concern with the constraints on practical computation led him to observe that

> The differences from our point of view between the single and compound symbols is [sic] that the compound symbols, if they are too lengthy, cannot be observed at one glance. This is in accordance with experience. We cannot tell at a glance whether 9999999999999999 and 999999999999999 are the same. (OCN p. 250)

This rather mundane point illustrates the great care which Turing took to identify the constraints on the human capacity for computation and to factor them into his machine design. The difference between single and compound symbols is significant for the design of a machine because a machine which could distinguish 9999999999999999 from 999999999999999 at a glance would not be a faithful model of a human computant who cannot do this. Turing's concern was that if his machines were allowed to distinguish compound symbols in ways that humans cannot distinguish them the machines might possibly be able to compute numbers beyond the range of effective human computation and this would undermine the goal of his study which was to understand exactly those numbers which can be computed by people.

The intimate relationship between the Turing machine model and the human computant is poorly understood in cognitive science and, as a result, the Turing machine model is undervalued. As we saw in Chapter 1, even an enthusiast for computational methods like Steven Pinker misunderstands what Turing was trying to do when he says 'Turing merely wanted to prove that *some* arrangement of gadgets could function as an intelligent symbol-processor' (Pinker 1997, p. 68). In fact Pinker is doubly wrong. Not only was Turing concerned that the arrangement of gadgets should be constrained in the same ways as human computants are, he was also concerned that the gadgetry should not require intelligence. An effective computation is precisely one that requires nothing more than the ability to follow a rule or to be governed by functional states. It most definitely does not require the exercise of either intelligence or intuition. Pinker has mixed up Turing's work on effective computation with his later work on whether computers could be made to display intelligence.

If a machine were able to use an infinite number of symbols it would not be possible to construct a finite description of it, because each symbol has to be mentioned explicitly in the description. Turing did not discuss this point directly. The central importance of finite machine descriptions for the development of his theory makes it seem like a curious omission but it stems from the need to provide independent justification for the restriction to finite means. The point, again, is to show that the mechanical analysis follows from the way that humans compute. The machine models are convincing precisely because the analysis of the human case is convincing. If Turing had simply insisted on a finite symbol alphabet because otherwise his machine descriptions would be infinite he would have left open the possibility that the machines would fail to capture some aspect of the capacities of human computants. It was, in fact, implicit in Turing's analysis and later proved by Shannon (1956) that any effective calculation can be carried out by a machine using only a two-symbol alphabet.

## Perceiving the environment

Following the discussion of symbols, Turing began to analyse the contribution of the human computant to the process of calculation. He started by discussing the perceptual constraints on the connection between the computant and the environment.

> The behaviour of the computer at any moment is determined by the symbols which he is observing, and his 'state of mind' at that moment. We may suppose that there is a bound $B$ to the number of symbols or squares which the computer can observe at one moment. If he wishes to observe more, he must use successive observations. (OCN p. 250)

When Turing says 'We may suppose that there is a bound $B$ ...' he is saying in mathematical terminology what we all know from everyday experience, namely that there is a limit to the number of symbols that a human can observe in a single glance. You can't take in a complete page of print in a single glance. Thus the bound $B$ reflects a perceptual constraint on the computant. If we wished to put a specific value on $B$ we would need to consider facts about the nature of the human visual system, for example the narrow visual angle covered by the fovea (Palmer 1999, p. 31), and the resolving power of the human visual system but Turing did not need to be precise about this. He was not trying to model human perception exactly but to identify and work within the constraints which limit it. We know that humans can observe single symbols, so if a machine is limited to observing single symbols it will be working within the range of human capability.

## States of mind

The previously quoted passage continues:

> We will also suppose that the number of states of mind which need be taken into account is finite. The reasons for this are of the same character as those which restrict the number of symbols. If we admitted an infinity of states of mind, some of them will be 'arbitrarily close' and will be confused. Again the restriction is not one which seriously affects computation, since the use of more complicated states of mind can be avoided by writing more symbols on the tape. (OCN p. 250)

It was a bold step for Turing to assert that only a finite number of states of mind need be taken into account and it is a pivotal point of his analysis. Turing's justification for the point is, like his argument for a finite number of symbols, extremely brief. In fact it is more of an assertion than an argument. He simply says that an infinity of states of mind would lead to confusion between them. I think his point can be understood as an early commitment to the idea that the mind supervenes on the brain.

The supervenience relation means, roughly, that any change in mental state that can correctly be ascribed to an individual implies a corresponding change in the physical state of the brain because mental state changes are caused by brain state changes. The finitude of the mind follows from the finitude of the brain and the relation of supervenience between them, but the supervenience thesis does not entail that mental states are reducible to physical states of the brain. The concept of supervenience is discussed in detail by Kim (1993). At root, I think Turing's point about the finitude of the mind comes to this. If there is no mind without brain then distinct mental states have to be represented by distinct parts of the brain or combinations of them. Given that the brain has only a finite number of physical parts and combinations of parts this means that there can only be a finite number of distinguishable states of mind.

The logician Kurt Gödel objected to the suggestion that the mind has only a finite number of possible states and described it as an error. His views are discussed further in Chapter 13. The finite bound on the number of mental states is also in conflict with versions of the computational theory of mind which argue, in principle, on productivity grounds, for a countable infinity of mental states. The influential argument of Fodor and Pylyshyn (1988) is a clear example. The argument is discussed more fully in Chapters 16 and 17 but it is helpful to introduce it briefly here. It is clear that natural languages can encode indefinitely many propositions because complex propositions can be built up from a finite set of atomic elements such as words. This characteristic is described as 'productivity'. It is assumed, by theorists who support the idea of a language of thought (cf. Fodor 1975; Fodor and

Pylyshyn 1988), that thinking is also productive for the same reasons, namely that complex thoughts are built up from a fixed set of conceptual atoms. This picture is compatible with the idea that mental representations are symbol structures. The productivity argument is related to 'systematicity' arguments and to the idea that inference is explicable in proof-theoretic terms. Turing's characterization of states of mind as elements of a fixed, finite set of functional entities with specified relations among them is fundamentally at odds with the whole edifice of productivity, systematicity and proof-theoretic arguments that depend on the postulation of a language of thought. The symbol structures with which a Turing machine interacts are outside the mind, not part of it.

Turing's assertion that more complicated states of mind can be avoided by writing more symbols on the tape confirms the view that the tape was not intended to model part of the mind. If sequences of symbols on the tape were parts of states of mind writing more symbols would not reduce the complexity of those states. It would, if anything, increase them.

### The actions of the computant

Having specified the sets of symbols and states of mind to be used in the construction of computing machines and having considered the perceptual constraints on the computant, Turing then turned to the computant's actions.

> Let us imagine the operations performed by the computer to be split up into 'simple operations' which are so elementary that it is not easy to imagine them further divided. Every such operation consists of some change of the physical system consisting of the computer and his tape. We know the state of the system if we know the sequence of symbols on the tape, which of these are observed by the computer (possibly with a special order), and the state of mind of the computer. We may suppose that in a simple operation not more than one symbol is altered. Any other changes can be split up into simple changes of this kind. The situation in regard to the squares whose symbols may be altered in this way is the same as in regard to the observed squares. We may, therefore, without loss of generality, assume that the squares whose symbols are changed are always 'observed' squares. (OCN p. 250)

This passage sets out the simple, one step at a time, operations that are characteristic of Turing machines. It is clearly right to suppose that the writing or alteration of a single symbol is the elementary visible operation in paper and pencil calculation no matter how complex the eventual end result. It is just possible to imagine someone writing symbols with both hands simultaneously or using a pen with multiple nibs like the tines of a fork, but the natural way to carry out a calculation is one symbol at a time. Turing does not at this stage say that we can assume that only one square is observed. He hints at the idea that operations involving states of mind may be decomposed into simple operations as well but says no more about such operations at this stage beyond making the implicitly anti-dualist point that every simple operation involves a change of a physical system.

Turing says that we know the state of the system if we know three things; the complete sequence of symbols on the tape, which symbols are observed and the computant's state of mind. This information constitutes what we have called a 'complete configuration'. The state of mind is clearly, although implicitly, taken to be just those aspects of the computant's mental activity that are relevant to the task at hand. This is a key point and one that is essential to the project of mechanization. In the normal course of a calculation very few of us are wholly focused on what we are doing. We get bored, we experience changing emotions, ideas about other topics interrupt the train of thought and so forth. None of these features of everyday experience is part of the essence of calculation and Turing ignores them all. He also ignores everything else that in a wider analysis might be thought to be part of the system. The table on which the paper rests; the chair on which the computant sits; the room containing the table and chair: all these are irrelevant to the computational task.

The care with which Turing thought through the analysis is further shown by the fact that he explicitly considers whether the tape squares whose symbols are changed are to be counted among the observed squares. This is like asking whether the room in which a mini-mind finds itself is the room in which its actions take effect. A less careful analyst might not even have noticed that there was a question to be asked here because it seems obvious that to write a symbol on a square one must be observing it. But it is certainly possible for a human computant to write a symbol on a sheet of paper that is not currently being observed (one might write with closed eyes or in the dark) and it is important for a water-tight analysis to consider whether such a possibility might somehow extend the scope of effective computation. Turing concludes that it does not and that no loss of generality results from changing symbols on observed squares only. This simplifies the construction of a computing machine. One final point is worth brief mention. When Turing talks about the symbols which are observed by the computant he adds the parenthetical remark that they may be observed 'with a special order'. Presumably what he has in mind here is that the interpretation of a complex symbol, 1101 for example, depends on whether one takes the least significant digit to be at the left or at the right. If 1101 is interpreted as a binary numeral with the least significant digit at the right the decimal value is 13; with the least significant digit at the left it is 11. Having dealt with changes of symbols, Turing goes on to consider how the computant may switch attention from one set of observed squares to another.

> Besides these changes of symbols, the simple operations must include changes of distribution of observed squares. The new observed squares must be immediately recognizable by the computer. I think it is reasonable to suppose that they can only be squares whose distance from the closest of the immediately previously observed squares does not exceed a certain fixed amount. Let us say that each of the new observed squares is within L squares of an immediately previously observed square. (OCN p. 250)

The new squares are required to be immediately recognizable because if they were not, the switch of attention could not be thought of as an elementary operation. Turing opts to define the potentially tricky concept of 'immediate recognizability' in terms of a bound L which links newly observed squares to previously observed ones. If we wished to find a maximum value for L we would need, as with B, to consider a variety of empirical matters, such as facts to do with the acuity of the visual system, the size of tape squares and the symbols printed on them. But Turing is not obliged to specify L precisely as long as the behaviour of the machine clearly operates within the range of the capabilities of the human computant. The squares immediately to the right and left of a currently recognized square are obviously immediately recognizable and they can be reached with L set to one. Other squares can be reached by further moves, one square at a time, so the bound L can be fixed at one without impairing recognizability.

There is one further aspect to immediate recognizability that requires analysis. This is the idea that squares marked by particular symbols might be immediately recognizable. Turing carefully distinguishes two cases.

> Now if these squares are marked only by single symbols there can be only a finite number of them, and we should not upset our theory by adjoining these marked squares to the observed squares. If, on the other hand, they are marked by a sequence of symbols, we cannot regard the process of recognition as a simple process. This is a fundamental point and should be illustrated. In most mathematical papers the equations and theorems are numbered. Normally the numbers do not go beyond (say) 1000. It is, therefore, possible to recognise a theorem at a glance by its number. But if the paper was very long, we might reach Theorem 157767733443477; then, further on in the paper, we might find '… hence (applying Theorem 157767733443477) we have …'. In order to make sure which was the relevant theorem we should have to compare the two numbers figure by figure, possibly ticking the figures off in pencil to make sure of their not being counted twice. (OCN p. 251)

The technique of comparing two strings of symbols element by element is a technique that Turing uses in the universal machine. A final catch-all proposal is that any other kind of immediate recognizability can be allowed 'so long as these squares can be found by some process of which my type of machine is capable' (OCN p. 251).

Having exhaustively thought through the means needed to mechanize the observable aspects of a computation, Turing then considers the changes of mental state that may also be needed to sustain the process from one step to the next. Changes of state of mind, that is, state transitions, are discussed only in the context of symbol changes and switches of attention. 'It may be that some of these changes necessarily involve a change of state of mind' (OCN p. 251). From this he arrives at the conclusion that the most general single operation must be of one of two kinds; (a) a possible change of symbol and a possible change of state of mind; (b) a possible change of observed squares and a possible change of state of mind. Turing repeats the point that the operation which is actually carried out is determined by the current state of mind of the computant and by the symbols currently being observed. He notes that 'In particular, they determine the state of mind of the computer after the operation is carried out' (OCN p. 251).

## The construction of a machine to do
## the work of a computant

Finally we come to the conclusion of the analysis and its application to the construction of a machine.

> We may now construct a machine to do the work of this computer. To each state of mind of the computer corresponds an '$m$-configuration' of the machine. The machine scans $B$ squares corresponding to the $B$ squares observed by the computer. In any move the machine can change a symbol on a scanned square or can change any one of the scanned squares to another square distant not more than $L$ squares from one of the other scanned squares. The move which is done, and the succeeding configuration, are determined by the scanned symbol and the $m$-configuration. (OCN pp. 251–2)

Turing machines generally respect the most constrained bounds possible, with $B = 1$ and $L = 1$. The newly observed square is always immediately to the right or left of the previously observed square. Turing does not say how the $m$-configurations of a machine are related to each other, nor indeed how they interact with symbol structures on the tape of the machine. That is a matter for the detailed analysis of particular tasks. It is entirely clear, however, that the machine architecture is designed specifically to respect the constraints which limit the computational powers of human computants no matter what task they are engaged in. Turing machines have finite mini-minds because human memory is 'necessarily limited' and they have infinite tapes because a fixed amount of paper is not an intrinsic limitation on human calculation.

The correspondence between Turing's machines and the examples of situated mini-minds considered in Chapter 5 is straightforward. The $m$-configurations of the Turing machine correspond to the functional states of a mini-mind. The single square of tape that the machine scans corresponds to the room that the mini-mind is in. The newly observed square corresponds to the room that the mini-mind moves to. The symbols written and changed correspond to the sheep and dogs that appear and disappear. Please note also that there is no mention in Turing's work of a Turing machine consulting a machine table or having a pointer to indicate its current $m$-configuration. Turing means what he says: the move which is made and the succeeding configuration are determined by the scanned symbol and the $m$-configuration, not by an explicit rule that mentions them.

# 7 Turing's Example Machines

In Section 3 of 'On Computable Numbers', Turing described two machines that illustrate some aspects of the design of the universal machine. The two machines are situated mini-minds essentially like those discussed in Chapter 5 but Turing's terminology and notation are somewhat different. Anyone who wishes to follow the technical detail in OCN needs to understand how Turing's notation works. However, some readers may wish to understand Turing's constructions without reading the original paper themselves. I have, therefore, approached the machines in OCN in four ways. I have provided verbal descriptions, state diagrams, traces and discussion of Turing's own notation. The verbal descriptions outline what the machines do, the state diagrams and traces of process behaviour provide full details as in Chapters 3–5 and I also discuss Turing's notation and his machine tables. These are interesting for the insight they give into Turing's way of tackling the complexities involved in the universal machine. Before getting into the detail there are some matters of terminology to discuss.

## *m*-configurations, configurations and complete configurations

Turing uses the term 'configuration' in three contexts. An *m*-configuration is an internal state of the control automaton of a Turing machine. The term is shorthand for 'machine-configuration'. It is analogous to a 'state of mind' of a human computant. *M*-configurations are the functional states of mini-minds.

Configurations are 'ordered pairs' consisting of an *m*-configuration and a symbol. As we have seen, Turing uses the term in exactly the way that it has been used in the earlier chapters of the book. Turing describes an arbitrary configuration as '$q_n, \mathfrak{S}(r)$'. The symbol $\mathfrak{S}$ is 'S' in a font called Fraktur. Turing used Fraktur throughout OCN to represent the *m*-configurations of machines, but it is hard to read and, as his biographer put it, turns much of the paper into 'a thicket of obscure German Gothic type'. I have maintained the Gothic connection by using, instead of 𝕱𝕽𝖆𝖐𝖙𝖚𝖗, a font called **Franklin Gothic Demi**, which is easier to read. For example, **(q1,0)** is the ordered pair consisting of the *m*-configuration **q1** and the symbol 0.

A complete configuration is a complete description of a Turing machine at a given moment. It consists of a record of all the symbols on the tape, an indication of which square on the tape is the currently scanned square, and an indication of the current $m$-configuration. Given this information, if one also has the description of how the machine functions, it is possible to describe its future behaviour in complete detail by writing down successive complete configurations. The changes of the machine and tape between one complete configuration and the next are called the 'moves' of the machine. Complete configurations play an important part in the processing of the universal machine. Turing uses the term in the way it was introduced in Chapter 5.

## Infinite tapes

Infinite tapes have already been discussed but there are some useful further points to make about them. The tapes of Turing machines can be finite, one-way infinite, or two-way infinite. A finite tape is one which is of a certain fixed length (capacity) and has two distinct ends. A machine could, as it were, fall off either end. The computational theory of mind proposes that the human mind is functionally equivalent to a Turing machine with a finite tape. A one-way infinite tape has one fixed end and is infinite in extent in the other direction. One-way infinite tapes can, in principle, be infinite either to the left or to the right of the fixed end. All the machines which Turing describes in OCN use one-way infinite tapes which extend to the right of the fixed end. The linear environments introduced in Chapter 5 are one-way infinite. Two-way infinite tapes have no fixed ends. They extend indefinitely in both directions from any given square. It can be shown that the storage capacity of a one-way infinite tape is equivalent to that of a two-way infinite tape and it is not hard to prove that this is so. Minsky (1967) gives the proof. It is not necessary to think of the tape of a Turing machine as being infinitely long at the start of a computation, just as it is not necessary to think of a human computant being equipped with an infinite number of sheets of paper at the start of a computation. What is required is simply that more tape (paper) be made available as and when it is needed.

## Symbols of the first and second kinds

The contents of the tapes of Turing machines are symbols of various kinds. Turing distinguished two kinds of symbols which he called symbols of the first kind and symbols of the second kind. Symbols of the first kind are also, and more usually, called 'figures'. Figures are used for the digits of the number computed by a Turing machine. In Turing's scheme, 0 and 1 are the only symbols of the first kind. Any other symbol that gets printed (and there may be many) is a symbol of the second kind. Turing machines work as follows:

> If the machine is supplied with a blank tape and set in motion, starting from the correct initial *m*-configuration, the subsequence of the symbols printed by it which are of the first kind will be called the *sequence computed by the machine*. The real number whose expression as a binary decimal is obtained by prefacing this sequence by a decimal point is called the *number computed by the machine*. (OCN p. 232)

It is clear from this that a given Turing machine outputs just a single, multi-digit number. This, of course, is quite unlike a practical computer which typically churns out lots of numbers. What is less immediately clear is that a Turing machine will output its number with infinite precision if it never stops producing figures. This leads to an important theoretical point. In general, for practical computation, we want machines that halt having completed their task. Computer programs which don't halt (with the exception of operating systems) are generally in a pathological state which was not intended by the designer of the program. Turing, by contrast, makes a distinction between machines which produce an infinite number of figures and those which don't.

### Circle-free and circular machines

For theoretical purposes Turing was interested in machines which go on for ever and never stop producing figures. These are the 'healthy' Turing machines and all the others are 'pathological'. Turing introduced the terms 'circular' and 'circle-free' to distinguish them. Healthy Turing machines are circle-free and pathological ones are 'circular'. Circle-free machines are needed to compute numbers like $\pi$ which have endless decimal expansions. A machine is circular if 'it reaches a configuration from which there is no possible move, or if it goes on moving, and possibly printing symbols of the second kind, but cannot print any more symbols of the first kind' (OCN p. 233). Clearly a circular machine could not compute a number like $\pi$.

### Organization of the tape: *F*-squares and *E*-squares

Turing adopted the convention of printing figures on alternate squares of the tape leaving the others for workspace. We can think of the first square as number 1, the second as number 2 and so on. Figures are printed only on the odd numbered squares which Turing called *F*-squares. Once a figure has been printed it is never erased and the figures on *F*-squares form a continuous sequence with no gaps. The even numbered squares Turing called *E*-squares and the symbols on them may be erased. *E*-squares provide workspace. It is useful to be able to represent the appearance of a sequence of symbols on a tape graphically but without too much fuss. For this purpose I have modified the notation introduced in Chapter 5 where the # was used to represent an empty tape square. From now on, unless it is necessary to use the # for clarity, empty squares on the tape are represented by spaces. A sequence of figures on a segment of tape is represented as follows:

        0  0  0  0  0  0  0  0

where the gaps represent *E*-squares, and a sequence with both figures and a symbol of the second kind (x in this case) as follows:

        0x0x0x0  0  0  0  0

The scanned square is indicated by a vertical bar as in Chapter 5 and the name of the current *m*-configuration or functional state is written next to it, again as in Chapter 5. Thus the expression below shows a complete configuration in which the *m*-configuration is **q1** and the configuration is **(q1, 0)**.

        0x0x0x0  0  0  0  0
            |**q1**

One other important convention should be noted at this point. *E*-squares are often used to 'mark' *F*-squares, and the symbols on them. A symbol on an *E*-square marks the *F*-square to its left (and the symbol on it, if the *F*-square is not blank). Thus in the segment below, the 1 is marked with x.

        0  0  0  0  1x0  0  0

Marking is extensively used in the design of the universal machine and provides a partial solution to the problems caused by the one-dimensional nature of a Turing machine's tape. Markers on *E*-squares serve the same sorts of purposes as the ticks, dots or pencil strokes crossing through a number that may be used in the course of a paper and pencil calculation.

### Turing's first machine: TM1

Turing described two example machines in OCN before tackling the universal machine. They were chosen to include most of the key features that need to be understood to make the operations of the universal machine comprehensible.

**Table 7.1**   The machine table for TM1

| Configuration | | Behaviour | |
|---|---|---|---|
| *m*-config | Symbol | Operations | Final *m*-config |
| b | # | P0,R | c |
| c | # | R | e |
| e | # | P1,R | k |
| k | # | R | b |

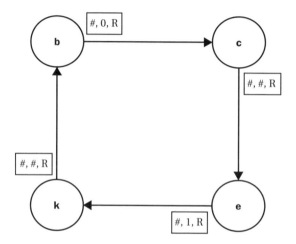

**Figure 7.1**   The state transition diagram for TM1.

Turing's first example machine, TM1, prints (on *F*-squares) the infinite sequence 010101 … The ellipsis '…' is a standard way of indicating an infinite continuation. Turing's machine table for the machine is shown in Table 7.1.

The first column shows the *m*-configurations of the machine. The second column shows the symbol on the scanned square. In the symbol column '#' represents the fact that the scanned square is blank. The third column of the table describes what the machine does. 'P0' means 'print 0' on the current scanned square, 'P1' means 'print 1' and 'R' means 'move one square to the right'. The final column of the table indicates the *m*-configuration to which the machine makes a transition after carrying out the actions described. The machine is started in *m*-configuration **b**, scanning the first square of a blank tape.

The state diagram for TM1 is shown in Figure 7.1. You have probably noticed by now that the machine of Figure 7.1 is essentially the same as the mini-mind of Figure 5.1 although Turing's machine outputs 0s and 1s rather than sheep and dogs. The state diagram for Figure 7.1 uses a slightly different convention for representing inputs and outputs. They are all gathered in a box. The first symbol represents the input, the second the output and the third the movement. The reason for this will become clear when Turing's second machine is examined.

### Turing's second machine: TM2

Turing's second example machine, TM2, is rather more complex than TM1. It computes the sequence 0010110111 ... The machine is useful, technically, because it illustrates the 'marking' process in action but it also has a more significant feature. TM2 outputs increasingly long sequences of 1s, punctuated by 0s. If the sequences of 1s are thought of as representations of integers in unary notation, the sequence can be interpreted as 0,1,2,3, ... For this sequence to be computed by a machine with a finite control mechanism the earlier parts of the sequence have to be used to produce the later parts. There is, therefore, an essential interaction between the control automaton and the sequence of digits on the tape. TM2 has five $m$-configurations. Its machine table is shown in Table 7.2 and its state diagram in Figure 7.2.

The machine table shows that TM2 departs from the convention that a Turing machine has only one action associated with each configuration. This convention is necessary in the context of the universal machine because without it the uniform representation of instructions is impossible, but it need not otherwise be obeyed provided that the actions of the machine are fully specified. Because there may be multiple printings and moves for a configuration, it makes the state diagram clearer to put all the relevant material in a box by the transition arrow. The first symbol is always the single input symbol. Where a box has more than one line, each line represents a separate input and set of actions. We will examine TM2 in detail. A clear

**Table 7.2**  The machine table for TM2

| Configuration | | Behaviour | |
| --- | --- | --- | --- |
| $m$-config | Symbol | Operations | Final $m$-config |
| b | # | Pe,R,Pe,R,P0,R,R,P0,L,L | o |
| o | 1 | R,Px,L,L,L | o |
| | 0 | | q |
| q | 0 or 1 | R,R | q |
| | # | P1,L | p |
| p | x | E,R | q |
| | e | R | f |
| | # | L,L | p |
| f | Any | R,R | f |
| | # | P0,L,L | o |

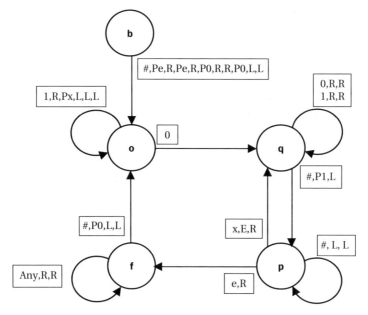

**Figure 7.2**   The state transition diagram for TM2.

understanding of how it works will help those who wish to understand the universal machine. The initial *m*-configuration **b** is used only at the start of the machine's processing. It marks the end of the tape with the pair of symbols 'ee', one on the first *F*-square, the other on the first *E*-square, and writes the first two 0s. Thereafter, the operations of the machine can be divided into sections each of which involves a cycle of processing through states **o**, **q**, **p**, and **f**. At the start of each section, the machine in *m*-configuration **o** examines the last figure printed. In every cycle, except the first, the figure will be a 1. If it is a 1, the *E*-square to its right is marked with 'x', and the figure next to the left is then examined. Each 1 found by the machine in this leftward motion is marked, a process which is terminated when a 0 is encountered. At this point, any 1s from the previous section's processing will have been marked and a transition is made to **q**. The machine moves to the right until it encounters the first blank *F*-square. The machine prints 1 on this square and makes a transition to **p**. The machine then moves leftward on *E*-squares. In this motion it will find the rightmost 'x' if there is one. If an 'x' is found, it is erased and a transition is made back to **q** which will result in a further 1 being printed on the first available *F*-square. Further cycles through **p** and **q** result in a 1 being printed at the end of the tape for each 1 which was marked with an 'x'. Each marker is erased when it is found. If this were not done, the machine would cycle endlessly through **p** and **q** printing an infinitely long sequence of 1s. After all the markers have been erased, and the marked 1s have been copied to the end of the tape, the machine moving left in **p** will eventually encounter the 'e' on the second square of the tape. It is this that, as it were, 'tells' the machine that all the 1s from the previous section have been copied. This information is implicit. There is nothing that says explicitly 'All the 1s have been copied.' It is simply the case that the configuration **(p,** e) is only instantiated when all the 1s have in fact been copied. A transition is made to **f** and the machine moves right until the first blank $F$-square is encountered. The machine prints 0 on this square to complete the actions of this section of processing and then moves two squares to the left. A transition to **o** then initiates the next section of processing. A graphical representation may help to make the machine's activities clear. At the end of the third section of processing, the state of the machine, immediately after the transition to **o**, is as shown below.

```
ee0 0 1 0 1 1 0
             |o
```

After two more moves, both 1s printed in the previous section's processing will have been marked and the machine will be scanning the 0 to the left of them.

```
ee0 0 1 0 1x1x0
           |o
```

The configuration **(o,** 0) causes a transition to **q** in which the machine makes successive moves to the right, two squares at a time, until the first blank $F$-square is found two squares beyond the rightmost figure.

```
ee0 0 1 0 1x1x0##
                |q
```

Then 1 is printed on the square, the machine moves one square to the left to align itself with the $E$-squares and a transition is made to **p**.

```
ee0 0 1 0 1x1x0 1
               |p
```

After one move the first marker is found.

```
ee0 0 1 0 1x1x0 1
             |p
```

This is erased, the machine moves one square right to align itself with the $F$-squares and transition is made to **q**.

```
ee0 0 1 0 1x1 0 1
               |q
```

The machine finds the next blank *F*-square, prints 1 on it, moves one square left and makes a transition to **p**.

```
ee0 0 1 0 1x1 0 1 1
                |p
```

The process is then repeated for the remaining marker.

```
ee0 0 1 0 1 1 0 1 1 1
                |p
```

The machine now makes successive moves to the left in **p**, until it encounters the 'e' on the second square.

```
ee0 0 1 0 1 1 0 1 1 1
  |p
```

This causes a move one square right to align the machine on *F*-squares, and a transition is made to **f**.

```
ee0 0 1 0 1 1 0 1 1 1
   |f
```

A series of moves right finds the first blank *F*-square, on which 0 is printed, the machine moves two squares left to remain aligned on *F*-squares, and a transition is made to **o** to start the next section of processing.

```
ee0 0 1 0 1 1 0 1 1 1 0
                   |o
```

There are some similarities between the way that TM2 constructs the sequence and the way that a human computant might do it but the principal point is that the machine functions under the human-like constraints discussed in Chapter 6. The process of marking and ticking off 1s is certainly analogous to a possible human process, although it is likely that a human computant would cross through each 1 from the previous segment as it was copied rather than using a marker as TM2 does. The similarity stops, however, at the point where all the markers have been erased. The human computant, who observes a number of squares simultaneously, does not need to engage in the wasteful process of moving all the way to the left end of the tape to check that there are no more markers. TM2 has to do this because it observes only one tape square at a time. If the environment were a linear sequence of rooms as in Chapter 5, a human computant carrying out TM2's processing would also have to traverse the whole environment to be sure that all markers had been accounted for. It is easy to modify TM2 to change this part of its processing which becomes increasingly wasteful as the printed sequence grows. One way to do this is to introduce a second marker which is printed by the machine in state **o** to mark the 0 which terminates the section of tape from which 1s are copied. The marker is then sensed by the machine in **p** at the appropriate time. Turing was not concerned about matters of this kind because his goal was to understand effective computability not efficient computability.

> **Exercise 7.1** Add instructions to TM2 to prevent the time wasting traverse at the end of each section of processing.

Having described the two machines discussed in this chapter, Turing then introduced a notation for defining processes which enabled him to build the complex processes needed for the universal machine from simple foundations. His functional notation is the topic of Chapter 8.

# 8 Turing's Functional Notation

The topic of this chapter is the notation that Turing developed to construct more complex machines than those discussed thus far. The notation is of interest not just because Turing used it to construct the universal machine but more generally because it contributes to our understanding of the significance of notations for developing complex ideas. It is well known, for example, that although the classical civilization of Ancient Greece produced masterly work in geometry, Greek mathematicians developed essentially no number theory or algebra because they lacked convenient notations to do so. Algebra and number theory were developed primarily by Hindu mathe-maticians who used and extended the place system for numbers which had been invented by Babylonian mathematicians. Turing did not use the graph-ical technique of state diagrams which we have used to display the structures of mini-minds. Instead he developed a functional notation for describing mini-minds which allowed him to combine simple processes to produce more complex ones and also to separate the structure of a process from its inputs and outputs. Like any other notation, Turing's has its strengths and weaknesses. Its principal strength is that it provides a very compact way of representing complex machine processes by linking simpler ones together. The principal weakness of the notation is a consequence of its compactness. It can be very difficult to unpack the behaviour of a complex process. Readers will perhaps wish to know that Turing's notation is not now used to describe machine processes. Turing himself used it in only two papers that I am aware of, the one other than 'On Computable Numbers' being a paper, published in 1937, which demonstrated the equivalence of his concept of computability with Alonzo Church's concept of effective calculability. Some readers may therefore wish to skim most of this chapter. They will, however, need to look at the state diagrams for the elementary components of the universal machine presented here.

### Skeleton tables and *m*-functions

Turing's functional notation is introduced and explained with the help of examples in section 4 of OCN. The section starts with what Turing called 'skeleton tables'. They provide, if you will excuse the pun, the bones of the universal machine. They separate the fixed parts of processes from the variable parts and provide ways to link processes sequentially. Consider, by way of introduction, the mini-mind of Figure 5.1 and Turing's first example machine TM1, Figure 7.1. The functional states of these two machines have different names and the inputs and outputs are different but the structure of the two processes is identical. The skeleton table is Turing's way of expressing the common core of such processes. It is a machine table with variables. Some of the variables represent the inputs and outputs of the process, others represent links to the starting states of other processes. A skeleton table is somewhat like a parameterized subroutine in a modern programming language. The point, as Turing put it, is that there are 'certain types of process used by nearly all machines, and these, in some machines, are used in many connections' (OCN p. 235). Turing's first skeleton table is shown in Table 8.1. It describes a symbol-finding process that is a fundamental component of the universal machine.[2]

Turing's description of the machine described in Table 8.1 is clear and succinct; 'From the $m$-configuration $\mathfrak{f}(\mathfrak{C}, \mathfrak{B}, \alpha)$ the machine finds the symbol of form $\alpha$ which is farthest to the left (the 'first' $\alpha$) and the $m$-configuration then becomes $\mathfrak{C}$. If there is no $\alpha$ then the $m$-configuration becomes $\mathfrak{B}$' (OCN p. 236). The symbol finder was designed to work with a tape which has

**Table 8.1**   The skeleton table for Turing's leftmost symbol-finding process **f(C,B,$\alpha$)**

| m-config | Symbol | Behaviour | Final m-config |
|---|---|---|---|
| | e | L | f1(C,B,$\alpha$) |
| f(C,B,$\alpha$) | not e | L | f(C,B,$\alpha$) |
| | # | L | f(C,B,$\alpha$) |
| | $\alpha$ | | C |
| f1(C,B,$\alpha$) | not $\alpha$ | R | f1(C,B,$\alpha$) |
| | # | R | f2(C,B,$\alpha$) |
| | $\alpha$ | | C |
| f2(C,B,$\alpha$) | not $\alpha$ | R | f1(C,B,$\alpha$) |
| | # | R | B |

---

[2] Turing made a number of mistakes in 'On Computable Numbers'. Some of these were noted by the logician Emil Post and corrected in an appendix to a paper, Post (1947). Post's paper was reprinted in Davis (1965) and the appendix with the corrections has more recently been reprinted in Copeland (2004, section 2.2). I have incorporated Post's corrections in the versions of Turing's tables used in this book. I have also substituted a small number of the symbols Turing used with others which are more convenient. The changes have no effect on the functioning of the processes described.

'ee' on its first two squares and conforms to the convention that there are no breaks in the sequence of symbols on *F*-squares. If the tape is not organized in this way, the finder will not function correctly.

The symbol finder has three *m*-configurations of its own, **f(C,B,$\alpha$)**, **f1(C,B,$\alpha$)** and **f2(C,B,$\alpha$)**. These three *m*-configurations specify the internal structure of the process. Two of the three variable parameters **C**, and **B**, are also *m*-configurations; they specify the functional states to which the symbol finder can make a transition when its processing is complete. The third parameter, $\alpha$, represents the symbol for which a search is made. If $\alpha$ is found, a transition is made out of the symbol finder to **C**. If $\alpha$ is not found the transition is to **B**. Turing's notation is slightly confusing, initially, because **f(C,B,$\alpha$)** refers both to the first *m*-configuration of the symbol finder and also to the whole process. In the latter guise, the expression **f(C,B,$\alpha$)** is called an *m*-configuration function or *m*-function. **f(C,B,$\alpha$)** is an expression that represents a class of mini-minds that find symbols. Particular members of the class are constructed by substituting specific values for the parameters, **C, B** and $\alpha$. The notation is powerful because the *m*-configuration (functional state) parameters can themselves be *m*-functions (mini-minds). A state transition diagram for the symbol finder is shown in Figure 8.1.

The symbol finder finds the leftmost token of the symbol $\alpha$ if there is one on the tape. It is a fundamental component of the universal machine because almost every operation of that machine can ultimately be expressed in terms of searches for symbols and copying of symbols. In Figure 8.1 the parameters are dropped from the names of the three *m*-configurations that define the symbol finder. The dashed circles represent the fact that the *m*-configurations **C** and **B** are not part of the process itself, but part of the context in which the process occurs. The first *m*-configuration **f** moves the machine to the leftmost square of the tape. The machine then moves rightwards, checking each square for an occurrence of $\alpha$. It uses two *m*-configurations, **f1** and **f2** to do this in order to check for the occurrence of two consecutive blank squares. Given the convention for tape use that

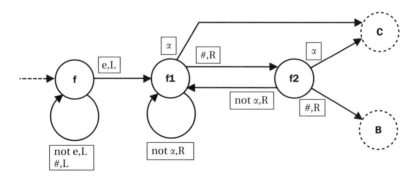

**Figure 8.1**   The state diagram for **f(C,B,$\alpha$)**.

Turing adopted, successive blank squares mean that the end of the marked portion of the tape has been reached. If the target symbol $\alpha$ has not been found by then the search has failed. Although Turing was not trying to simulate human behaviour with this $m$-function it is clear that a human who wanted to find the first occurrence of a given symbol on a one-dimensional tape would have to carry out a search that was of essentially the same character, starting from the left end of the tape and working rightwards.

## Building composite $m$-functions by linking

The symbol finder can be used to show how composite processes are specified using $m$-functions. Suppose that one wished to find the first instance of $\alpha$, followed by the first instance of $\beta$, if an $\alpha$ has been found. The first instance of $\alpha$, if there is one, can be found by a symbol finder **f(C,B,$\alpha$)**. To find $\beta$ if $\alpha$ has been found, a second instance of the symbol finder is substituted for the appropriate parameter of **f(C,B,$\alpha$)**. The parameter is **C** because it represents the functional state to which a transition is made if the symbol finder finds $\alpha$. Making the substitution gives the expression **f(f(C,B,$\beta$),B,$\alpha$)**. This describes a process consisting of two linked symbol finders. Its state diagram is shown in Figure 8.2. No confusion arises from the fact that there are two $m$-configurations labelled **f**, two labelled **f1** and so on. Each $m$-configuration has a unique place in the composite process. In Figure 8.2 the terminating $m$-configuration **B** of the composite process is the same for the two component instances of the symbol finder, but there is no requirement that it must be.

Suppose, instead, that the search for $\beta$ were to be made if the search for $\alpha$ failed. In that case, the composite $m$-function would be **f(C,f(C,B,$\beta$),$\alpha$)**, in which the second instance of the symbol-finder replaces parameter **B**. The state diagram is shown in Figure 8.3.

Figures 8.2 and 8.3 demonstrate the basic technique of linking mini-minds to make composites. Both the strengths and weaknesses of the notation are

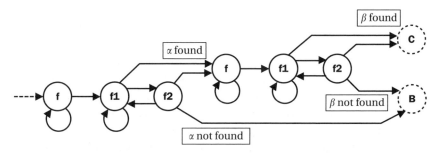

**Figure 8.2**    The state diagram for **f(f(C,B,$\beta$),B,$\alpha$)**.

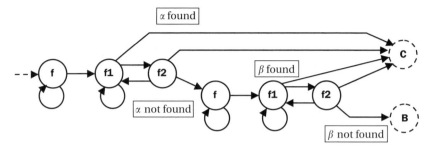

**Figure 8.3**    The state diagram for **f(C,f(C,B,β),α)**.

illustrated. The strength is that composite process specifications are compact and easy to define. The weakness is that the notation can already be seen to be hard to read. One of the principal difficulties is that the sequential linkage of processes is expressed by nesting. The second instance of the symbol finder is contained within the definition of the first. This makes it look like a component of the first symbol finder rather than its successor. Programmers who are familiar with conventional high level programming languages will also see that the order of evaluation is the reverse of the familiar order. One works from the outside in, rather than from the inside out.

> **Exercise 8.1**    Use Turing's notation to write down the expression for a composite symbol finder which first searches for an instance of $\alpha$. If it succeeds it searches for a second instance of $\alpha$; if it fails it searches for an instance of $\beta$.

### Defining *m*-functions in terms of other *m*-functions

Turing took the process of defining *m*-functions a step further by using previously defined *m*-functions in the skeleton tables of new *m*-functions. A simple example is the skeleton table for an *m*-function whose purpose is to erase the leftmost instance of a given symbol if one is found. The skeleton table for the eraser is shown in Table 8.2. It is fairly easy to see that the major part of this *m*-function is its component symbol finder to which a single *m*-configuration has been added to erase the symbol found. The state diagram for the eraser, which shows this clearly, is shown in Figure 8.4.

Another example, which illustrates both the flexibility of the notation and the ease with which it can result in inscrutable *m*-functions is shown in Table 8.3. It is an *m*-function which erases all the instances of $\alpha$ on the tape. This is Turing at his elegant best but the result is initially hard to understand. He says, laconically, 'The last example seems somewhat more difficult to interpret than most' (OCN p. 237). Indeed, there's a hint of smoke and

**Table 8.2**   The skeleton table for the leftmost symbol eraser
**e(C,B,$\alpha$)**

| *m*-config | Symbol | Operations | Final *m*-config |
|---|---|---|---|
| **e(C,B,$\alpha$)** | | | **f(e1(C,B,$\alpha$),B,$\alpha$)** |
| **e1(C,B,$\alpha$)** | | E | **C** |

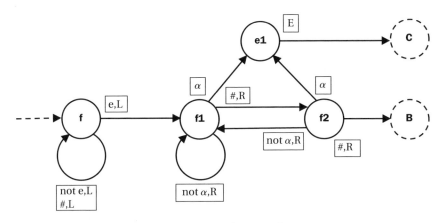

**Figure 8.4**   The state diagram for **e(C,B,$\alpha$)**.

**Table 8.3**   The skeleton table for the multiple symbol
eraser **e(B,$\alpha$)**

| *m*-config | Symbol | Operations | Final *m*-config |
|---|---|---|---|
| **e(B,$\alpha$)** | | | **e(e(B,$\alpha$),B,$\alpha$)** |

mirrors about the way in which a three-variable function which erases a
single instance of a symbol becomes a two-variable function which erases
multiple instances of the symbol and it is perhaps confusing to use the same
name. But let us investigate. The three-variable function **e(C,B,$\alpha$)**, which
erases a single symbol if one is found, has two state variables and one symbol variable inherited from the symbol finder which is its major component.
The two state variables **C** and **B** are the destinations of the transitions following success and failure respectively, in the search for the symbol. Turing's
recursive definition of the multiple symbol eraser makes **C**, the destination

of the transition when a symbol is found and erased, an internal part of the process. The recursion is implemented by a transition back to the first state of the symbol finder. There is, therefore, only one exit point from the multiple symbol eraser which is taken when all tokens of the symbol have been erased, and the symbol finder fails to find another token. Hence the multiple symbol eraser has only two variables rather than three. The straightforward nature of the process can be seen in the state diagram, shown in Figure 8.5.

The observant reader may have noticed that the definition of $e(B,\alpha)$ introduces an entirely unnecessary traverse of the tape, from the point at which a token of the target symbol has been erased to the left end and back again, at the start of each recursive call. After the first token has been found, there can, by definition, be no further tokens to the left of the currently scanned square. Any others must be to the right so further search to the left is wasted. Inspection of the state diagram in Figure 8.5 shows that if the transition went from **e1** back to **f1** rather than from **e1** back to **f** the resultant process would erase all tokens of the target symbol without unnecessary leftward traverses. This observation prompts a couple of thoughts. The first is methodological and relates to the notation. Turing was, presumably, well aware of this feature of $e(B,\alpha)$. He was, however, interested in effectiveness rather than efficiency. A transition from **e1** to **f1** rather than from **e1** to **f** cannot be achieved when $e(B,\alpha)$ is defined in terms of existing $m$-functions because it involves a transition to an internal component of $f(C,B,\alpha)$. Turing's notation does not allow such transitions. $m$-functions are encapsulated or modular. From the standpoint of effectiveness it is much safer to use a proven mechanism inefficiently than to construct a special-purpose machine which may contain errors. Wherever it was possible, Turing defined new $m$-functions in terms of existing, simpler ones. The second point to note is that the efficiency of a mechanism is dependent on the context in which it is deployed. The symbol

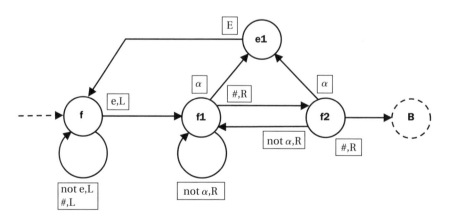

**Figure 8.5**   The state diagram for $e(B,\alpha)$.

finder is perfectly efficient in the context of the $m$-function which erases just the first token of the target symbol but inefficient in the context of multiple erasures. Suppose that the human cognitive system contains some mechanisms that have been copied and modified by processes of natural selection. It is possible that they too might function with different effectiveness depending on the context.

The use of parameterized expressions as both $m$-configurations and $m$-functions; the linkage of processes by substitution of $m$-functions for parameters and the definition of new $m$-functions in terms of existing definitions constitute the basic techniques of Turing's functional notation. In the design of the universal machine he used these techniques whenever it was possible to do so. The universal machine contains multiple instances of the same component processes particularly the leftmost symbol finder. Special purpose processes were constructed only when none of the existing stock of components would serve the required purpose. Chapter 10 discusses the components of the universal machine. Chapter 9 discusses Turing's format for standard descriptions which needs to be understood for a proper comprehension of the universal machine. Standard descriptions are the software of the universal machine.

# 9 Standard Descriptions and Description Numbers

## Introduction

Chapters 7 and 8 have discussed a number of Turing machines. One feature they all have in common is that what they compute is fixed. TM1 always computes the sequence 010101..., TM2 always computes the sequence 0010110111..., and the computations of the symbol finders and erasers discussed in Chapter 8 are fixed once values have been chosen for their parameters. The fundamental difference between these machines and modern computers is that modern computers can be programmed whereas simple Turing machines cannot. Turing's universal machine, which is discussed in Chapters 10–12, is a programmable machine. In that sense it is like a modern computer. In fact the universal machine can be thought of as one of the abstract ancestors of the modern digital computer. The mini-mind of the universal machine is a fixed, finite structure like any other mini-mind. The universal machine's program is the machine table of another Turing machine expressed in a particular way. The task of the universal machine is to interpret the machine tables of other Turing machines and hence to compute the numbers they compute.

Turing's functional notation provides a way of describing and linking machine processes. Turing used it to construct the complex processes of the universal machine from simple components such as the leftmost symbol finder discussed in Chapter 8. These processes constitute the 'hardware' of the universal machine and are discussed in detail in Chapter 10. In this chapter the software for the machine is discussed and its modus operandi is explained. In Chapter 11 the hardware and software are put together to explain the simulation cycle of the universal machine in outline and in Chapter 12, the cycle is examined in detail.

The software for the universal Turing machine is a special form of machine table called a 'standard description'. Machine tables provide the same information as state diagrams but present it in a different way. A standard description is a machine table, in the form of a linear string of symbols, which can be written on the tape of a Turing machine. The mini-mind of the universal machine is designed in such a way that when the standard description of an arbitrary Turing machine is written on its tape it can interpret that standard description and simulate the functioning of the machine described. The machine whose functioning is simulated is called the 'target' machine.

Standard descriptions have to satisfy two fundamental requirements. First, of course, the format has to be suitable for input to a Turing machine because the universal machine is one. This means that the standard description must use a fixed, finite symbol alphabet. Second, the standard description format must be capable of encoding the machine table of any Turing machine because a universal machine is, by definition, one which can simulate the functioning of any Turing machine. This second requirement leads naturally to a consideration of the scope of the simulations that the universal machine may be called upon to carry out. We consider this question first.

### How many Turing machines are there?

In Chapter 5 the formula $nmr^{nk}$ was used to calculate the number of machines with $n$ functional states, $m$ movements, $r$ outputs and $k$ inputs, assuming that no halt state was defined. The question at issue is how large these terms can become. There is no limit to the number of functional states a Turing machine can have provided that for each given machine the number is fixed and finite, nor are there limits on the size of the input and output alphabets provided the alphabets are also specified in advance and of finite size. This means that $n$, $k$ and $r$ can be as large as needed. The number of possible movements $m$ can be no greater than three because a Turing machine moves left, right, or not at all. These considerations show that $nmr^{nk}$ can become indefinitely large but always has a specific value, and this can be used to show that there is a countable infinity of Turing machines.

This means that there are as many Turing machines as there are positive whole numbers, 'natural' numbers as they are sometimes called. There are infinitely many of these because counting starting from 1 and going on with 2,3,4,... never comes to an end. The natural numbers are countable because they form an ordered list and we know that for a given number $n$, the next number in the list is $n + 1$. The Turing machines are countable because they can be paired one to one with the natural numbers. For $n = 1$, $m = 1$, $r = 1$ and $k = 1$, $nmr^{nk} = 1$ so there is just one Turing machine definable with these resources. This is Turing machine number 1. That's a start, but to go further we need a systematic way of working through all the possibilities as $n,m,r$ and $k$ are increased. One way to do this is to work through all the permutations of numbers of states, movements, outputs and inputs. Thus

**Table 9.1**   A scheme for counting Turing machines

| $n$ | $m$ | $r$ | $k$ | $nmr^{nk}$ | Description numbers |
|---|---|---|---|---|---|
| 1 | 1 | 1 | 1 | 1 | 1 |
| 1 | 1 | 1 | 2 | 1 | 2 |
| 1 | 1 | 2 | 1 | 2 | 3–4 |
| 1 | 1 | 2 | 2 | 4 | 5–8 |
| 1 | 2 | 1 | 1 | 2 | 9–10 |
| 1 | 2 | 1 | 2 | 4 | 11–14 |
| 1 | 2 | 2 | 1 | 4 | 15–18 |
| 1 | 2 | 2 | 2 | 16 | 19–34 |
| 2 | 1 | 1 | 1 | 4 | 35–38 |
| 2 | 1 | 1 | 2 | 16 | 39–54 |
| 2 | 1 | 2 | 1 | 16 | 55–70 |
| 2 | 1 | 2 | 2 | 256 | 71–326 |
| 2 | 2 | 1 | 1 | 16 | 327–342 |
| 2 | 2 | 1 | 2 | 256 | 343–598 |
| 2 | 2 | 2 | 1 | 64 | 599–662 |
| 2 | 2 | 2 | 2 | 4096 | 663–4758 |

we could proceed with $n = 1$, $m = 1$, $r = 1$, $k = 2$, follow this with $n = 1$, $m = 1$, $r = 2$, $k = 1$ and so on. Table 9.1 gives the first 16 permutations of this scheme, the number of machines definable for each permutation, and the description numbers associated with them. It is clear from the discussion in Chapter 4 that the machines within a block can be listed, so a scheme like Table 9.1 provides an organized list of lists which has no end. This shows that there are infinitely many Turing machines but that the infinity is countable.

The observant reader may have noticed that the scheme of Table 9.1 assigns different numbers to machines than the schemes discussed in Chapter 4. That doesn't matter, provided it is always clear which numbering scheme is being used. Turing's scheme, discussed later in this chapter, is different again. The wider significance of issues to do with counting and listing Turing machines is discussed in Chapter 13.

## Standard descriptions

The problem faced by the designer of a universal machine can now be seen clearly. The universal machine is, itself, a Turing machine and thus by definition has a finite alphabet of symbols and a finite number of functional states. The reasons for these constraints were discussed in Chapter 6. Nevertheless, a universal machine is one which can simulate the processing of any given Turing machine by interpreting its machine table. It is over-whelmingly likely, however, that an arbitrary Turing machine chosen at random from the countable infinity will have symbols in its alphabet that are not in the alphabet of the universal machine. How then, can a machine be designed to simulate another machine which uses a different symbol alphabet?

The answer is that the machine table of the target machine must be expressed in terms of the alphabet of the universal machine. Universality is not, therefore, absolute. It is relative to a particular alphabet and coding scheme and this brings in its train the requirement to show, for a given alphabet and coding scheme, that every Turing machine can be translated into it. This is a powerful constraint on the design of a universal machine and it has major implications for psychology if the physical symbol systems hypothesis is correct. These implications are discussed in detail in Chapters 16 and 17.

Turing's standard description format is set out in Section 5 of 'On Computable Numbers'. The first point to note is that the *m*-configurations of a machine can always be renamed as **q1, q2,**… because the name of an *m*-configuration has no effect on its function. Turing stipulated that **q1** should always be used as the starting *m*-configuration. Second, the same reasoning and a similar technique can be used to rename the symbols that a machine uses. Turing used s0,s1,s2, … for this purpose, stipulating that s0 = blank, s1 = 0 and s2 = 1. We have seen these kinds of equivalence in operation already. The 'sheep and dogs' mini-mind of Figure 5.1 and Turing's first machine TM1, Figure 7.1, are functionally equivalent although their functional states have different names and their inputs and outputs are different. The operations column of a machine table can be standardized by noting that printing a blank is equivalent to erasing a symbol and that reprinting a symbol is equivalent to taking no action. Thus, incorporating all these elements, the machine table shown in Table 9.2 is functionally equivalent to that of TM1 and the 'sheep and dogs' machine of Figure 5.1, but expressed in the standard form. The translation into standard form is easily done for TM1, but TM2 is more complicated because some of its configurations have multiple operations associated with them. In such cases the machine has to be transformed into one which is functionally equivalent by adding more *m*-configurations. The transformed machine is called TM2S.

**Table 9.2**    The machine table for TM1 in standard form

| Configuration | | Behaviour | |
|---|---|---|---|
| *m*-config | Symbol | Operations | Final *m*-config |
| q1 | s0 | Ps1R | q2 |
| q2 | s0 | Ps0R | q3 |
| q3 | s0 | Ps2R | q4 |
| q4 | s0 | Ps0R | q1 |

Notice that what is at stake is input/output equivalence. TM2 and TM2S are functionally equivalent because they compute the same sequence. They are not equivalent in terms of their functional states and state transitions. Table 9.3 shows the machine table for TM2S, expressed in standard form. e becomes s3, and x becomes s4. The operations of state **b** of TM2 are carried out by **q1–q6** of TM2S, those of **o** by **q7**, those of **q** by **q11** and **q12**, those of **p** by **q8, q9, q10, q13** and **q14**, and those of **f** by **q15, q16** and **q17**.

Two more steps are needed to produce the standard description of a machine. First, the rows of the machine table are represented by a linear expression with the symbols of each row separated from the next with a semi-colon. The 'P' indicating 'Print' is redundant because the symbol to print is always in the same place in an instruction. Taking TM1 as an example, its machine table can be expressed as the symbol string

```
q1s0s1Rq2;q2s0s0Rq3;q3s0s2Rq4;q4s0s0Rq1;
```

**Table 9.3**   The machine table for TM2S

| Configuration | | Behaviour | |
| --- | --- | --- | --- |
| *m*-config | Symbol | Operations | Final *m*-config |
| q1 | s0 | Ps3R | q2 |
| q2 | s0 | Ps3R | q3 |
| q3 | s0 | Ps1R | q4 |
| q4 | s0 | Ps0R | q5 |
| q5 | s0 | Ps1L | q6 |
| q6 | s0 | Ps0L | q7 |
| q7 | s1 | Ps1N | q11 |
| q7 | s2 | Ps2R | q8 |
| q8 | s0 | Ps4L | q9 |
| q9 | s2 | Ps2L | q10 |
| q10 | s0 | Ps0L | q7 |
| q11 | s1 | Ps1R | q12 |
| q11 | s2 | Ps2R | q12 |
| q11 | s0 | Ps2L | q13 |
| q12 | s0 | Ps0R | q11 |
| q12 | s4 | Ps4R | q11 |
| q13 | s4 | Ps0R | q11 |
| q13 | s3 | Ps3R | q15 |
| q13 | s0 | Ps0L | q14 |
| q14 | s1 | Ps1L | q13 |
| q14 | s2 | Ps2L | q13 |
| q15 | s1 | Ps1R | q16 |
| q15 | s2 | Ps2R | q16 |
| q15 | s0 | Ps1L | q17 |
| q16 | s0 | Ps0R | q15 |
| q17 | s0 | Ps0L | q7 |

It would be complicated for a machine to interpret the decimal numbers used for states and symbols so the final step is to translate the linear expression into a form which uses unary numerals. Each representation of an *m*-configuration $q_i$ is replaced by D followed by A repeated $i$ times, and each representation of a symbol $s_j$ is replaced by D followed by C repeated $j$ times. q1 becomes DA, q2 becomes DAA, s0 becomes D, s1 becomes DC and so on. With this final step the standard description of TM1 is complete.

DADDCRDAA;DAADDRDAAA;DAAADDCCRDAAAA;DAAAADDRDA;

This line of text is worth looking at and thinking about for a few moments. There are several things to say about it. It is an encoding of Turing's first example machine TM1; it is an encoding, with additional translation of states and symbols, of the sheep and dogs mini-mind of Figure 5.1; it is a finite encoding of the infinite sequence 010101...; and it is a program for Turing's universal machine. Every Turing machine has a standard description. Each machine has a finite number of functional states which can be encoded as q1,q2,... and then as DA,DAA,... . A similar argument can be used with regard to the finite alphabet of the machine. Finally, as we have seen with TM2 and TM2S, an instruction which includes multiple actions is functionally equivalent to a set of instructions each of which carries out a single action. It is always possible to replace an instruction with multiple actions by a set of instructions with single actions and these can then be expressed in the standard description format.

## Description numbers

Turing used standard descriptions as the basis for description numbers. The scheme is straightforward. Turing expresses it thus:

> If finally we replace 'A' by '1', 'C' by '2', 'D' by '3', 'L' by '4', 'R' by '5', 'N' by '6', and ';' by '7' we shall have a description of the machine in the form of an arabic numeral. The integer represented by this numeral may be called a *description number* (D.N) of the machine ... . To each computable sequence there corresponds at least one description number, while to no description number does there correspond more than one computable sequence. The computable sequences and numbers are therefore enumerable. (OCN pp. 240–1)

Putting this into practice for the standard description of TM1 we get

31332531173113353111731113322531111731111335317

The value of description numbers as a way of exploring sets of mini-minds has already been discussed in Chapter 4. In general, the theoretical importance of representing computing machines as description numbers lies in the fact that it becomes possible to bring mathematical techniques to bear to analyse how these machines relate both to psychology and to some fundamental questions about mathematics itself. Since mathematics is a human activity, and computing machines are representations of parts of that activity, representing machines as numbers makes it possible to reflect human activity back on itself in a rigorous fashion. Kurt Gödel was able to prove some startling and unexpected theorems in 1931 using a self-referential technique and Turing was able to prove some equally powerful results in a similar fashion. Turing called the description number of a circle-free machine, a *satisfactory* number. The proof of the unsolvability of the halting problem, which is examined in Chapter 13, shows that there is no general process for determining whether a given number is satisfactory. Some theorists argue that this proof has significant psychological as well as mathematical implications.

Description numbers are, at this point, of less immediate importance to us than standard descriptions. As already noted, a universal machine works by interpreting the standard description of a target Turing machine. In Chapter 10 the component processes needed for this purpose are introduced.

# 10 Basic Components of the Universal Machine

## Introduction

The notation that Turing used to construct skeleton tables and $m$-functions and his format for standard descriptions have been discussed in Chapters 8 and 9. We turn now to a consideration of the component processes of the universal mini-mind. These processes can be thought of as its hardware. Its software is the standard description of a machine whose operations are to be simulated.

Three of the basic components of the universal mini-mind, the leftmost symbol finder, the single symbol eraser and the multiple symbol eraser were discussed in Chapter 8. Section 4 of 'On Computable Numbers' contains many other definitions of $m$-functions, some, but not all, of which are used in the design of the universal machine. Those that are used are discussed here. As the title of the chapter indicates, the processes described here are basic components. Like the components of many other kinds of machines they can be understood at a variety of levels as can the machines themselves. Consider, for example, the components of internal combustion engines, things such as pistons, valves, valve springs, camshafts, crankshafts, carburettors, exhausts, and so forth. People who design and make car engines know what all these components are and how they work down to the last detail. People who maintain car engines are supposed to know what all the components are, how they fit together, what kinds of things tend to go wrong and how to repair them. Some people who drive cars know roughly what the components are and how they work to transmit power to the wheels. Other people know nothing about the components but understand perfectly well what cars are for and how to use them. The components of Turing's universal machine can, similarly be understood at a variety of levels. Whatever level one considers them at, however, it is appropriate to think of these components as abstract specifications of parts that could be physically realized. If we were actually to build a universal machine they would constitute parts of its hardware even though their definitions are functional rather than physical. For most components I shall give a verbal description and a state diagram as well as Turing's table for the component and discussion of it where necessary.

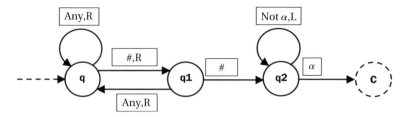

**Figure 10.1**    The state diagram for **q(C,α)**.

**Table 10.1**    Turing's table for **q(C,α)**

| *m*-config | Symbol | Operations | Final *m*-config |
|---|---|---|---|
| **q(C,α)** | | | **q(q1(C,α))** |
| **q1(C,α)** | $\alpha$ | | **C** |
| | not $\alpha$ | L | **q1(C,α)** |
| **q(C)** | Any | R | **q(C)** |
| | # | R | **q1(C)** |
| **q1(C)** | Any | R | **q(C)** |
| | # | | **C** |

## The rightmost symbol finder

The mini-mind that finds the leftmost token of a symbol is matched by one that finds the rightmost token **q(C,α)** relies on the convention that the sequence of symbols on *F*-squares is continuous. It also presupposes that there is at least one token of $\alpha$ on the tape. To find the rightmost token the mini-mind moves right until it finds two consecutive blank squares indicating that it has reached the end of the used part of the tape. It then moves left until a token of $\alpha$ is encountered. The state diagram for **q(C,α)** is shown in Figure 10.1.

Considering how simple the process is, the skeleton table, Table 10.1, is one of Turing's less felicitous uses of the *m*-functional notation but he probably found it perfectly readable himself. One of his contemporaries, Maurice Wilkes, who was an important figure in the British effort to develop digital computers in the late 1940s recounted a story about Turing when he received the Turing award in 1967.

> I remember that he had decided – presumably because someone had shown him a train of pulses on an oscilloscope – that the proper way to write binary numbers was backwards, with the least significant digit on

the left. He would, on occasion, carry this over into decimal notation. I well remember that once, during a lecture, when he was multiplying some decimal numbers together on the blackboard to illustrate a point about checking a program, we were all unable to follow his working until we realized that he had written the numbers backwards. I do not think that he was being funny, or trying to score off us; it was simply that he could not appreciate that a trivial matter of that kind could affect anybody's understanding one way or the other. (Wilkes 1987, p. 201)

### Printing figures

Thus far, the *m*-functions described have been concerned with finding and erasing symbols. *M*-functions to print symbols are also required. The basic *m*-function of this kind is **pe(C,$\alpha$)** which prints $\alpha$ on the first available blank *F*-square at the end of the tape. **pe(C,$\alpha$)** uses a symbol finder to position itself on the first square of the tape, which is an *F*-square, and then uses **pe1(C,$\alpha$)** to hop down the tape, two squares at a time, until it lands on a blank square. Given Turing's tape conventions, that square will be the first blank *F*-square, to the right of all *F*-squares with symbols on them. The target symbol is printed on it and a transition is made out of the printing process to **C**. The state diagram for **pe(C,$\alpha$)** is shown in Figure 10.2, and its skeleton table in Table 10.2. Figure 10.2 introduces a new convention. It represents the constituent symbol finder as a rectangular block with all of its internal structure hidden. This convention is used from now on.

There are several occasions during the processing of the universal machine when a pair of symbols needs to be printed at the end of the tape.

**Table 10.2**   Turing's table for **pe(C,$\alpha$)**

| *m*-config | Symbol | Operations | Final *m*-config |
|---|---|---|---|
| **pe(C,$\alpha$)** | | | **f(pe1(C,$\alpha$),C,$e$)** |
| **pe1(C,$\alpha$)** | Any | RR | **pe1(C,$\alpha$)** |
| | # | P$\alpha$ | **C** |

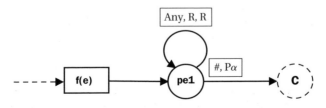

**Figure 10.2**   The state diagram for **pe(C,$\alpha$)**.

**Table 10.3**   Turing's table for **pe2(C,$\alpha$,$\beta$)**

| *m*-config | Symbol | Operations | Final *m*-config |
|---|---|---|---|
| **pe2(C,$\alpha$,$\beta$)** | | | **pe(pe(C, $\beta$),$\alpha$)** |

Turing achieves this by linking two instances of **pe(C,$\alpha$)** together to give an *m*-function whose skeleton table is shown in Table 10.3. This *m*-function shares the inefficiency of **e(B,$\alpha$)** because it makes a complete, unnecessary traverse to the left end of the tape and back from the point at which the first symbol is printed. It illustrates Turing's fundamental preference for using existing processes, where possible, rather than defining new ones even in cases like this where it would have been easy to define an efficient process.

## Copying marked symbols

TM2, see Figure 7.2, copies marked symbols as an essential part of its processing and much of the processing of the universal machine also consists of copying marked symbols. Turing defined a number of *m*-functions for these purposes. A symbol on an *F*-square is said to be marked by a symbol on the *E*-square immediately to its right and a useful process finds the marker and then moves one square to the left so as to be scanning the square containing the marked symbol. Turing introduced a very simple *m*-function **l(C)** which moves one square left from a given position and makes a transition to **C**, and used this in conjunction with a symbol finder to define **f*(C,B,$\alpha$)** whose skeleton table is shown in Table 10.4. **f*(C,B,$\alpha$)** was then used in an *m*-function **c(C,B,$\alpha$)** which copies the first symbol marked by $\alpha$ to the end of the tape. **pe(C,$\alpha$)** is also a component of the *m*-function. The skeleton table for **c(C,B,$\alpha$)** is shown in Table 10.5. The $\beta$ in the symbol column of Table 10.5 indicates that the symbol to be copied may, in principle, be any symbol in the machine's alphabet. This raises an implementation issue, when the *m*-function is used in a specific context, which is not immediately obvious from the skeleton table. Mini-minds have to be set to the fixed values with which they deal before they are used. They cannot take variable input. All possible choices for $\beta$ must, therefore, be made explicit when the skeleton table is implemented. Suppose, first, that $\beta$ can be one of two symbols, D or C. The state diagram for the resulting process is shown in Figure 10.3.

Figure 10.3 shows that *m*-configuration **c1** reads the marked symbol and directs processing either to **pe(D)** or to **pe(C)** depending on which of D or C was found on the scanned square. Two **pe($\alpha$)** processes are required because each can print only one symbol. If, therefore, $\beta$ the marked symbol, could be D, C or A the discrimination made by **c1** would have to be threefold, and three **pe(C,$\alpha$)** processes would be needed. The state diagram for this case is

**Table 10.4**   Turing's table for **f\*(C,B,$\alpha$)**

| *m*-config | Symbol | Operations | Final *m*-config |
|---|---|---|---|
| **f\*(C,B,$\alpha$)** | | | **f(I(C),B,$\alpha$)** |

**Table 10.5**   Turing's table for **c(C,B,$\alpha$)**

| *m*-config | Symbol | Operations | Final *m*-config |
|---|---|---|---|
| **c(C,B,$\alpha$)** | | | **f\*(c1(C),B,$\alpha$)** |
| **c1(C)** | $\beta$ | | **pe(C,$\beta$)** |

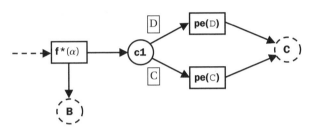

**Figure 10.3**   The state diagram for **c(C,B,$\alpha$)** when $\alpha$ marks either C or D.

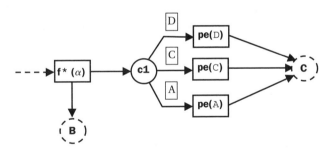

**Figure 10.4**   The state diagram for **c(C,B,$\alpha$)** when $\alpha$ marks D,C or A.

shown in Figure 10.4. The general principle is that all possible choices for symbols must be built in when an *m*-function is implemented.

### Copying marked symbols and erasing the markers

It is often the case when a marked symbol has been copied, that the marker needs to be erased. Turing modified the symbol copier **c(C,B,$\alpha$)** by adding an

**Table 10.6**   Turing's table for **ce(C,B,$\alpha$)**

| *m*-config | Symbol | Operations | Final *m*-config |
|---|---|---|---|
| ce(C,B,$\alpha$) | | | c(e(C,B,$\alpha$),B,$\alpha$) |

**Table 10.7**   Turing's table for **ce(B,$\alpha$)**

| *m*-config | Symbol | Operations | Final *m*-config |
|---|---|---|---|
| ce(B,$\alpha$) | | | ce(ce(B,$\alpha$),B,$\alpha$) |

eraser in place of *m*-configuration **C**. The skeleton table for **ce(C,B,$\alpha$)** is shown in Table 10.6.

Turing then used a recursive definition to change the single symbol copier/marker eraser into a multiple copier/eraser. The definition has the same recursive structure as the definition of the multiple symbol eraser **e(B,$\alpha$)** discussed in Chapter 8. The skeleton table for **ce(B,$\alpha$)** is shown in Table 10.7 and the state diagram, with three choices for the copied symbol $\beta$, is shown in Figure 10.5.

The universal machine uses **ce(B,$\alpha$)** *m*-functions with exactly these three choices for $\beta$. The role of these functions is described in more detail in Chapter 12. **ce(B,$\alpha$)** *m*-functions can be chained so as to copy all the symbols marked with one marker, followed by all those marked by another, erasing the markers in both cases. Turing defined **ce2(B,$\alpha$,$\beta$)** to do this as **ce(ce(B,$\beta$),$\alpha$)** and then **ce3(B,$\alpha$,$\beta$,$\gamma$)** as **ce(ce2(B,$\beta$,$\gamma$),$\alpha$)**.

## Comparing marked symbols

The universal machine makes many comparisons of pairs of marked symbols in the course of its processing. The basic piece of machinery to do this is the *m*-function **cp(C,A,E, $\alpha$, $\beta$)**. The skeleton table is shown in Table 10.8 and the state diagram in Figure 10.6. The state diagram shown in Figure 10.6 assumes, for simplicity, that the symbols to be compared will be either D or C. There are eight possible outcomes of the process. The two outcomes which lead to functional state **C** occur when both markers are found and the symbols they mark are the same. The five outcomes which lead to functional state **A** occur when there is a mismatch. Mismatches happen if the two marked symbols are not the same, or if one marker is found but not the other. The case where neither marker is found, is a match of a different kind and leads to outcome **E**. The universal machine uses a matching process where the alphabet has three symbols rather than two.

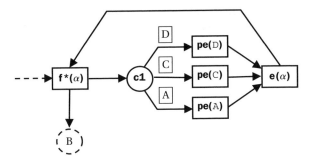

**Figure 10.5** The state diagram for **ce(B,α)** when α marks D,C or A.

**Table 10.8** Turing's table for **cp(C,A,E,α,β)**

| *m*-config | Symbol | Operations | Final *m*-config |
|---|---|---|---|
| **cp(C,A,E,α,β)** | | | **f\*(cp1(C,A,β),f(A,E,β),α)** |
| **cp1(C,A,β)** | γ | | **f\*(cp2(C,A,γ),A,β)** |
| **cp2(C,A,γ)** | γ | | **C** |
| | not γ | | **A** |

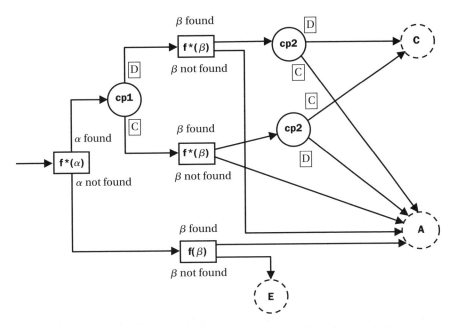

**Figure 10.6** The state diagram for **cp(C,A,E,α,β)** when the symbols marked by α and β can be either D or C.

**Exercise 10.1**    Construct the state diagram for **cp(C,A,E,$\alpha$,$\beta$)** when the two sequences to be compared can contain tokens of three symbols D, C and A rather than just D and C.

## Comparing marked symbols and erasing the markers

Turing defined two processes for comparing marked symbols and erasing the markers if the comparison showed the marked symbols to be the same. The first process adds two single symbol erasers to the comparison process of Table 10.8 in place of $m$-configuration **C**. **cpe(C,A,E,$\alpha$,$\beta$)** compares the symbols marked by $\alpha$ and $\beta$ and erases the markers if the symbols are the same. Table 10.9 shows the skeleton table and Figure 10.7 the state diagram.

**Table 10.9**    Turing's table for **cpe(C,A,E,$\alpha$,$\beta$)**

| $m$-config | Symbol | Operations | Final $m$-config |
|---|---|---|---|
| **cpe(C,A,E,$\alpha$,$\beta$)** | | | **cp(e(e(C,C,$\beta$),C,$\alpha$),A,E,$\alpha$,$\beta$)** |

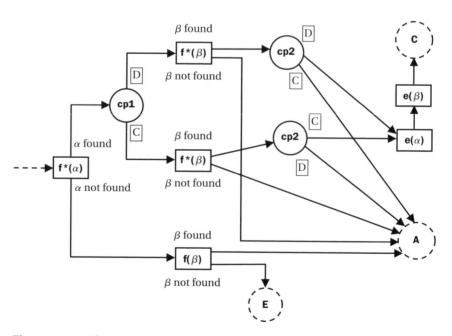

**Figure 10.7**    The state diagram for **cpe(C,A,E,$\alpha$,$\beta$)** when the symbols marked by $\alpha$ and $\beta$ can be either D or C.

The second process uses the, by now familiar, strategy of recursive definition to transform **cpe(C,A,E,$\alpha$,$\beta$)** from a process which compares one pair of symbols and erases the markers if they match, to a process which compares multiple pairs and erases their markers for as long as matching pairs are found. This definition has the same type of recursive structure as **e(B,$\alpha$)** and **ce(B,$\alpha$)**. Table 10.10 shows the skeleton table and Figure 10.8 the state diagram. **cpe(A,E,$\alpha$,$\beta$)** has two exit points. **A** is taken when the matching process fails, **E** when it succeeds. The latter exit point indicates that two complete sequences of symbols have been found to match.

**Table 10.10**  Turing's table for **cpe(A,E,$\alpha$,$\beta$)**

| *m*-config | Symbol | Operations | Final *m*-config |
|---|---|---|---|
| **cpe(A,E,$\alpha$,$\beta$)** | | | **cpe(cpe(A,E,$\alpha$,$\beta$),A,E,$\alpha$,$\beta$)** |

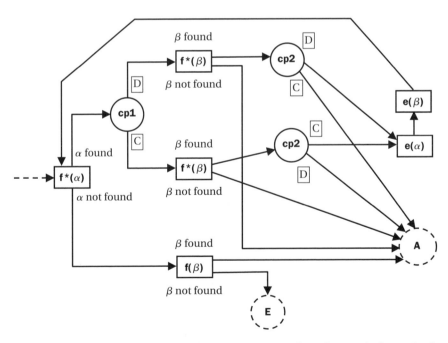

**Figure 10.8**  The state diagram for **cpe(A,E,$\alpha$,$\beta$)** when the symbols marked by $\alpha$ and $\beta$ can be either D or C.

**Table 10.11**   Turing's table for **con(C,$\alpha$)**

| *m*-config | Symbol | Operations | Final *m*-config |
|---|---|---|---|
| **con(C,$\alpha$)** | Not A | R,R | **con(C,$\alpha$)** |
| | A | L,P$\alpha$,R | **con1(C,$\alpha$)** |
| **con1(C,$\alpha$)** | A | R,P$\alpha$,R | **con1(C,$\alpha$)** |
| | D | R,P$\alpha$,R | **con2(C,$\alpha$)** |
| | None | PD,R,P$\alpha$,R,R,R | **C** |
| **con2(C,$\alpha$)** | C | R,P$\alpha$,R | **con2(C,$\alpha$)** |
| | Not C | R,R | **C** |

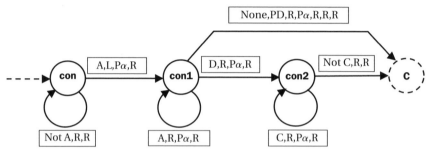

**Figure 10.9**   The state diagram for **con(C,$\alpha$)**.

## Marking configurations

One more process which plays an important part in the processing of the universal machine is more specialized than those discussed thus far. It needs to be considered in the context of standard descriptions. The standard description format for an *m*-configuration is D followed by one or more As, and the standard description format for a symbol is D, followed by zero or more Cs: D by itself being the standard description representation of a blank square. Configurations are, therefore, sequences of symbols such as DAD which represents the configuration (**q1**,#) and DAADC which represents the configuration (**q2**,0). Configurations are crucially important because they determine the behaviour of Turing machines and Turing defined a process **con(C,$\alpha$)** which marks a configuration in standard description format with $\alpha$. Its skeleton table is shown in Table 10.11 and its state diagram in Figure 10.9.

We have now considered all the major components that Turing used in the design of the universal machine. There are other specialized processes still to be described that are best understood in the context of the detailed discussion of the universal machine in Chapter 12. Chapter 11 explores Turing's simulation strategy in outline.

# 11 Simulation

## Introduction

Turing's universal machine is a wonderful, hugely imaginative, invention. Its processing is intricate, effective and longwinded, all at the same time. The machine has, in a sense, two different identities and can be understood in two different ways. In one sense it is just another Turing machine, with a mini-mind, a symbol alphabet and a tape. Its behaviour is governed by its configurations. In another sense, it is a second order machine, a simulator of other Turing machines, and its behaviour is governed by the standard description of the Turing machine it is simulating. Turing's remarkable achievement was to demonstrate that a single machine could properly be described in both of these ways simultaneously. In this chapter, the simulation cycle of the universal machine is described in outline. To dramatize the presentation and, I hope, to clarify the distinction between the two ways of describing its behaviour, the simulation cycle is presented from two different standpoints. The everyday Turing machine aspect is described from the inside, as it were, using the imaginary environment of windowless rooms introduced in Chapter 5. The reader is invited to participate in the processing of the machine as it goes about its square by square business. The simulation aspect is described from the outside, from the standpoint of an observer who can see the whole tape rather than just the current square available to the mini-mind of the machine. The details of the processes involved are discussed in Chapter 12. The emphasis in this chapter is on the structure of the simulation cycle as a whole.

## The simulation cycle in outline

The processes executed by the universal machine constitute nine distinct groups, each of which is defined by a top level $m$-function. The flow of processing through these $m$-functions is shown in Figure 11.1. Processing starts with **b** which writes out the first complete configuration of the target machine to the right of the standard description (SD). This provides the universal machine with its first search key. There is then a cycle of processing through **anf, kom** and **kmp**. This cycle identifies the instruction in the SD of the target machine which matches the current configuration of the target machine. **anf**

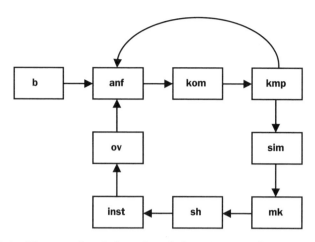

**Figure 11.1**  The top level functional description of Turing's universal machine.

starts the work by marking the configuration in the most recent complete configuration and **kom** marks the nearest (i.e. rightmost) instruction in the SD that has not yet been examined. The two marked sequences are then compared, symbol for symbol by **kmp**. If the match fails, the markers are cleared and a transition is made back to **anf** to initiate the marking and attempted matching of the next instruction. Eventually, the matching process will succeed and a transition is made from **kmp** to **sim**. The purpose of **sim** is to mark those parts of the matched instruction in the SD of the target machine which refer to the operations to be carried out and which indicate the next *m*-configuration of the target machine. The **mk** processes mark the most recent complete configuration into four different sections. Taken together, the marked portions of the matched instruction and those from the last complete configuration, enable the universal machine to construct the next complete configuration. **sh** examines the matched instruction to determine whether the target machine prints 0 or 1. If it does the appropriate symbol is printed at the end of the tape. The new complete configuration is constructed by **inst** which copies the marked parts of the instruction and last complete configuration. The construction process has to take account of the way in which the target machine would have moved relative to its tape. Finally, **ov** tidies up the tape and makes a transition to **anf** to initiate a new processing cycle. A complete cycle from **anf** to **anf** simulates a single move of the target machine. It is, roughly speaking, equivalent to a single fetch-execute cycle in a stored program computer.

### Observation and participation

At the start of a processing cycle, the tape of the universal machine is blank except for the standard description of the target machine, the machine it is to simulate, which is written on *F*-squares. In what follows, TM1 is used as the target machine. We begin from the standpoint of the observer.

*Observer*

The tape of the universal machine at the start of a simulation of TM1 appears as follows:

```
ee; D A D D C R D A A ; D A A D D R D A A A ; D A A
                      | b
A D D C C R D A A A A ; D A A A A D D R D A *
```

The standard description of the target machine is written on *F*-squares of the universal machine's tape. To facilitate processing the semicolons separating instructions in the standard description have been moved from the end to the beginning of each instruction, there are two tokens of 'e' marking the first *F*-square and *E*-square of the tape and the standard description is terminated with an asterisk on the *F*-square following the final symbol of the description. The environment is a linear sequence of squares but will be described as rooms when we adopt the perspective of the participant. The environment appears as two lines on the page simply because of the constraints of page size. The first 'e' is in square (room) number 1 and the * is in square (room) 97. The odd numbered squares (rooms) are equivalent to *F*-squares, the even numbered ones to *E*-squares. The vertical bar indicates the position of the mini-mind which is in functional state **b**. We have chosen, arbitrarily, to start with the mini-mind in room 23. It doesn't matter. It could have been anywhere on the tape, not necessarily within the region inscribed with the standard description of the target.

*Participant*

Imagine if you will, as in Chapter 5, that you wake yet again from a dreamless sleep and find yourself in a room of the kind described there. Your perception is bounded by the walls of the room. Figure 11.2 shows roughly how the situation appears to you. There is a semi-colon clearly inscribed on the back wall of the room.

*Observer*

The universal machine is simulating TM1 which is functionally equivalent to the first sheep and dogs example of Chapter 5. The sheep and dogs example starts with the machine in the 'sheepish' state but this functional state, or its TM1 equivalent, is not a functional state of the universal mini-mind. The environment contains the standard description of TM1 but nothing else. In particular there is no indication, in the standard description, of the target machine's starting state. The distinction drawn in Chapter 5 between configuration-governed and rule-governed activity is now of practical significance. A universal machine is governed by its configurations like any other Turing machine, but it is required to function as though it were rule-governed

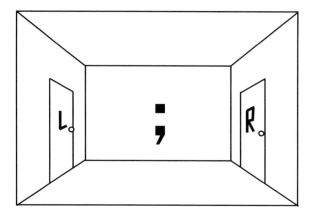

**Figure 11.2**    The appearance of room 23.

and the set of rules it is to follow is a standard description. The universal mini-mind has to use its own configurations to set up what is needed to begin the simulation task. This is what is called a 'bootstrap' sequence in computer jargon. The starting configuration for a target machine is always (q1,#) which is DAD in the alphabet of standard descriptions. The bootstrap sequence, *m*-function **b** in Figure 11.1, takes the universal mini-mind through the moves needed to write DA on the *F*-squares immediately following the standard description. Its behaviour is initially controlled by a leftmost symbol finder looking for the * at the end of the standard description.

*Participant*

Having registered the symbol on the back wall of the room you find that you feel 'e'ish. You want to find a token of 'e'. Leaving unchanged everything that you encounter in the rooms that you pass through, you start to move left-wards looking at the back wall of each room. In due course you encounter an 'e'. This causes you to move one more room to the left and you find yourself again looking at an 'e'. You now want to find a token of * and you start moving rightwards through the rooms inspecting each to see if it has an * written on the back wall. Whatever you find you leave unchanged. In due course you find that you are in a room with an * on the wall. Leaving the * unaltered you move two rooms to the right. There you take a pen from your pocket and write a big colon on the wall. Unfortunately, because you are a simple universal mini-mind, you do not understand how privileged you are to be allowed to write on walls. Having written the colon you again move two rooms further to the right and write a D on the wall, followed by an A two rooms further on beyond that.

*Observer*

The observer looking at the whole environment now sees the following:

```
ee; D A D D C R D A A ; D A A D D R D A A A ; D A A
A D D C C R D A A A A ; D A A A A D D R D A * :
D A
   | anf
```

The mini-mind of the universal machine is positioned at the end of the tape having written : DA on the first three blank *F*-squares. The standard description of TM1 has not been consulted but activity has been possible because of Turing's stipulation that all machines start in state **q1** scanning a blank square. The mini-mind now embarks on the processing of *m*-function **anf** which completes the bootstrap sequence by appending a D to complete the representation of the starting configuration of TM1 and then marking the configuration with tokens of 'y'.

*Participant*

As you contemplate the 'A' on the back wall of the room you feel a desire to find an * again and you move left until you find yourself in a room with an * on the wall. You now find yourself wanting to find an A to the right of where you are, so you move to the right until you find yourself looking at one. From there you move one room left, write a 'y' on the wall of the empty room you find yourself in and go back into the room on the right which has the A in it. From there you move one room right again, write another 'y' in the empty room you find yourself in and move right again. The room you find yourself in is also empty, you write a D on the wall, move one room to the right, which again is empty, and write a 'y' on the wall there. You then move three rooms further to the right.

*Observer*

To the watching observer the environment now appears as follows:

```
ee; D A D D C R D A A ; D A A D D R D A A A ; D A A
A D D C C R D A A A A ; D A A A A D D R D A * :
DyAyDy###
            | kom
```

The bootstrap sequence has been completed. In addition to the standard description of TM1 we also see its starting configuration written in standard description format and marked with tokens of 'y'. The configuration marking process was described in Chapter 10. The fact that the mini-mind is three squares to the right of the final 'y' is a consequence of the fact that its behaviour has been under the control of an instantiation of the *m*-function **con(C,**α**)** which is used for a variety of purposes most of which require this kind of positioning. It has no functional significance in the current context.

Configurations, as we have repeatedly seen, determine the behaviour of Turing machines. The universal machine now has the means to find the instruction of the target machine it has to execute because the configuration DAD uniquely determines that instruction. Inspection of the standard description allows the observer to see that it happens to be the first on the tape, DADDCRDAA. The observer can see that this is the instruction to follow because it is the only one in the standard description which starts with DAD. The configuration is, in effect, an index to the instruction. Instructions have two parts, the configuration (in this instance) DAD, and the actions DCRDAA. However, as the observer also knows, the universal machine can see the symbol in only one room at a time and cannot, therefore, tell which instruction is to be followed. Indeed, of course, the universal machine has no idea that it is following instructions at all. What it is actually doing is simply following the dictates of its configurations. What is needed, therefore, is a square by square process which will 'find' the instruction automatically. The reader, as observer, may quite correctly be beginning to feel that this will be a lengthy process. It will, but we won't prolong the description too far here. It's worth pointing out, however, that the need to work on a square by square basis is a good illustration of why computers have to work at electronic speeds. They are somewhat more efficient than Turing's universal machine but still have to execute billions of elementary instructions in order to achieve results that appear useful to the user.

### Participant

You now want to find a semi-colon and move off to the left inspecting the rooms you pass through to see if there is a semi-colon on the wall. You find one fairly quickly. Moving to the room on the right you write a 'z' on the wall and go back into the room with the semi-colon in it. You now start moving to the right two rooms at a time looking for an A. When you find one you move to the room on its left, write an 'x' on the wall and move back to the room with an A. Then you start a process moving to the right looking for either an A or a D. If you find an A you move to the room on its right, write an 'x' on the wall, move to the right again and repeat the process. If you find a D you also move to the room on its right and write an 'x' on the wall but then, instead of repeating the process you look for a C. While looking for a C you find a D instead and move two rooms to the right.

### Observer

The observer now sees the following pattern of symbols in the environment:

```
ee; D A D D C R D A A ; D A A D D R D A A A ; D A A
A D D C C R D A A A A ;zDxAxAxAxAxDxD R D A * :
                                      |kmp

DyAyDy
```

The universal machine has marked the configuration of the rightmost instruction in the standard description with 'x's. The environment is now set up for a process which compares the configurations marked with 'x' and 'y', square by square, to see if they match. If they do, the correct instruction of the target machine has been identified. The observer can see at a glance that the configurations in the example don't match but the universal machine can't see this because of its limited perception.

### Participant

You now want to find an 'e' so you move to the left until you encounter one and then move one room further left. Now you want to find an 'x' so you move to the right until you encounter one. This makes you move one room to the left. The room has a 'D' on the wall. You now want to find an 'e' again so you move to the left until you find one, and then move one room further left. Now you want to find a 'y' so you move to the right until you find one. This makes you move one room to the left. The room has a 'D' on the wall. This makes you want to find an 'e' again, so you move to the left until you do so, and, as before, you then move one room to the left. Now you want to find an 'x' so you move to the right until you find it. You erase the 'x'. Now, yet again, you want to find an 'e'. Moving left you repeat the moves that find the 'e' and then move left. Now you want to find a 'y' and you move right until you do so. You erase the 'y'.

### Observer

The observer now sees the following pattern of symbols in the environment:

```
ee; D A D D C R D A A ; D A A D D R D A A A ; D A A
A D D C C R D A A A A ;zD AxAxAxAxDxD R D A * :
D AyDy
 | kmp
```

The laborious process that the universal machine has just gone through has compared the first symbol marked by 'x' with the first symbol marked by 'y'. They have been found to match and the markers have been erased. Most of the time has been spent shuttling left and right along the tape because the basic process in the universal machine's repertoire is the leftmost symbol finder $f(C,B,\alpha)$. The next pair of symbols compared will also be found to match but the third pair will not. At this point the universal machine erases all the remaining 'x' and 'y' markers on the tape and makes a transition from **kmp** back to **anf** (see Figure 11.1). The next instruction is then marked and compared with DAD. This comparison also fails, as does a third cycle.

The fourth matching cycle succeeds and the universal machine makes a transition from **kmp** to **sim** to continue the simulation cycle. At this point the environment appears as follows:

```
ee;zD A D D C R D A A ;zD A A D D R D A A A ;zD A A
A D D C C R D A A A A ;zD A A A A D D R D A * : D A
D##
    |sim
```

The appropriate instruction in the standard description is now identified by the leftmost 'z' and its actions have to be carried out to simulate the first move of TM1. The actions prescribed are DC, R and DAA which mean 'Print 0, move right, make a transition to state **q2**. The first of these instructions is reasonably straightforward because it is a simple print instruction. The remaining actions are more complicated to deal with because they indicate how TM1 would move and change state if it were carrying out the task rather than how the universal machine has to behave in order to simulate these actions of TM1. The movement and change of state of TM1 have, therefore, to be represented in a form which the universal machine can use to continue its simulation. The discussion in Chapter 5 introduced the concept of a 'complete configuration' which is a record of everything on the tape of a Turing machine plus an indication of its current functional state and the current scanned square. This information includes the configuration which determines the next move of the machine. The solution that Turing adopted for the universal machine was to write each complete configuration of the target machine on the tape in standard description format and to use the information in this complete configuration to find the configuration of the next instruction to execute. This was done by an intricate process of marking and copying elements from the instruction being executed and from the previous complete configuration. The **sim** *m*-function starts this process by marking the newly identified instruction of the target machine to prepare it for later copying. Once this has been completed the environment appears as follows:

```
ee; D A D DuCuRuDyAyAy; D A A D D R D A A A ; D A A
A D D C C R D A A A A ; D A A A A D D R D A * : D A
D##
    |mk
```

The **mk** *m*-function does essentially the same job with respect to the most recent complete configuration of the target machine. When it has finished it writes a colon on the first available *F*-square to separate the complete configuration from everything that follows it. In the present case, **mk** leaves no markers so when the transition to **sh** is made the environment appears as follows:

```
ee; D A D DuCuRuDyAyAy; D A A D D R D A A A ; D A A
A D D C C R D A A A A ; D A A A A D D R D A * : D A
D :
     |sh
```

*Participant*

You want to find an 'e' so you move to the left until you do so, and then left again. Now you want to find a 'u' so you move to the right until you do so. You now move three rooms to the left where you find a 'D'. This makes you move four rooms to the right where you find a 'C'. This makes you move two rooms to the right where you find an 'R'. This makes you want to find an 'e' so you move to the left until you do so, and then left again. You now move right, two rooms at a time, inspecting the second room of each pair, until you find one that is empty. You write a '0' on the wall. Now you want to find an 'e' so you move to the left until you do so, and then left again. You now move right, two rooms at a time, inspecting the second room of each pair, until you find one that is empty. You write a colon on the wall.

*Observer*

The environment now appears as follows:

```
ee; D A D DuCuRuDyAyAy; D A A D D R D A A A ; D A A
A D D C C R D A A A A ; D A A A A D D R D A * : D A
D : 0 :
         |inst
```

The universal machine has carried out the first print instruction of TM1. It now has to write the next complete configuration of TM1 on the tape in standard description format. This is a lengthy process which is carried out by the **inst** *m*-function. When it is finished the environment appears as follows:

```
ee; D A D D C R D A A ; D A A D D R D A A A ; D A A
A D D C C R D A A A A ; D A A A A D D R D A * : D A
D : 0 : D C D A A ##
                    |ov
```

The final part of the simulation cycle uses the *m*-function **ov** to remove any markers that might be left on *E*-squares. In the present case there are no markers and when it finishes its work and makes a transition to **anf** the environment is unchanged:

```
ee; D A D D C R D A A ; D A A D D R D A A A ; D A A
A D D C C R D A A A A ; D A A A A D D R D A * : D A
D : 0 : D C D A A##
```
                        | **anf**

At this point, the universal machine has completed the simulation of one move of TM1. It has identified and executed the instruction (**q1**,#) → (0,R **q2**) and is ready to begin the process of identifying the next instruction to follow.

Several points about simulation are noteworthy. First, as already observed, simulation is relative to a particular type of encoding. Turing's universal machine uses standard descriptions, other universal machines use other encodings. Readers who would like to see a different universal machine design are recommended to look at Minsky (1967). Minsky's universal machine is also discussed in Feynman (1996). Simulations are not all equal in terms of practicality, time taken or aesthetic appeal. Second, the capacity to simulate does not imply the capacity to reproduce exactly the behaviour of the machine simulated. Turing's universal machine computes the same sequence of digits as the machine it simulates but does so in an entirely different way. Third, as the discussion of this chapter shows, a universal machine does not, in any sense, have to have any understanding of or insight into the machine it is simulating. A universal machine is a Turing machine like any other and its immediate behaviour is entirely locally caused. Finally though, despite its square by square operations and complete lack of insight, there is a sense in which the capacity to simulate makes Turing's universal machine as powerful as any computer ever built. Nothing that has ever been computed on any computer is beyond the scope of Turing's machine provided that the desired computation can be presented in standard description format. In Chapter 12 we look in detail at the nine high level *m*-functions of Turing's universal machine.

# 12 The Universal Machine in Detail

Chapters 10 and 11 introduced the major functional components of Turing's universal machine and the method of simulation employed. Some aspects of the structure and processing of the machine were treated sketchily in the interests of brevity and readability. This chapter provides full details of the universal machine. Despite its historical importance and intrinsic interest, however, the level of detail is not essential for the issues discussed in the rest of the book and readers with notation fatigue may wish to return to it later.

### Initiating a computation

The processing of the universal machine is started by the *m*-function **b** which adds the sequence : D A to the end of the tape. It does this by using a symbol finder to locate the symbol * which marks the end of the SD of the target machine. The machine table for the *m*- function is shown in Table 12.1 and its state diagram in Figure 12.1.

It is apparent immediately that the universal machine does not itself conform to the standard description format. It has multiple behaviours

**Figure 12.1**   The state diagram for **b** which begins the processing of the universal machine.

**Table 12.1**   Turing's table for **b**

| *m*-config | Symbol | Operations | Final *m*-config |
|---|---|---|---|
| b | | | f(b1,b1,*) |
| b1 | | R,R,P:,R,R,PD,R,R,PA | anf |

defined for *m*-configuration **b1**. This serves to highlight the distinction between the universal machine and the target machine which it simulates. It is the description of the target machine that has to be given in standard form. When the transition to **anf** is made, the tape is marked as shown below:

```
ee; D A D D C R D A A ; D A A D D R D A A A ;
D A A A D D C C R D A A A A ; D A A A A D D R D A *
: D A
      | anf
```

## Marking and matching configurations

The process of marking and matching configurations is carried out by a processing loop that cycles through **anf**, **kom** and **kmp**. Cycles of processing round this loop find the current instruction of the target machine. It was an oversight on Turing's part, not to append the final D, which indicates that the target machine would be scanning a blank square, to complete the representation of the first configuration of the target machine.[3] This is done by **anf** which also marks the configuration. The skeleton table for anf is shown in Table 12.2 and its state diagram in Figure 12.2.

**Table 12.2**   Turing's table for **anf**

| *m*-config config | Symbol | Operations | Final *m* |
|---|---|---|---|
| anf |  |  | q(anf1, *) |
| anf1 |  |  | con(kom, y) |

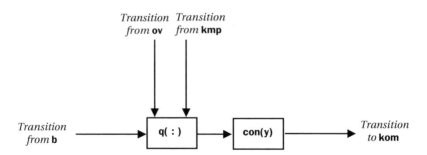

**Figure 12.2**   The state diagram for **anf**.

---

[3] This was the most important problem identified by Emil Post. He corrected it by modifying the *m*-function **con(C,α)**.

After processing by **anf** is completed, the tape is as shown below:

```
ee; D A D D C R D A A ; D A A D D R D A A A ; D A A
A D D C C R D A A A A ; D A A A A D D R D A * :
DyAyDy###
        | kom
```

The universal machine now has to find the matching configuration in the standard description of the target machine. This process is started by **kom** whose machine table is shown in Table 12.3 and state diagram in Figure 12.3.

  **kom** makes a traverse to the left until the first unmarked semicolon is found, indicating an instruction in the SD of the target machine that has not yet been tried for a match with the current configuration. The semicolon is marked with 'z' and the configuration immediately to the right with 'x'. On completion a transition is made to **kmp**.

**Table 12.3**  Turing's table for **kom**

| $m$-config | Symbol | Operations | Final $m$-config |
|---|---|---|---|
|  | ; | R,Pz,L | con(kmp,$x$) |
| **kom** | z | L,L | **kom** |
|  | not z nor ; | L | **kom** |

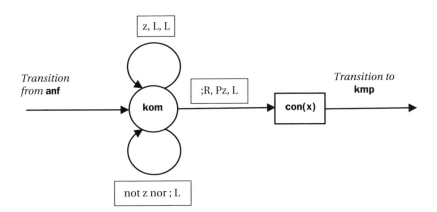

**Figure 12.3**  The state diagram for **kom**.

```
ee; D A D D C R D A A ; D A A D D R D A A A ; D A A
A D D C C R D A A A A ;zDxAxAxAxAxDxD R D A * :
```
                                                    | **kmp**
```
DyAyDy
```

**kmp** compares marked configurations and erases the markers for each pair of matching symbols. Its skeleton table is shown in Table 12.4. Turing made two mistakes in his definition of **kmp**. It is clear what his intention was but he did not have the luxury of a computer on which to test the correctness of his definitions and neither he nor the otherwise hawk-eyed Emil Post spotted that his definition of **kmp** makes reference to an undefined eraser function and incorrectly makes the transition on failure of matching to **kom** rather than to **anf**. The version of the process given here functions correctly.[4] The state diagram for **kmp** is shown in Figure 12.4. It is an extended version of the $m$-function of Figure 10.8.

**Table 12.4**   Turing's table for **kmp**

| $m$-config | Symbol | Operations | Final $m$-config |
|---|---|---|---|
| **kmp** | | | **cpe(e(e(anf, y), x), sim, x, y)** |

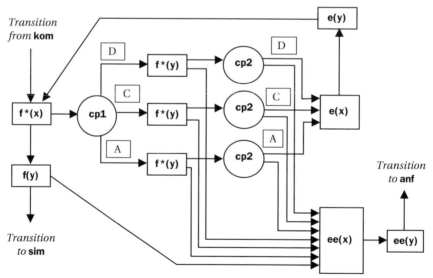

**Figure 12.4**   The state diagram for **kmp**.

---

[4] Copeland (2004, section 2.4) shows that this mistake had, in fact, been spotted and corrected by Donald Davies who was working at NPL in 1947. I discovered the error, independently, when writing a program to emulate the functioning of Turing's universal machine.

The comparison process is set up for D,C and A which are the three symbols out of which configurations in standard description format are constructed. The comparison *m*-function is augmented by two pairs of eraser *m*-functions. If the match succeeds for a pair of symbols, their markers are erased by the pair of *m*-functions labelled **e(x)** and **e(y)** in the state diagram. The first and second symbol pairs in the current example would be successfully matched in this way and a transition made back to **f\*(x)** to continue the process from the situation shown below:

```
ee; D A D D C R D A A ; D A A D D R D A A A ; D A A
A D D C C R D A A A A ; zD A  AxAxAxDxD  R D A  *  :
D A Dy
   | f*(x)
```

If a pairwise match fails, as happens in the next cycle, the transition on failure is made to **ee(x)** which removes all tokens of 'x'. This makes a transition to **ee(y)** which removes the remaining 'y' marker and makes a transition to **anf** with the tape as shown.

```
ee; D A D D C R D A A ; D A A D D R D A A A ; D A A
A D D C C R D A A A A ; zD A A A A D D R D A  *  :
D A D#
    | anf
```

The marker 'z' is left in place, indicating the fact that the instruction to its right has been tried. If this marker were not in place, the universal machine would cycle endlessly trying and failing to match the rightmost instruction. Two further attempted matching cycles for the next two instructions also fail. The fourth cycle finds the correct instruction, matches each pair of symbols and makes a transition to **sim** when further searches for 'x' and 'y' markers by **f\*(x)** and **f(y)** fail. The latter search uses **f(y)** rather than **f\*(y)** because if there is no 'x' marker, the significant question is whether there is a 'y' marker not whether there is a marked symbol. If there is a 'y' marker the match fails whatever symbol is marked. The tape condition at this point is

```
ee; zD A D D C R D A A ; zD A A D D R D A A A ; zD A A
A D D C C R D A A A A ; zD A A A A D D R D A  *  :
D A D##
        | sim
```

## Marking the tape in preparation for writing the next complete configuration

In order for the universal machine to construct the next complete configuration of the target machine, the successfully matched instruction

**Table 12.5**   Turing's table for **sim**

| *m*-config | Symbol | Operations | Final *m*-config |
|---|---|---|---|
| **sim** | | | **f\*(sim1,sim1,**$z$**)** |
| **sim1** | | | **con(sim2,**#**)** |
| **sim2** | A | | **sim3** |
| | not A | L,Pu,R,R,R | **sim2** |
| **sim3** | not A | L,Py | **e(mk,**$z$**)** |
| | A | L,Py,R,R,R | **sim3** |

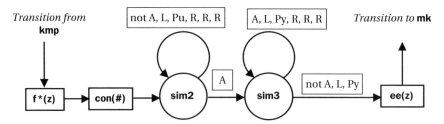

**Figure 12.5**   The state diagram for **sim**.

and the most recent complete configuration have to be marked so that the appropriate parts can be copied. **sim** does this for the matched instruction. The table for **sim** is shown in Table 12.5 and its state diagram in Figure 12.5.

Processing begins with a search for the first 'z' which is immediately to the left of the matched instruction:

```
ee;zD A D D C R D A A ;zD A A D D R D A A A ;zD A A
   |sim1
A D D C C R D A A A A ;zD A A A A D D R D A * :
D A D
```

The marking of the configuration with blanks is carried out so as to position the machine in the right place to mark out the rest of the instruction which is what is needed for the next complete configuration. Turing could, of course, have designed a special process for this purpose, but this is another instance of his preference for using an existing process wherever possible. **con(sim2,**#**)** is ideal for the purpose although this is, presumably, a side effect and not something that Turing had planned from the outset.

```
ee;zD A D D C R D A A ;zD A A D D R D A A A ;zD A A
          |sim2
A D D C C R D A A A A ;zD A A A A D D R D A * :
D A D
```

**sim2** marks the instructions to be carried out with 'u' and makes a transition to **sim3**;

```
ee;zD A D DuCuRuD A A ;zD A A D D R D A A A ;zD A A
                  |sim3
A D D C C R D A A A A ;zD A A A A D D R D A * :
D A D
```

**sim3** marks the final $m$-configuration with 'y'.

```
ee;zD A D DuCuRuDyAyAy;zD A A D D R D A A A ;zD A A
                      |e(mk,z)
A D D C C R D A A A A ;zD A A A A D D R D A * :
D A D
```

All the 'z' markers are then erased and a transition is made to **mk** to mark out the last complete configuration.

```
ee; D A D DuCuRuDyAyAy; D A A D D R D A A A ; D A A
A D D C C R D A A A A ; D A A A A D D R D A * :
D A D##
        |mk
```

The machine table for **mk** is shown in Table 12.6 and its state diagram in Figure 12.6.

In the most general case, **mk** marks out the last complete configuration on the tape into four sections which represent the configuration, the symbol immediately to the left of the configuration (if there is one), all other symbols further to the left (if any) and all symbols to the right of the

**Table 12.6**  Turing's table for **mk**

| $m$-config | Symbol | Operations | Final $m$-config |
|---|---|---|---|
| mk | | | q(mk1,:) |
| mk1 | not A | R,R | mk1 |
| | A | L,L,L,L | mk2 |
| mk2 | C | R,Px,L,L,L | mk2 |
| | : | | mk4 |
| | D | R,Px,L,L,L | mk3 |
| mk3 | not : | R,Pv,L,L,L | mk3 |
| | : | | mk4 |
| mk4 | | | con(l(l(mk5)), #) |
| mk5 | Any | R,Pw,R | mk5 |
| | None | P: | sh |

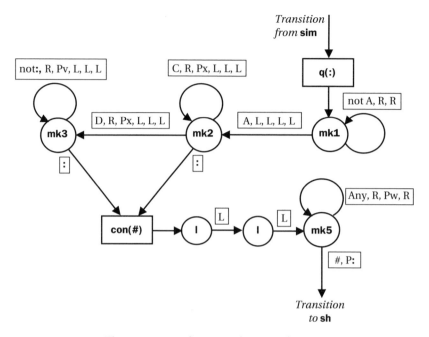

**Figure 12.6**   The state diagram for **mk**.

configuration (if any). The process is not seen fully in the simulation of TM1, but an example which shows the general form is the string DCCDC-DAAADCDDCC which we now consider. If this were the final complete configuration on the tape, it would be bounded by a colon on the left and by blank squares on the right.

```
:  D  C  C  D  C  D  A  A  A  D  C  D  D  C  C##
                                        | mk
```

**mk** is implemented by **q(mk1,:)** which leaves the machine scanning the colon.

```
:  D  C  C  D  C  D  A  A  A  D  C  D  D  C  C
| mk1
```

Anything to the left of the representation of the *m*-configuration has to be divided into two parts, the symbol immediately to the left of the *m*-configuration and everything else. The easiest way to do this is to work from right to left starting from the representation of the *m*-configuration. **mk1** moves the machine to the right until the first 'A' of the *m*-configuration is found, and then backtracks four squares and makes a transition to **mk2**.

```
:  D  C  C  D  C  D  A  A  A  D  C  D  D  C  C
            | mk2
```

**mk2** marks the representation of a single symbol, if there is one, with 'x' and makes a transition to **mk3**. If there is no symbol the transition is to **mk4**.

```
: D C C DxCxD A A A D C D D C C
     |mk3
```

**mk3** marks any other symbols further left on the tape with 'v' and makes a transition to **mk4** when the colon is encountered.

```
: DvCvCvDxCxD A A A D C D D C C
|mk4
```

**mk4** marks the configuration with blanks. This ensures that it will not be copied and also positions the machine in the right place to mark any symbols to the right of the configuration.

```
: DvCvCvDxCxD A A A D C D D C C
                        |mk5
```

**mk5** completes the process by marking all the remaining symbols with 'w'. A colon is then printed on the next $F$-square before a transition is made to **sh**.

```
: DvCvCvDxCxD A A A D C DwDwCwCw:
                               |sh
```

The point of the **mk** processes is to mark the last complete configuration of the target machine in such a way that it can be used by **inst** to construct the next complete configuration. The universal machine then uses this information to control the simulation of the next step of the target machine. Continuing, now, with the example of the simulation of TM1, when the transition to **sh** is made, the tape appears as follows:

```
ee; D A D DuCuRuDyAyAy; D A A D D R D A A A ; D A A
A D D C C R D A A A A ; D A A A A D D R D A * :
D A D :
     |sh
```

## Printing figures

The function of a Turing machine is to compute a sequence of figures (0 and 1) and the function of a universal machine is to simulate the computation of a sequence by a Turing machine. It is, therefore, essential for the universal machine to know when the machine it is simulating would print a new figure. This knowledge is possible because the representations of 0 and 1 in standard description format are DC and DCC by stipulation. Once the marking process has been completed, the universal machine checks to see if the target machine prints a new figure and, if so, that is done at the end of the tape. This process is carried out by the **sh** *m*-functions. The machine table is shown in Table 12.7 and the state diagram in Figure 12.7.

**Table 12.7**    Turing's table for **sh**

| *m*-config | Symbol | Operations | Final *m*-config |
|---|---|---|---|
| **sh** | | | **f(sh1,inst,u)** |
| **sh1** | | L,L,L | **sh2** |
| **sh2** | D | R,R,R,R | **sh3** |
| | not D | | **inst** |
| **sh3** | C | R,R | **sh4** |
| | not C | | **inst** |
| **sh4** | C | R,R | **sh5** |
| | not C | | **pe2(inst,0 , : )** |
| **sh5** | C | | **inst** |
| | not C | | **pe2(inst,1 , : )** |

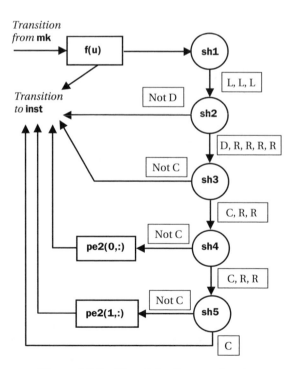

**Figure 12.7**    The state diagram for **sh**.

The instructions that the target machine is to carry out have been marked with 'u' by **sim3**. The leftmost of these markers is found by **sh**, a transition is made to **sh1** which moves the machine three squares left, and the instruction checking process is then begun in earnest by **sh2**.

```
ee; D A D DuCuRuDyAyAy; D A A D D R D A A A ; D A A
        |sh2
A D D C C R D A A A A ; D A A A A D D R D A * :
D A D :
```

The move three squares to the left by **sh1** is puzzling until one realizes that in standard description format, every instruction has a print operation in order to achieve uniformity of representation. Thus the standard description of an instruction in which a machine passes over a square containing a previously printed figure, contains an instruction to reprint that figure. The universal machine has, therefore, to distinguish new printings from re-printings. It is only new printings that should trigger the universal machine to print a figure. The way to find out is to check if the currently scanned square of the target machine is blank. If it is, its representation will be the single symbol 'D' which will be three squares to the left of the first marker 'u'. Hence the three moves left. Any other symbol scanned by **sh2** means that the instructions do not include a new printing and therefore the checking process can be discontinued. In the TM1 example processing continues with **sh3**.

```
ee; D A D DuCuRuDyAyAy; D A A D D R D A A A ; D A A
        |sh3
A D D C C R D A A A A ; D A A A A D D R D A * :
D A D :
```

The cases of interest are those in which the print symbol is either DC or DCC, that is, 0 or 1. These are picked out by **sh4** and **sh5**. If the print symbol is DC the universal machine prints 0 followed by a colon at the end of the tape, and if it is DCC, a 1 followed by a colon is printed. Otherwise nothing is printed and a transition is made directly to **inst**. In the current example, the machine encounters 'R' when in **sh4**.

```
ee; D A D DuCuRuDyAyAy; D A A D D R D A A A ; D A A
        |sh4
A D D C C R D A A A A ; D A A A A D D R D A * :
D A D :
```

This causes a transition to **pe2(inst,**0**, :)** after which a transition to **inst** is made.

```
ee;  D  A  D  DuCuRuDyAyAy;  D  A  A  D  D  R  D  A  A  A  ;  D  A  A
A  D  D  C  C  R  D  A  A  A  A  ;  D  A  A  A  A  D  D  R  D  A  *  :
D  A  D  :  0  :
                | inst
```

## Printing the next complete configuration

The final large scale activity that the universal machine carries out to complete the simulation of a move of the target machine is to write out its next complete configuration. This is put together from marked portions of the tape. The process is managed by the **inst** *m*-functions.[5] The machine table for **inst** is shown in Table 12.8.

   **inst** begins by positioning the machine so that it is scanning the symbol marked by the rightmost marker 'u'. This symbol indicates the direction in which the target machine moves relative to its tape.

```
ee;  D  A  D  DuCuRuDyAyAy;  D  A  A  D  D  R  D  A  A  A  ;  D  A  A
                | inst1
A  D  D  C  C  R  D  A  A  A  A  ;  D  A  A  A  A  D  D  R  D  A  *  :
D  A  D  :  0  :
```

The symbol can be L, R or N and its identity determines the way the next complete configuration is put together. **inst1** erases the marker 'u' and makes a conditional branch to the appropriate **inst1**($\alpha$) *m*-function.

```
ee;  D  A  D  DuCuR  DyAyAy;  D  A  A  D  D  R  D  A  A  A  ;  D  A  A
                | inst1(R)
A  D  D  C  C  R  D  A  A  A  A  ;  D  A  A  A  A  D  D  R  D  A  *  :
D  A  D  :  0  :
```

**Table 12.8**   Turing's table for **inst**

| *m*-config | Symbol | Operations | Final *m*-config |
|---|---|---|---|
| inst | | | q(l(inst1,u)) |
| inst1 | $\alpha$ | R,E | inst1($\alpha$) |
| inst1(L) | | | ce5(ov,v,y,x,u,w) |
| inst1(R) | | | ce5(ov,v,x,u,y,w) |
| inst1(N) | | | ce5(ov,v,x,y,u,w) |

---

[5] Donald Davies included a correction to **inst** to resolve the problem referred to in note 3. See Copeland (2004, pp. 123–4). Presumably Davies was unaware of Post's correction to **con(C,**$\alpha$**)**. With Post's correction, Turing's table for **inst** works properly and Davies' correction is not needed.

**ce5(ov,**v , y , x , u , w**),** which implements **inst1**(R), is a chain of five linked **ce(B,**α**)** processes, **ce(ce(ce(ce(ce(ov, w), u), x), y), v).** One **ce(B,**α**)** process is needed for each marker because the marker has to be fixed when the process is implemented. To understand what **inst** does we first note that a complete configuration of the target machine, in standard description format, includes representations of all the symbols on its tape, the position of its mini-mind and its current functional state. A complete configuration of TM1, for example, whose trace appears as

```
0  1  0  1#
          | ov
```

is DCDDCCDDCDDCCDAAAAD in standard description format. Notice that the representations of the squares of the tape of TM1 are implicit. The first square of its tape is represented by DC because the square has a 0 on it, whereas the second square is represented by D because it is blank. The vertical bar and state name are represented by DAAAA which is positioned immediately to the left of the representation of the scanned square which is also blank in this instance. The new complete configuration may record a move left or right, a state change and a change to the contents of the scanned square. Everything else remains unchanged. Symbols marked with 'v' represent everything to the left of where the action takes place and are always copied first. Those marked with 'w' represent everything to the right of the action and are copied last. 'x' marks the representation of the symbol on the square to the left of the scanned square in the last complete configuration, 'u' marks the representation of the symbol that is printed during the current move of the target machine and 'y' marks the representation of its next *m*-configuration. To simulate a move left, the marked symbols need to be printed in the order, 'y', 'x', 'u'. For no move the order is 'x', 'y', 'u', and for a move right, the order is 'x', 'u', 'y'. The state diagram for **inst** is shown in Figure 12.8. It is a large scale instance

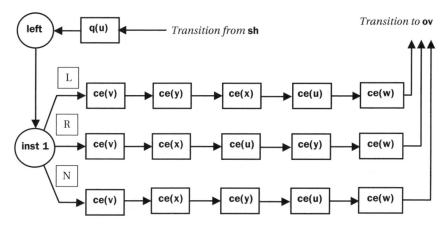

**Figure 12.8**   The state diagram for **inst**.

of the technique for remembering multiple symbols described in Chapter 5, Figure 5.4. To continue with the example simulation of TM1, which moves right, the updated tape appears as follows.

```
ee; D A D D C R D A A ; D A A D D R D A A A ; D A A
A D D C C R D A A A A ; D A A A A D D R D A * :
D A D : 0 : D C D A A##
                      | ov
```

## Housekeeping

The final task, before the transition back to **anf** to start a new simulation cycle, is a simple housekeeping exercise. Any markers that have not previously been erased are removed. The *m*-function **ov** which carries out this task, is defined in terms of an eraser *m*-function **e(C)**. The machine table for **ov** is shown in Table 12.9 and its state diagram in Figure 12.9.

After the housekeeping process the tape is ready for the simulation of the next step of the target machine.

```
ee; D A D D C R D A A ; D A A D D R D A A A ; D A A
A D D C C R D A A A A ; D A A A A D D R D A * :
D A D : 0 : D C D A A##
                      | anf
```

**Table 12.9**    Turing's table for **ov**

| *m*-config | Symbol | Operations | Final *m*-config |
|------------|--------|------------|------------------|
| **ov**     |        |            | e(anf)           |
| **e(C)**   | e      | R          | e1(C)            |
|            | not e  | L          | e(C)             |
| **e1(C)**  | Any    | R,E,R      | e1(C)            |
|            | None   |            | C                |

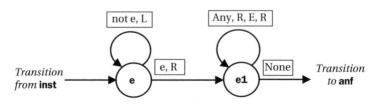

**Figure 12.9**    The state diagram for **ov**.

## Further processing cycles

On its next processing cycle, the universal machine has DAAD as the search key. This matches the second instruction in the SD, DAADDRDAAA which instructs the machine to move right and leave the scanned square blank. At the end of this instruction, the tape of the universal machine appears as follows;

```
ee; D A D D C R D A A ; D A A D D R D A A A ; D A A
A D D C C R D A A A A ; D A A A A D D R D A * :
D A D : 0 : D C D A A D : D C D D A A A## 
                                        | anf
```

Third and fourth processing cycles by the universal machine complete the simulation of a cycle of processing by TM1 through **q1, q2, q3, q4** and return to the point where the target machine is once again in **q1** scanning a blank square.

```
ee; D A D D C R D A A ; D A A D D R D A A A ; D A A
A D D C C R D A A A A ; D A A A A D D R D A * :
D A D : 0 : D C D A A D : D C D D A A A D : 1 : D C
D D C C D A A A A D : D C D D C C D D A## 
                                        | anf
```

The simulation continues indefinitely from this point. The universal machine uses the configuration from the most recent complete configuration to find the relevant instruction in the SD of the target machine. The instruction is then carried out and a new complete configuration constructed to provide the basis for the next move. A record is kept, not just of the sequence computed by the target machine but of every step it takes. The process is reminiscent of a program which keeps track of every key stroke made by its user. In this respect, Turing's universal machine has a very modern feel to it. It is, of course, massively inefficient and, if each move takes a unit of time, it becomes steadily slower, because the amount of tape it has to traverse in order to reach the standard description of the target machine increases as successive complete configurations are added to the record. However, with unlimited space and time available, this is not a matter for theoretical concern.

# 13 Turing's Unsolvability Proofs

The design for the universal machine was a remarkable achievement. It is part of the theoretical foundation of computer science and, as discussed briefly in Chapter 2, the concept of a universal machine is central to the physical symbol systems hypothesis about the nature of intelligence. The universal machine changed forever the idea that a machine is an inflexible system whose behaviour is determined solely by the parts out of which it is made and the way in which they are put together. The universal machine shows that a machine with fixed hardware can be made to behave in a variety of ways by changing the program that controls its behaviour. A program is equivalent to the standard description of a Turing machine and there is a countable infinity of Turing machines so the conclusion to draw is that there is also a countable infinity of programs and hence limitless scope for behavioural flexibility. A rather natural question to ask given this vast panorama of possibilities, is whether there is anything that a universal Turing machine can't do. The answer is 'Yes'. There are limitations and Turing gave proofs in 'On Computable Numbers' of three things that universal machines can't do. These proofs are examined shortly. Before that, it is appropriate to say a few words about 'Turing's Thesis' and how it relates to 'Church's Thesis'.

## Turing's thesis

Turing's investigation of computable numbers was undertaken, in part, to find a formal counterpart to the informal concept of 'effective calculation'. What does it mean to say that a number is 'naturally computable'? The attempt to find a satisfactory formal counterpart to an informal idea is not something that is amenable to proof, and for this reason, as Turing himself said, 'All arguments which can be given are bound to be, fundamentally, appeals to intuition, and for this reason rather unsatisfactory mathematically' (OCN p. 249). Turing was convinced, however, that he had captured the essence of rule-governed computation and agreement is widespread that he had. There are other, in some ways very different, formalizations of the concept of effective calculability and all of them describe the same set of entities. We don't want to talk about proofs with regard to the informal concept so we describe the relationship between Turing machines and human computation in terms of 'Turing's thesis' which proposes that Turing machines can compute all and only those numbers which can be produced by a human computant working according to fixed rules but with unlimited resources of paper, pencils and time. Turing's thesis is often compared with Church's thesis which proposes that the effectively calculable functions are recursive, and some authors refer to the 'Church–Turing thesis' because the two are ultimately equivalent. A careful description of the Church–Turing thesis is given by Sieg (1999). An earlier paper, Sieg (1994) provides a thorough account of the relationship between Church's work and Turing's and discusses more of the mathematical background. An issue over which care is needed is the scope of the thesis in any of its forms. It has been claimed, for example, that all machines are covered, that Church and Turing showed that the functioning of any machine could be simulated by a universal Turing machine.

It should be clear from the earlier chapters of the book that this is by no means obvious. Turing's analysis was specifically concerned with what can be computed by a machine working according to fixed rules and under constraints derived from the limitations on humans. The universal machine is strictly serial and its functional states are discrete. Gandy (1980) showed that Turing's analysis could be extended to parallel, discrete machines, but the extension of the thesis to all machines would be justified only if it could be shown that any conceivable machine could be described in standard description format. Copeland (1997, 2002) claims that there are machines which are physically realizable in principle and which compute functions that cannot be computed by any Turing machine. Copeland's own thesis is highly debatable but it supports the idea that caution is needed in claiming more for the concept of universality than is justified by Turing's own work. Readers interested in theoretical exploration of the scope for machines that are claimed to compute uncomputable functions may also wish to look at Siegelmann (1999) and at the collection of papers edited by Teuscher (2004).

## Uncomputable numbers

The universal machine demonstrates that it is possible to carry out a huge range of tasks with a single mechanism and our everyday experience with the many applications of programmable computers, which are essentially practical versions of universal machines, bears out the astonishing degree of flexibility of machines instantiating their principles of operation. Indeed, it is probable that our everyday understanding of the concept of a machine has changed substantially over the past 50 years and will continue to do so as more applications are developed. It is striking, therefore, that a primary use for Turing's universal machine was to prove that some sequences were not computable and that some problems could not be solved in a finite number of steps. OCN contains three important results of this kind. First Turing proved that there was no Turing machine which could decide in a finite number of steps whether a given number was the description number of a circle-free machine. This proof is more generally known as the proof of the unsolvability of the halting problem for Turing machines.[6] Second, he used this result to prove that there can be no machine which can decide, given the standard description of an arbitrary machine *M*, whether *M* ever prints a given symbol, 0 for example. Finally, using the first two results, he was able to prove that Hilbert's Entscheidungsproblem was unsolvable. That is to say, he proved that there was no machine which could decide whether an arbitrary given formula of Hilbert's functional calculus was provable. These proofs are different from Gödel's well known incompleteness theorems, and they have interesting characteristics that deserve discussion. One important question is whether the provable limitations on the capacities of Turing machines support an argument to show that minds cannot be machines. Gödel's results have been used to support such arguments. An early argument by J.R. Lucas (1961) has been widely discussed and, more recently, Roger Penrose has developed an argument which combines elements of Gödel's and Turing's results. Gödel's theorems and Turing's proof of the unsolvability of the halting problem both include crucial self-referential constructions. I shall return to a consideration of this issue after describing Turing's proofs.

## The unsolvability of the halting problem

Turing's first negative result arises from his defence of the claim that the computable sequences are enumerable. The basic question concerning enumeration is whether it is possible to count the members of a particular class of objects. We have already encountered, in Chapter 9, the simple, but powerful, idea that objects can be counted if a list can be made of them such that they can be paired with the natural numbers. Each computable sequence $\gamma$ is determined by a machine which computes $\gamma$ and each such machine is defined by its description number. In Chapter 9 a scheme for numbering Turing machines was introduced which showed that they can be counted. Each computable sequence has at least one description number corresponding to it, but no description number corresponds to more than one

---

[6] Copeland (2004, pp. 36–40) argues that it is not, strictly speaking, accurate to describe this proof as a proof of the unsolvability of the halting problem. He calls the problem the 'satisfactoriness' problem and attributes the term 'halting problem' to Martin Davis. However, in Turing's terminology, a number is satisfactory if it is the description number of a circle-free machine, which is one that never stops producing figures, and is unsatisfactory otherwise. There is, therefore, a clear sense in which Turing's problem is a type of halting problem.

computable sequence. A given sequence may have more than one description number because it might be computed by more than one machine. The two versions of TM2 (Chapter 7, Table 7.2; Chapter 9, Table 9.3) have different description numbers but compute the same sequence 0010110111 ... . The fact that the computable sequences are enumerable shows that in total there is a countably infinite number of them. The reason why this is important can be understood by reflecting on Turing's goal which was to understand which of the real numbers were 'calculable by finite means'. Georg Cantor had proved in the late nineteenth century that there were uncountably many real numbers. An uncountable infinity is definably larger than a countable infinity. Thus, it follows from the demonstration that the computable numbers are countably infinite that there must be some real numbers that cannot be computed by Turing machines.

Each description number defines a computable sequence and each computable sequence has one or more description numbers. This shows that the computable sequences are also enumerable. It appears at first sight, however, that a diagonal argument can be used to show that the computable sequences are not enumerable. The diagonal argument was developed by Cantor in the late nineteenth century to show that the real numbers are not enumerable. Cantor had shown, using the listing technique, that the integers and the rational fractions are enumerable. The diagonal argument showed that the real numbers could not be put in a list. The proof used the classic technique of *reductio ad absurdum* in which you assume what you want to disprove and derive a contradiction from the assumption. Suppose that the real numbers, represented as infinite sequences of digits, were enumerable. Then it would, in principle, be possible to make a list of them. Somewhere in the list would be the $k$-th real number which might appear in the list as

$k$    29817263847362387346 ...

and somewhere further on would be the $k+n$-th real number which might appear as

$k+n$    39283823749362347861 ...

If the real numbers are enumerable then the list must contain them all. However, it is possible to construct a real number which is definitely not on the list. To do this, inspect the first digit of the first number on the list and write down something different as the first digit of the new number. Then inspect the second digit of the second number on the list and write down something different for the second digit of the new number. This procedure, carried through inexorably, produces a number which is not on the list because it differs from the first in its first digit, the second in its second digit, the $n$-th in its $n$-th digit and so on. It follows from this that the starting premise that the real numbers can be listed must be false and, therefore, that they are not countable.

It looks as though a similar technique can be used to show that the computable sequences are not enumerable either, contrary to the claim derived from their description numbers. The idea is to list the sequences rather than their description numbers and then to construct a sequence $\beta$ which differs from the first sequence in its first digit, from the second sequence in its second digit, from the $n$-th sequence in its $n$-th digit and so on for all the computable sequences. The sequence $\beta$ appears to be computable because a method for producing it has been described but it differs from each enumerated sequence by at least one digit and this shows that the computable sequences are not enumerable.

The flaw in this argument, as Turing showed, is the assumption that it is always possible to compute the $n$-th digit of the $n$-th computable sequence. For this to be so, the machine whose description number is $n$ must be circle-free and Turing proved that there is no general process for deciding that this is the case in a finite number of steps. Thus there is no guarantee, for an arbitrary description number $n$, that the machine it describes will produce an $n$-th digit. The putative diagonal argument fails to distinguish the description numbers of machines, which are enumerable, from the individual elements of the sequences they produce.

This constitutes a point of some psychological interest. It shows that there is an essential distinction between structural accounts of machines in terms of description numbers and behavioural accounts in terms of computed sequences. The fact that we can give a complete, finite, structural description of a machine does not show that we can thereby also fully describe its behaviour in a finite way.

Turing's proof shows that the diagonal argument does not work, but it is also significant for what it shows about Turing machines, namely that it is not possible to devise a single machine which can tell from an arbitrary description number, whether the machine described is circle free. Like Cantor, Turing uses a *reductio ad absurdum* argument. The proof starts from the assumption that we can, as he puts it, 'invent' a machine $D$ which can decide if a given number is 'satisfactory'. A number is satisfactory if it is a description number of a circle-free machine. $D$ is combined with the universal machine $U$, to make a composite machine $H$. $H$ works through the integers 1, 2,... using $D$ to test each in turn to see if it is satisfactory. For each satisfactory number found a counter $k$ is incremented. Then the satisfactory number is interpreted as the standard description of a machine $M$ and the universal machine component of $H$ runs $M$ to calculate its first $k$ figures and the $k$-th of them is written down as the next figure of the sequence computed by $H$.

It can be seen from this description that if $D$ works as hypothesized then $H$, the combination of $D$ and the universal machine, is circle-free. Each integer tested is found by $D$ to be satisfactory or unsatisfactory. If it is unsatisfactory it is discarded and $H$ moves on to test the next integer. If the integer tested is satisfactory, the machine it describes is circle-free and the simulation by $U$ will produce a $k$-th digit in a finite number of steps. The proof that $D$ cannot be possible rests on the consideration of what happens when $H$ evaluates the integer which is its own description number. The test by $D$ should, for the reasons just discussed, conclude that the number is satisfactory. $H$ should then execute its own description to produce the first $k$ digits of its own output and write down the $k$-th of these. However, the way that $H$ works prevents it from ever producing a $k$-th digit. Any programmer who has inadvertently written a recursive call which puts a procedure into an infinite loop will readily understand the nature of the problem. Having written down $k-1$ digits by simulating the first $k-1$ circle-free machines, $H$ now has to calculate the $k$-th digit of the sequence it computes by simulating its own operations. But $H$ as we have just seen, 'works through the integers 1, 2, … using $D$ to test each in turn to see if it is satisfactory. For each satisfactory number found, a counter $k$ is incremented …' This means that $H$ has to re-run the $k-1$ machines it has already simulated, in order to get to the number $k$. But when it gets there, it will, of course, have to simulate its own operations again, and then again and again. The recursion never bottoms out, because each nested simulation of $H$ works through $k-1$ digits and then makes a further recursive call to itself, and so on *ad infinitum*. $H$ is clearly circular and will never write down a $k$-th digit. But this contradicts the original claim that $H$ is circle-free. Thus neither verdict is possible and this proves that there cannot be a machine $D$.

It is important to be clear about what the proof does not show. It does not show that the problem of determining whether a given machine is circle free can never be solved. It is perfectly clear, for example, that the two Turing machines examined in Chapter 7 which produce the sequences 010101 … and 0010110111 … are circle free and it is clear from our understanding of the universal machine that it too is circle free when interpreting the standard description of either of those machines. The proof also tells us nothing about whether there exists a machine whose status is not determinable. It shows only that there is no single machine which can answer the question with complete generality no matter what machine it is required to assess.

The self-referential nature of the proof is intriguing and it is interesting to note that Gödel's incompleteness theorem also uses a self-referential construction but it is not clear precisely what the significance of self-reference is. It is, perhaps, germane to note that in both cases it is behaviour which is crucial. Gödel's proof rests on constructing a formula which cannot be proven, that is, which cannot be reached by a finite sequence of inferences from the axioms, and Turing's proof rests on showing that the putative machine $H$ can never print the $k$-th digit of its own sequence. If one focuses on structure, by contrast, self-reference does not seem to cause the same problems. It is, for example, possible to construct a Turing machine whose output is its own description in symbolic form. Two interesting papers by Lee (1963) and Thatcher (1963) provided the first demonstrations of self-describing machines and Minsky (1967) outlines how a self-describing Turing machine works. It is also logically possible, as von Neumann (1948) showed, for a machine to construct an exact replica of itself if it is given access to a store of elementary parts.

## The unsolvability of the printing problem

It is perhaps not surprising that there should be no general process for determining whether an arbitrary machine is circle free, but Turing's second proof is very striking. Turing proved that there can be no machine $E$ which, when supplied with the standard description of an arbitrary machine $M$, will determine whether $M$ ever prints a given symbol (0 for example). The proof is striking because the problem seems, on the face of it, so simple to solve. Suppose we want to know whether a machine ever prints 0. First, we examine the machine to see if it has 'Print 0' as part of one of its instructions. If it doesn't the answer is obvious; the machine never prints 0. If there is a 'Print 0' instruction it will be part of the action associated with a given configuration and it ought, one might think, to be possible to determine from the structure of the machine whether the relevant configuration will ever be instantiated.

The proof that a single machine cannot be specified to solve the printing problem rests on the demonstration that if there is such a machine $E$ then there is a general process for determining whether $M$, the machine to be assessed, prints 0 infinitely often. The behaviour of printing 0 infinitely often is clearly associated with the question of whether a machine is circle free. A solution to the printing problem implies a solution to the halting problem and this is already known to be insoluble.

Turing tackled the problem of constructing $E$ via another machine $F$ which, in effect, monitors the number of zeroes produced by $M$. $F$ takes the standard description of $M$ and transforms it into a machine $M_1$ which prints the same sequence as $M$ except that the first 0 printed by $M$ is changed to some other character, say *. Thus if $M$ printed ABA01AAB0010AB, $M_1$ would print ABA*1AAB0010AB. $F$ applied to $M_1$ would produce $M_2$ whose output would be ABA*1AAB*010AB, and so on indefinitely. Turing tells the reader that $F$ can be constructed but does not describe how the construction is achieved. It is an interesting exercise to consider how it might be done. $E$ and $F$ are combined to obtain a new machine $G$ which works as follows when supplied with the description number of a machine $M$. $F$ is used first to write down the standard description of $M$. $E$ then tests $M$ to see if it ever prints 0. If $M$ never prints 0 then $G$ prints 0. $F$ then transforms $M$ to $M_1$ and the process is repeated. Suppose $M$ is a machine which prints exactly 151955 zeroes. Then, after 151955 transformations by $F$, $M$ will have been transformed into a machine $M_{151955}$ in which every 0 has been replaced by *. When $M_{151955}$ is tested by $E$ it will be found never to print 0. Consequently, $G$ will itself print 0 to record this finding. An observer who watches $G$ before this point has been reached and sees that it has not yet printed 0 can infer that each of the $M_i$ tested thus far has printed 0 at some point but cannot tell whether this will continue indefinitely or whether, as in the example, there is a value $n$ for which $M_n$ never prints 0.

Suppose, however, that $G$ itself, with $M$ as input, is tested by $E$. By hypothesis, $E$ can determine if $G$ ever prints 0. If $E$ reports that $G$ never prints 0, we can infer that $M$ prints 0 infinitely often. The connection with the halting problem becomes immediately apparent when we note that a similar process can be used to determine whether $M$ prints 1 infinitely often. If we combine the tests for 0 and 1 we have a machine to determine whether $M$ prints an infinite number of figures of the first kind, that is, we have a machine to determine whether $M$ is circle-free. Because we already know this is impossible, we conclude that there cannot be a machine $E$. Again it is important to note that what is ruled out is a single machine which can inspect an arbitrary standard description and determine whether the machine described ever prints a particular symbol. It does not, of course, rule out deciding whether or not this is true for a particular machine. For many machines the answer can be found by inspection of the standard description or by running them for a period. It is striking, however, that such an apparently straightforward task should be beyond the capacity of a single machine. The proof demonstrates the scope of the original proof that the halting problem is unsolvable.

## The unsolvability of the Entscheidungsproblem

Turing used his first two negative results to tackle Hilbert's Entscheidungsproblem which he also showed to be unsolvable. The question at issue is whether there is a single machine or, equivalently, a general process to determine whether a given formula of the predicate calculus is provable. This is quite distinct from the incompleteness result proved by Gödel. It was shown by Gödel that an unprovable formula could be constructed for any formal system of sufficient power, such as the predicate calculus, thus answering positively the question 'Does this system contain unprovable formulae?' Turing asked the question, 'Given an arbitrary formula of a system such as the predicate calculus, is it possible to tell by mechanical means whether the formula is provable or not?' The proof that it is not possible is based on a formal construction that is rather intricate and Turing made a number of mistakes in the details of its presentation which were pointed out by Paul Bernays and rectified in a correction which was published after the main paper. The details are not important for present purposes. Turing began by showing that the description of any Turing machine, *M*, could be translated into formulae of the predicate calculus and that the moves of *M* could be represented as steps in a proof. He then showed how to construct a formula which expressed the proposition 'In some complete configuration of *M*, 0 appears on the tape.' He called this formula Un(*M*). The connection between this formula and the printing problem is readily apparent. The formula asserts that *M* prints 0 at some point in its computation and we know that there is no general process for establishing that this is so. Turing then proved two things:

(a) If 0 appears on the tape in some complete configuration of *M* then Un(*M*) is provable.

(b) If Un(*M*) is provable, then 0 appears on the tape in some complete configuration of *M*.

(a) and (b) together demonstrate that *M* prints 0 if and only if Un(*M*) is provable. Proving Un(*M*) is thus equivalent to determining whether *M* ever prints 0 and we already know that there is no general mechanical process to do this. It follows that there is no general process to determine if a formula of the predicate calculus is provable and this shows that the Entscheidungsproblem cannot be solved.

## Unsolvability proofs and the nature of the mind

A general question which arises from Turing's negative proofs about the capacities of Turing machines is whether human minds can do things that machines provably cannot. If so, then we have a convincing demonstration that the mind is not a computing machine. A widely discussed argument is based on the famous theorem, proved by Kurt Gödel and published in 1931, which has already been mentioned. Gödel showed that any formal system which was powerful enough to express basic arithmetic concepts could be made to yield unprovable propositions, that is, formulae which are syntactically correct but which cannot consistently be derived from the axioms of the system.

The outcome of Gödel's work was a proposition that said of itself that it was not provable in PM (the formal system of Russell and Whitehead's Principia Mathematica). Gödel then showed that the proposition was indeed unprovable and it followed that what it asserted was true. Thus, said Gödel, 'the proposition that is undecidable *in the system PM* still was decided by metamathematical considerations' Gödel (1931, p. 599). The point that has been taken up by anti-mechanist commentators is that a human reader of

Gödel's argument can see that the proposition which is undecidable within PM is nevertheless true. That is said to show that the human mind transcends the limitations of PM. Gödel also showed that the limitations of a particular formal system can be overcome by adding its undecidable proposition as an axiom. However, the second level formal system thus arrived at would have its own undecidable proposition. A third level system could be defined by adding the undecidable proposition of the second system to its axioms but the third system would also yield an undecidable proposition. In his paper on ordinal logics which was published in 1939 Turing explored the question whether it was possible to overcome the incompleteness phenomena globally by transfinite iteration of the principles that serve to overcome it locally (cf. Feferman 2001). He showed that this could not be done in the general sense he had hoped to achieve.

The most recent attempts to show that the mind cannot be a computer have been made by the physicist Roger Penrose in a series of articles and books (Penrose 1989, 1994, 1997). The heart of Penrose's attempt is a hybrid argument based on both Gödel's and Turing's results. Penrose begins with the idea of a computational procedure $A$ which, when it terminates, provides a demonstration that another computation $C(n)$ does not stop. This is equivalent to demonstrating that a particular Turing machine is circle-free so we can couch the argument in terms of Turing machines. In particular, we can think of both $A$ and $C(n)$ as Turing machines. We know, already, from Turing's first negative proof that there is no general process for determining that a given Turing machine is circle-free, but that is not what Penrose has in mind. He says, 'I am certainly not requiring that $A$ can always decide that $C(n)$ does not stop when in fact it does not, but I do insist that $A$ does not ever give us wrong answers' (Penrose 1994, p. 73). The possibility of a machine which can tell whether some other machines are circle-free is not ruled out by Turing's result and that is effectively what Penrose has in mind.

We now consider how $A$ might be used. We know from Turing's work that an effective listing of all the possible computations can be made. It can be done, for example, by listing all the description numbers in ascending numerical order. We can then take $A$ and apply it to each Turing machine in turn. If $A$ halts when applied to a particular Turing machine $M$, then we know that $M$ will never halt, that is, we know that $M$ is circle-free. Because $A$ is a Turing machine, it appears somewhere on the list and it is reasonable to ask what happens when $A$ is presented with its own description number to evaluate. $A$ is constructed such that if it halts then its target does not halt. Thus we arrive at the proposition '*If A halts then A does not halt.*' It is clear that we must deduce from this that $A$ does not halt because otherwise we are caught in a contradiction. Penrose concludes that 'we know something that $A$ is unable to ascertain. It follows that $A$ *cannot* encapsulate our understanding' (Penrose 1994, p. 75). The fundamental result is the same as Turing's but it includes the reader as an observer in the same way that Gödel's argument included the reader as an observer who could see that the unprovable proposition was true. The final step in Penrose's argument is to ask us to imagine that *A* 'encapsulates *all* the procedures available to human mathe- maticians for convincingly demonstrating that computations do not stop' (Penrose 1994, p. 73). The point of this step is to extend the argument to cover not just a particular computational procedure *A*, but every possible computation. If *A* does indeed have that character then it follows that we can understand something that no computational procedure can understand.

The argument appears watertight for any given *single* procedure *A*, and is what would be expected because Penrose uses self-reference in essentially the same way as Turing did in the proof of the unsolvability of the halting problem and as Gödel did in the incompleteness theorems. The novel aspect of Penrose's argument is the proposed extension of *A* from a single procedure to a whole class of procedures, or, equivalently, from a single Turing machine to the whole class of Turing machines which carry out halting tests.

It is here I think that Penrose's argument can be challenged and the precise nature of what Turing proved is important to the challenge. Turing showed that there is no single process that can successfully determine whether or not an arbitrary Turing machine halts, but it remains possible that a machine which defeats one halting-tester will be successfully tested by another. Penrose wants, and needs, to combine all the different testers together as a single procedure which would then be defeated when applied to itself. There is clearly no problem, in principle, in combining two given machines to make a hybrid, and if two machines can be combined so can 20 or 200. So indeed can any finite, specified collection of machines. Suppose, however that the number of possible halting-testers is infinite. Penrose considers the issue (Penrose 1994, pp. 77–8) in the course of responding to a range of possible objections to his argument. He accepts that if the collection is infi- nite there would have to be a way of generating a list of the procedures in some algorithmic way. If this can be done then their executions can be inter- leaved in a computable way. The argument turns, therefore, on the question whether it is possible to list algorithmically an infinite collection of procedures for determining that computations do not terminate. Penrose assumes that it is possible but does not say how it could be done.

I think it is reasonable to doubt that there is a general process for deter- mining whether a given procedure is a halting-tester. We already know that there is no general process for determining whether an arbitrary machine ever prints zero or any other given symbol and that there is no general process for determining whether an arbitrary machine halts or not. In order to have an algorithm to list the halting-testers we would have to have a crite- rion for halting-testerhood. The criterion could not be specified in terms of halting or printing a given symbol because no general process based on either of these characteristics is possible. I suppose one cannot absolutely rule out there being some appropriate, independent criterion but it seems improbable. If this is correct then Penrose's argument loses its bite because it does not generalize as he wishes from a specified single procedure for determining if computations halt to all possible procedures for testing halting.

## Gödel and Turing

Gödel and Turing took very different views on the question of whether the mind is mechanical or not. Gödel thought that it was not and that Turing was in error in supposing so. In a comment on Turing reported by Hao Wang (1974, p. 325) he said

> Turing ... gives an argument which is supposed to show that mental procedures cannot carry any farther than mechanical procedures. However, this argument is inconclusive, because it depends on the supposition that a finite mind is capable of only a finite number of distinguishable states. What Turing disregards completely is the fact that *mind, in its use, is not static, but constantly developing* ... . Therefore, although at each stage of the mind's development the number of its possible states is finite, there is no reason why this number should not converge to infinity in the course of its development.

Wang noted, in his own comments on this passage, that in conversation Gödel accepted the validity of Turing's argument given the assumption that there is no mind apart from matter. He felt, however, that the assumption was a prejudice of our times and was likely to be disproven in due course.

Turing's path to a mechanist view is not entirely clear despite the commitment in OCN to a finite bound on the number of states of mind. His biographer, Andrew Hodges, suggests that Turing's work on ordinal logics, which was done after OCN was published, recognized the possibility of non-computable mental activity. 'The evidence is that at this time he was open to the idea that in moments of "intuition" the mind appears to do something outside the scope of the Turing machine' Hodges (1997, p. 22). Hodges suggests that it was Turing's wartime experience with the mechanical aids which helped to break the German naval Enigma codes that finally convinced him of the mechanist approach to mind.

> I would suggest ... it was at this period that he abandoned the idea that moments of intuition corresponded to uncomputable operations. Instead, he decided, the scope of the computable encompassed far more than could be captured by explicit instruction notes, and quite enough to include all that human brains did, however creative or original. (Hodges 1997, p. 29)

The reader interested in this part of Turing's life will also find it useful to read Hodges (2001). It is quite clear that at later points in his life Turing was firmly committed to a mechanist view of the mind. He knew, of course, that the negative proofs that he and Gödel had established could be used to argue that minds were not machines but he took a robust stance with regard to such uses. In his famous paper *Computing Machinery and Intelligence* (Turing 1950), he says of computers:

> Whenever one of these machines is asked the appropriate critical question and gives a definite answer, we know that this answer must be wrong, and this gives us a certain feeling of superiority. Is this feeling illusory? It is no doubt quite genuine, but I do not think too much importance should be attached to it. We too often give wrong answers to questions ourselves to be justified in being very pleased at such evidence of fallibility on the part of the machines. Further, our superiority can only be felt on such an occasion in relation to the one machine over which we have scored our petty triumph. There would be no question of triumphing simultaneously over *all* machines. (Turing 1950, p. 445)

The unsolvability proofs are an important part of a rounded understanding of what Turing achieved. The fact that there are limits to what a universal machine can do, and the fact that proofs about these limits use self-referential constructions are both matters which should be of interest to psychologists. Self-reference appears to be bound up with questions about consciousness and understanding which are of great importance for a complete psychological theory. Even if it does turn out that some aspects of mentality cannot be captured by computational methods as Penrose argues, it does not follow that there is no place for computational thinking in psychology.

# 14 Von Neumann Computer Architecture

## Introduction

Turing's universal machine focuses attention on the fundamental role of variable environmental structure in extending the behavioural scope of a fixed, finite, mechanism. The mini-mind of the universal machine is, like the mini-mind of any other Turing machine, a fixed mechanism and the universal machine gains its remarkable behavioural flexibility from its environmental links. It uses environmental structure, in the form of standard descriptions, to determine its behaviour and that behaviour is variable because the standard description can be changed from one occasion to another. The universal machine design suggests that the environment is equally significant for humans even if the human mind is not a fixed mechanism like the mini-mind of a universal machine. The moment by moment contact modelled by the successive configurations of a universal machine and the way in which the functional states of the mini-mind and the format of standard descriptions are co-designed suggest equally important and intricate links between humans and their environments. One might expect, therefore, that a psychological theory based on Turing's analysis of computation would be ecological in character and would seek to understand how functional states are instantiated in the brain, which environmental inputs they are attuned to, what the structure of those inputs is and how behaviour unfolds in a continuous sequence of perception-action cycles.

Surprisingly, perhaps, such a theory has not been developed although the need for it has had tacit recognition in various quarters. J.J. Gibson's ecological approach, the situated action framework, and the emphasis on real environments in mobile robotics are all pointers in this direction but no one working from these perspectives has seen that Turing provided a fundamental formal framework within which the development of the theory might take place. Indeed, some approaches which lay particular stress on the role of the environment, such as Gibson's ecological approach, are actively hostile to computational thinking. Still more surprisingly, the computational theory of mind which has been attributed to Turing is, essentially, a model of the internal structures of the mind and does not treat the external environment as a fundamental part of the system in the way that Turing did.

The simple explanation for the mismatch between where Turing's analysis and theory seem to point and what has actually been developed is that computational thinking in psychology has been based on von Neumann architecture rather than on the architecture of Turing machines. This chapter discusses the fundamental characteristics of von Neumann computer architecture and explains how it relates to the architecture of the universal machine and to current computational thinking about the mind. By way of an introduction, a further model of computation which Turing presented in 'On Computable Numbers' is discussed.

## Turing's instruction note model

Turing's fundamental concern was, we should recall, not psychological but mathematical. He wished to know which numbers could be computed by a human working in a routine fashion with paper and pencil. The machine model was intended to be able to compute all and only the numbers computable by a human working in the way described. The perceptual and motor constraints under which the human worked were important in determining the way the machine was built but the primary interest was in the numbers themselves.

Turing may possibly have perceived the involvement of 'states of mind' in the model as a weakness and he supplemented it with two further models in sections 9.II and 9.III of OCN. The model in section 9.II expresses computable numbers in terms of formulae of the predicate calculus. It is not discussed further here except to note that it might be considered a precursor to, or basic justification for, the Logic Theorist program developed by Newell, Shaw and Simon in the 1950s.

Turing's third model links the first two. He said it could be seen as a modification of the first or a corollary of the second. The analysis is based on the concept of a 'note of instructions' which is, Turing says, 'a more physical and definite counterpart' of the state of mind. The analysis is still based on the constraints that govern the activities of a human computant but uses them to construct a computing machine in a very different way. Turing starts by saying

> We suppose, as in [the analysis of section 9.I discussed in chapter 6], that the computation is carried out on a tape; but we avoid introducing the 'state of mind' by considering a more physical and definite counterpart of it. It is always possible for the computer to break off from his work, to go away and forget all about it, and later to come back and go on with it. If he does this he must leave a note of instructions (written in some standard form) explaining how the work is to be continued. This note is the counterpart of the 'state of mind'. (OCN p. 253)

The human computant has a new, peripheral role in this model. In the Turing machine, the elements of each new configuration result from the actions of the previous instruction. The computation of a sequence is a continuous process in which a configuration causes a set of actions which produce the next configuration and so forth. The computant is fundamental to the process because states of mind form part of each configuration and thus are part of the definition of the sequence being computed. In the instruction note model, by contrast, the states of mind of the computant are used to interpret the note of instructions but no longer form part of it.

> [T]he state of progress of the computation at any stage is completely determined by the note of instructions and the symbols on the tape. That is, the state of the system may be described by a single expression ... consisting of the symbols on the tape followed by $\Delta$ ... and then by the note of instructions. This expression may be called the 'state formula'. We know that the state formula at any given stage is determined by the state formula before the last step was made, and we assume that the relation of these two formulae is expressible in the functional calculus. In other words, we assume that there is an axiom $\mathfrak{A}$ which expresses the rules governing the behaviour of the computer, in terms of the relation of the state formula at any stage to the state formula at the preceding stage. If this is so, we can construct a machine to write down the successive state formulae, and hence to compute the required number. (OCN pp. 253–4)

Hodges (1983, p. 107) describes the difference between the analyses of section 9.I and section 9.III in these terms. 'The first put the spotlight upon the range of thought within the individual – the number of "states of mind". The second conceived of the individual as a mindless executor of given directives.' In the analysis of section 9.III the human mind is no longer an integral part of each instruction. In fact the computant is sufficiently detached that the calculation can be put aside and forgotten between steps. The state formula is, in essence, a program plus an indication of where the computation has got to. The note of instructions is rather like the program counter in a modern computer. It keeps track of where the computation has got to and enables the next step to be taken.

The key point, for present purposes, is that the note of instructions replaces the states of mind of the computant and the role of the computant is changed from active participant in the computational process to interpreter of the program and of the note of instructions. This opens up the possibility that the computant can be removed entirely from the process and replaced by an interpreter which can carry out the same functions. It is this model which has been implemented in stored program computers of the familiar kind. Anyone who has observed the extraordinary development of computers over the past twenty years or so will be aware that the technology is dynamic and changing but in some respects the basic organization of computers still follows the principles worked out by John von Neumann and his colleagues in the late 1940s and early 1950s. This chapter discusses the hardware 'architecture' of von Neumann computers and Chapter 15 discusses software. The term 'architecture' is most commonly understood in its application to buildings but in recent years it has also frequently been applied to both the software and hardware of computers. The hardware architecture of a computer is the set of parts it contains and the connections between them. To understand why von Neumann architecture has the characteristics it has, it is valuable to know a little about the ENIAC, the machine whose construction and operating principles stimulated von Neumann's thinking.

## The ENIAC

In 1943 the Moore School of Electrical Engineering at the University of Pennsylvania was commissioned to construct an electronic computer for the United States Army. The machine was formally accepted by the US Government in 1946 and operated successfully until it was retired to the Smithsonian museum in 1955. The ENIAC (Electronic Numerical Integrator and Computer) was, by modern standards, a physical giant but a computational midget. It was 100 feet long, 10 feet high, 3 feet deep and weighed 30 tons. In operation it consumed 140 kilowatts of power. The clock functioned at 100 kilohertz and the machine performed some 330 multiplications per second. For all its impressive size, it had storage for only 20 ten digit decimal numbers. Nonetheless, it represented a huge step forward both in the sophistication and reliability of its engineering and in its speed of operation which was some 500 times faster than its closest electro-mechanical rival, the IBM Automatic Sequence Controlled Calculator (Goldstine 1972, p. 117). The ENIAC owed its speed to the use of electronic rather than electro-mechanical components which was both controversial and risky at the time. Some engineers claimed that the necessary reliability could not be achieved and that the machine would never operate successfully. By proving the doubters wrong, the engineers led by J.P. Eckert and J.W. Mauchly ushered in the modern era of computing.

The ENIAC was a parallel machine in which many operations proceeded simultaneously. The machine had 30 basic units. Twenty accumulators for the 20 numbers mentioned earlier, one multiplier, one combined divider and square-rooter, three function table units which provided additional storage for fixed data, an input unit and an output unit, two control units and a master programmer which provided overall direction for the parallel operations of the machine.

The major problem with the ENIAC was programming. 'This was a highly complex undertaking and was one of the reasons why it was to be a unique machine. This aspect of the machine was unsatisfactory, as the evolutionary process was to reveal.' Goldstine(1972, p. 160). The difficulty lay in the fact that the ENIAC had to be reconfigured physically, by means of numerous switches and a plugboard, every time a new calculation was to be done.

> [T]here was no concept of a single stored program that described the whole algorithm, and which was subsequently executed by a fixed computer architecture – this important idea of the stored program computer was implemented first in the next generation of computers.
>
> In contrast, the architecture of the ENIAC was rearranged for each problem, by using the plugboard to rewire the connections between the units. One could say that the algorithm was literally wired into the computer … . However, the time was not ripe for this type of parallel architecture in the 1940's … . The difficulty of programming parallel computers is a recurring theme that is still with us today. (Hockney and Jesshope 1988, pp. 9–10)

Programming parallel computers is still a formidable task. The ENIAC was, in effect, a re-configurable, special-purpose Turing machine. Rewiring the plugboard and sequencing the accumulators was equivalent to reorganizing the state transitions of the Turing machine.

## John von Neumann and the stored program concept

In 1947, von Neumann, who had learned about the ENIAC after a chance meeting with Goldstine, showed 'how to convert it into a centrally programmed computer in which all the programming could be done by setting switches on the function tables' Burks (1966, pp. 7–8). This meant that the machine was, in effect, turned into a primitive stored program computer. It was a significant development. As Goldstine (1972, p. 233) says 'Although it slowed down the machine's operation, it speeded up the programmer's task enormously. Indeed, the change was so profound that the old method was never used again.' Because of its very high operating speed, the scope of the ENIAC was potentially much greater than its designers had originally supposed, but it suffered from two major flaws. The programming problem has already been noted. The other flaw was its very small storage capacity, which made it unsuitable for problems which generated large amounts of intermediate data.

Von Neumann, as a consultant to the EDVAC (Electronic Discrete Variable Computer) project, with other contributors, produced various reports from 1945 onwards, dealing with the logical design of high speed computers, in which proposals were put forward to overcome the difficulties experienced with the ENIAC. The first, and perhaps the most influential, was the 'First

Draft of a Report on the EDVAC' von Neumann (1945), which outlined what has since become known as 'von Neumann architecture'.[7]

## The design of the EDVAC

The draft report on the EDVAC argued for a number of features in a high speed computer. First, because the machine would be used primarily for calculations it should have specialized arithmetic organs. 'Since the device is primarily a computer, it will have to perform the elementary operations of arithmetic most frequently … . It is therefore reasonable that it should contain specialized organs for just these operations.' (Aspray and Burks 1987, p.18). The arithmetic processors, known collectively as the central arithmetic unit **CA** would constitute one distinct part of the computer. Although Turing machines compute numbers there are no arithmetic processors as such in a Turing machine. This illustrates from the start that the principles underlying von Neumann architecture represent a shift from the analysis of human computation with which Turing was concerned to the problems of designing an efficient practical instruction interpreter.

The second part would be a device which exercised central control **CC** over the sequencing of operations. This marks a radical departure from the design of the ENIAC. In the new design, it was anticipated that the instructions to the machine would be stored in the same way as its data, that is, as numbers in the memory, rather than being wired in as they were in the ENIAC. This is the stored program concept. Thus the EDVAC and its successors were designed to function in broadly the same way as universal Turing machines although OCN was not mentioned in the EDVAC design document. It was anticipated that the stored program principle would lead both to faster programming and to faster program execution times. **CA** and **CC** together constituted the control device **C** which is functionally analogous to the control automaton of a Turing machine. It is noticeable, however, that **C** is viewed entirely in terms of arithmetic, logic and sequence control and not at all in terms of 'states of mind'. It is, therefore, better thought of in terms of the instruction note model. The practical orientation is completely dominant as one would expect. The design of **C** implies the existence of a machine language, which the 'First Draft' refers to as an 'order code'. It is analogous to the standard description language used by Turing's universal machine.

The third requirement was for a large memory **M**. This was needed to enable the machine to hold the program instructions and to deal with

---

[7] The 'First Draft' engendered a controversy about who was responsible for the stored program concept. von Neumann's name was the only one on the report which was prepared by him, and was not initially intended for circulation beyond the group whose ideas it collated. Other members of the group, in particular Eckert and Mauchly, felt that their contributions were not recognized when the report was made public.

complex numerical problems (various types of partial differential equations being specifically mentioned) which might need large amounts of storage for intermediate results. **M**, although finite, is functionally analogous to the tape of a Turing machine and a great deal of attention was paid to the way in which communications between **C** and **M** were to be handled.

In addition to **C** and **M**, the computer would need an input device **I** and an output device **O** which would manage the transfer of information between the high speed internal components of the computer and an external recording medium **R**, which would use punched cards, magnetic tape or wire, or some other suitable technology. It was envisaged that communications would, as a rule, be between **R** and **M** and not between **R** and **C**. **R** can be thought of as an extension of **M** and thus, in a sense, analogous to the tape of a Turing machine, but there is nothing in the Turing machine architecture analogous to **I** or **O**.

A major preoccupation of the designers of the EDVAC was finding a suitable way of using the computer to control its own external storage so as to minimize human intervention. As Rosen (1969, p. 14) says 'The early scientific computers were designed in accordance with a philosophy that assumed that scientific computing was characterized by little or no input or output.' von Neumann argued that once a machine had been given the instructions for a particular task, 'it must be able to carry them out completely and without any need for further intelligent human intervention.' While this is exactly the sort of arrangement which is suitable for high speed calculations, it is much less satisfactory as the basis for a model of the cognitive system which is characterized by the constancy of its interactions with the external environment and by the sensitivity and range of its input and output systems. It is also fundamentally different from the Turing machine which communicates with its environment by scanning and printing during each step of a computation.

## The case for serial processing

The parts of a computer described above, **C**, **M**, **I**, **O** and **R** which, as noted, is an extension of **M**, constitute the structural heart of the von Neumann architecture. **C** is what we think of today as the CPU, **M** is the main memory, **I** and **O** are peripherals such as the keyboard, mouse and monitor, and **R** is secondary memory which is familiar in the form of hard disks, floppy disks and CD-ROMs. A schematic representation of the parts of a von Neumann computer is shown in Figure 14.1.

All the components have become faster and more sophisticated in modern computers but are functionally much the same as the elements of von Neumann's original design. The most important remaining feature in the 'First Draft' is the argument for serial as opposed to parallel processing.

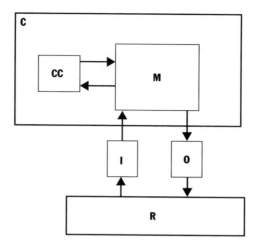

**Figure 14.1**   The components of von Neumann architecture.

As has already been noted, the ENIAC was designed as a parallel machine, but was eventually configured to operate as a serial machine in order to ease the complex task of programming it, a task which remains difficult in parallel machines today. Parallelism provides an excellent way of increasing the throughput of a machine with relatively slow components but it means that the machine requires more of those components.

> This way of gaining time by increasing equipment is fully justified in non vacuum tube element devices, where gaining time is of the essence, and extensive engineering experience is available regarding the handling of involved devices containing many elements … . For a vacuum tube element device on the other hand, it would seem that the opposite procedure holds more promise. (von Neumann 1945, p. 363)

The argument is founded on the state of the technology and engineering experience in 1945. The vacuum tube was a bulky, expensive and error-prone piece of equipment. Thus it was wise to use as few as possible. On the other hand it was extremely fast by the standards of the day. von Neumann reported that the fastest relays available had reaction times of 5 milliseconds at best, and more commonly 10 milliseconds or more, whereas the reaction times of vacuum tubes could feasibly be made as short as 1 microsecond. Thus a single vacuum tube device operating serially might in principle give about the same performance as some 5000 relay devices operating in parallel. These figures led to the eminently sensible conclusion,

> The device should be as simple as possible, that is, contain as few elements as possible. This can be achieved by never performing two operations

simultaneously, if this would cause a significant increase in the number of elements required. (von Neumann 1945, p. 364)

In the relatively few pages of the 'First Draft', von Neumann, with his incisive insights and customary clarity of expression, set down principles which heavily influenced the logical design of computers thereafter. The argument that substantial performance gains could be had by improving the speed of components rather than multiplying their numbers went against the conventional wisdom of the time but has been fully justified. It is an entirely different question whether the principles of von Neumann architecture provide a satisfactory foundation for a theory of cognitive computation. The brain appears to operate with very large numbers of relatively slow components functioning in parallel, exactly the opposite of von Neumann's proposal. von Neumann made some brief but significant remarks about correspondences between the parts of the proposed architecture and the human brain. He suggested that **C** and **M** together 'correspond to the *associative* neurons in the human nervous system' and that **I** and **O** are 'the equivalents of the *sensory* or *afferent* and the *motor* or *efferent* neurons.' This is fundamentally different from Turing's proposal in which only the finite control, the analogue of **C,** corresponds to the mind. Von Neumann's proposal amounts, in effect, to the suggestion that the brain is organized as a universal machine with a finite memory which is not a one-dimensional tape but a complex set of neural structures. The plausibility of this suggestion is considered further in Chapters 16 and 17. In Chapter 15 we consider the organization of software. To introduce this a little more consideration needs to be given to the relationship between the control **C**, and the memory **M** of a von Neumann computer.

## Internal organization of von Neumann architecture

A von Neumann computer is functionally equivalent to a high speed, encapsulated universal Turing machine plus input and output systems for communicating with the external environment. The Turing machine + I/O organization, as a whole, is theoretically significant for cognitive science but there are also theoretically significant aspects of the organization of just that part of the architecture which is functionally equivalent to a Turing machine.

In order to achieve the high speeds needed for practical computation, the relationship between the control mechanism and the memory has to be different from the relationship between the mini-mind of a Turing machine and its tape, because the organization of the memory as a one-dimensional tape makes the Turing machine architecture much too slow for most practical computations, even if it were to be implemented electronically. The solution, adopted in modern von Neumann architecture computers, is a memory in which each location is accessible in the same, fixed amount of time. This is what is called 'random access' memory. If the mind is the software of a von Neumann computer, the brain must implement memory in essentially the same way. The term 'random' is somewhat misleading because one rarely wants to access the memory randomly but it captures the idea that at any step in a computation, any one memory location can be accessed as easily as any other. This is about as far removed as it is possible to get from the organization of the memory of a Turing machine where a move in a computation can access only two memory locations other than the currently scanned square. The two fundamental requirements for a random access memory are (i) the memory consists of a fixed, finite number of locations and (ii) there is a hard-wired physical connection between the control and each memory location. The general principle is illustrated in Figure 14.2 which shows eight units. Each bi-directional arrow in Figure 14.2 stands for a hard-wired link between the control mechanism and a unit of memory. The control unit sends a message on the wire to a particular memory unit saying, in effect, 'What symbol are you storing?' and the memory unit sends a message back saying 'The symbol is $\alpha$'. It must also be possible for the control to send a message saying 'Erase $\alpha$', or 'Replace $\alpha$ with $\beta$'. This is significantly different from the arrangement that would be needed to realize the control of a universal Turing machine where access to the memory is made by physical movement of the control or the tape and the contents of the scanned square are read directly. For a memory with only eight units, individual hard-wired links are a plausible solution to the memory access problem but for a memory with many millions of units the amount of wiring required quickly becomes prohibitive and in real computers, memory access is managed via an addressing scheme. If the memory units are given addresses in the form of binary numbers eight units can be addressed with three binary digits. The addresses are 000, 001, 010, 011, 100, 101, 110, 111. The digits of these addresses can be transmitted in parallel over three wires and that is

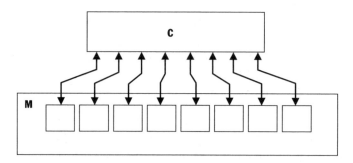

**Figure 14.2**   Schematic representation of the relationship between control and memory in a von Neumann computer.

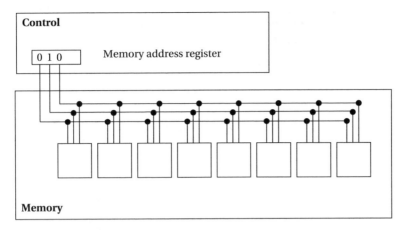

**Figure 14.3** Schematic representation of an addressing scheme for an eight-unit memory.

essentially how the task is managed. Figure 14.3 shows an eight unit memory and a control unit equipped with a memory address register (MAR).

When the control needs to access a particular memory unit, the address is put in the MAR and sent out as a signal on the address lines. Each memory unit is equipped with decoding hardware which responds to the address signal. Every memory unit receives the address signal and the one that matches it prepares for action. With an eight-unit memory, the addressing scheme saves five wires. This is modest, but for larger memories the savings quickly become much more significant. A memory with a million units requires only twenty address lines thus saving more than 999,900 wires.

The action taken is either to send what is in the memory location to the control (a read operation by the control) or to receive something from the control for storage in the memory location (a write operation). Data transfer operations use different wiring in order to prevent confusion between addresses and data. Data are almost always stored in binary form in a computer and are generally transmitted in parallel so the number of wires needed is determined by the number of different patterns that can be stored in a memory unit. Figure 14.4 shows the additional data transfer wiring needed to access the memory on the assumption that $16 = 2^4$ patterns can be stored in each location. Eight, sixteen, thirty-two and sixty-four bit data paths are commonly used in modern computers rather than the four bit path shown.

Exactly what happens depends on whether a read or write operation is to be performed. If the operation is 'read', the memory buffer register (MBR) is cleared, and the value in the location whose address has been activated is transferred to the MBR where it is then available to the control. If the operation is 'write', the value to store is loaded into the MBR and transferred to the

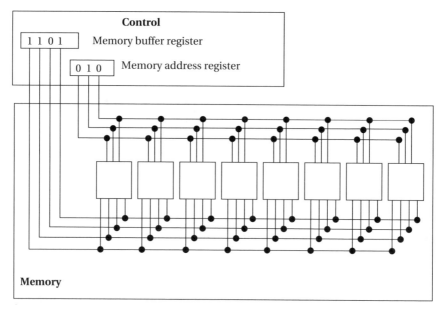

**Figure 14.4**   Schematic representation of address and data wiring for an eight-unit, four-bit memory.

active memory location, replacing whatever was there before. The enormous savings in wiring that can be achieved by using address and data lines instead of unique hard wired connections are only possible if signals can be transmitted and read with extremely high reliability. An error of a single bit in an address will result in the wrong location being accessed and an error of a single bit in a read or write operation will result in incorrect values being transferred. It is simply not known whether the brain uses addressing mechanisms anything like these or distinguishes between instructions and data. Thus it is also not known whether the von Neumann architecture is at all plausible as a model of the functional organization of the human nervous system. Reasons for thinking that it is not are discussed in Chapter 17. The assumption that the brain does provide the type of hardware that is needed for universal computation has led cognitive scientists to exploit the notion of 'virtual' architecture and to think of the mind in terms of software that 'runs' on the hardware of the brain. Chapter 15 considers the organization of software in more detail.

To close this chapter, a brief comparison of Turing's model of the mind and that derived from von Neumann architecture may be helpful. Turing, as is clear from earlier chapters, modelled the mind as a system of functional states. Such systems have been called mini-minds in this book. States are defined purely in terms of their relationships to each other and to their inputs and outputs. Turing said nothing at all about how they might be implemented. The relations between functional states are fixed when the machine is defined and there can be only finitely many of them. The mini-mind of a Turing machine is distinct from its, potentially infinite, tape.

In a von Neumann computer, the control and the memory are both finite and the relation between them is such that the control has access to each memory location in essentially equal time. von Neumann suggested that the control and memory together corresponded to the 'associative' neurons in the human brain. The concept of associative cortex has largely been superseded by more advanced knowledge of brain function but the important point made by von Neumann is that human memory is like symbolic computer memory. This provides a way of thinking about the implementation of functional states which is not Turing's way but which is central to the physical symbol systems hypothesis. Turing machines, as is clear from the discussion in earlier chapters, have two kinds of memory. There is the symbolic memory of the tape and the memory for fixed choices arising from multiple paths through the fixed structure of functional states. It is the latter that models human memory in Turing's scheme. The distinction effectively disappears in von Neumann architecture. Functional states, according to this view, are implemented as combinations of symbol structures and control structures.

# 15 Virtual Architecture

In Chapter 14 von Neumann computer architecture was discussed with an emphasis on hardware. The use of an addressing scheme to couple a finite memory with the central processor is one of the most important characteristics of the architecture. The combination of an addressing scheme and the high speed electronic components of a von Neumann machine have significant consequences for the kinds of software that can be implemented in a practical way. This chapter discusses the nature of software in a von Neumann computer and the ways in which software concepts have been used to develop hypotheses about the mind. One key concept, virtual architecture, was mentioned towards the end of Chapter 14. The concept of virtual architecture includes both data structures and control regimes.

## Standard descriptions as virtual machines

A useful starting point which relates the discussion to Turing's work is the concept of a standard description for a universal Turing machine. A standard description, as introduced in Chapter 9, is the symbolic representation of a Turing machine in a form designed to be used by a specific universal machine. Standard descriptions make it possible for a universal machine to simulate any of the countable infinity of Turing machines. A standard description is a purely symbolic representation of a Turing machine but it provides a universal machine with all the information needed to simulate the machine described. For that reason a standard description can be described as a 'virtual' machine. The virtual machine concept has two related facets. It refers, by way of something like a standard description, to a machine whose structure is represented abstractly for use by a universal machine and it refers to the behaviour of the universal machine as it interprets and acts on the description. If we take TM1 as an example, the standard description of TM1 constitutes a virtual machine and the universal machine behaves as though it were TM1 when it produces the same sequence as TM1 by simulating it.

The core concept of virtual architecture, simulation via software, is thus present in the universal Turing machine but there is an important extension of the concept in stored program computers which is not obvious in 'On Computable Numbers'. This is the idea that machines with different hardware structures and control regimes can be simulated. The target machines which Turing's universal machine simulates are all Turing machines with the same architecture of tape and control but it is quite straightforward to use digital computers to simulate machines with different hardware. Connectionist architectures, for example, which would be parallel if constructed in hardware, are routinely simulated using serial computers.

Because of its serial nature, a von Neumann computer carries out one machine language operation at a time and single machine language operations do very simple things like accessing a specific location in the memory and loading its contents into a register in the CPU. Machine language operations are equivalent to Turing's elementary processes of scanning, printing and moving and it is typically the case that lots of elementary processes are needed to carry out even simple tasks at higher levels. Virtual architectures provide these tasks as their elementary processes and thus shield the user from needing to know how they are implemented by virtual machines lower down the chain. Turing's $m$-functions are instances of virtual machines in this sense. $f(C,B,\alpha)$, for example, is a virtual machine that finds the first instance of $\alpha$ if there is one. Finding a symbol is not an operation which is available at the level of direct operations on the tape. Scanning, printing and moving exhaust the repertoire of Turing machines at the most basic level.

## Hierarchies of virtual machines

Modern computers typically have a number of links in a chain of virtual machines mediating the interaction between the user at one end and the hardware of the computer at the other. The principal reason for using virtual machines in this way is that they allow the user to specify tasks in ways that are 'natural' for humans. The symbols that actually drive the hardware, the 'machine language' or 'machine code' of a computer, are sequences of ones and zeros. It is notoriously easy to make mistakes when writing machine code and notoriously difficult to remember which sequence of zeros and ones does what. This explains why there are virtual machines at all, but not why there is a chain of them linking the user to the hardware. The answer is that there are tasks at many different levels which are best handled by thinking of the computer in different ways. The user wants to think of the computer as a word-processor at one moment, as a digital photographic processor at another, as a link to the Internet at a third and so forth. Each of these virtual machines has common requirements in terms of handling files and windows, communicating with the memory and the processor and so on. These tasks are handled at the level of a virtual machine called the operating system. The operating system virtual machine makes standard facilities, like handling files and windows, available to the developers of the applications virtual machines. The operating system itself, may draw on, or be written in, the languages of other virtual machines. Operating systems can be written in programming languages like C which are themselves virtual machines. Almost nobody ever writes binary code directly. The lowest level generally used by programmers is a virtual machine defining what is called an assembly language. This is a language that provides mnemonic codes for the machine language operations themselves. The assembly language for the Intel 8086 processor, for example, which is a distinguished ancestor of the hair-raisingly speedy Pentium processors commonly encountered in today's computers, has an instruction called HLT which halts the processor. In binary, the instruction is 11110100. It is obviously much easier to remember that HLT means 'halt'. A functioning computer, such as the machine on which I am writing this chapter, can therefore be thought of as a hierarchy of machines. At the bottom of the hierarchy is the hardware machine which moves binary digits around between the memory, the processor and the various peripheral devices that enable communication with the user. Above this physical machine is a layered system of virtual machines. Each layer has its primitive operations defined in terms of sequences of operations at the next lower level and offers services to the layer above. The topmost layer is the virtual machine which is visible to the user.

The concept of a hierarchy of virtual machines is very helpful in understanding why a computer typically has different kinds of software but Turing's universal machine shows that only two levels are absolutely necessary for full mechanical flexibility, one hardware level and one software level. The hardware level for a universal machine is its mini-mind and its tape; the software level is the standard description of a target machine. The equivalent two levels for a von Neumann computer would be its hardware and a program written in its machine language.

## The mind as virtual machine

The wonderfully enticing idea that gradually became established as a working hypothesis in psychology from the 1950s onwards was the idea that the relation between brain and mind could be understood as a relation between physical and virtual architectures. The brain provides the physical architecture and the mind the virtual architecture. The mind can be understood in terms of programs or standard descriptions running on the neural computer. If it's true, this idea answers two fundamental questions. It answers the ancient question about the relationship between mind and brain. The mind is a pattern of organization imposed on the brain by the symbolic representations that constitute its virtual machines. It also answers the question about how a finite organ like the brain can produce apparently limitless flexibility of behaviour. It can do this, the physical symbol system hypothesis claims, because it is organized as a practical version of a universal machine.

The idea that mind stands to brain in essentially the relation that the software of a von Neumann computer stands to its hardware has two highly significant, related theoretical consequences. It implies that the brain is organized like the hardware of a von Neumann computer and this, if true, implies that psychology is independent of neuroscience. Many authors have made the latter point:

> There is a major lesson for cognitive science [in computational thinking], which has been drawn by a number of authors, notably Miller, Galanter, and Pribram (1960, chapter 14), Putnam (1960), Fodor (1968), and Oatley (1978): the mind can be studied independently from the brain. Psychology (the study of the programs) can be pursued independently from neuro-physiology (the study of the machine and the machine code). The neuro-physiological substrate must provide a physical basis for the processes of the mind, but granted that the substrate offers the computational power of recursive functions, its physical nature places no constraints on the patterns of thought. This doctrine of *functionalism*, which can be traced back to Craik, and even perhaps ultimately to Aristotle, has become commonplace in cognitive science. (Johnson-Laird 1983, p. 9)

The reason why the physical nature of the brain 'places no constraints on the patterns of thought' is that if it is organized as a universal machine it can simulate any of the countable infinity of different special purpose machines and each of these has its own logic. In order, for example, to understand a word processor or a computer game, one has to look at the user manual for the word processor or the game rather than at the manual for the hardware of the computer. The latter tells you nothing at all about the logic of particular programs which can be run on the computer. Furthermore, provided that there is a suitable hierarchy of virtual machines, the same top level program can be run on different hardware architectures. Thus there is, apparently, a dual independence of software from hardware. Multiple programs can be run on a given hardware architecture and the same program can be run on multiple hardware architectures.

## Virtual machines depend on the underlying hardware

What is striking with the hindsight of 20 years, is the emphasis on the independence idea and the lack of attention paid to the idea that the hardware of the brain must be like that of a von Neumann computer. The powerfully constraining requirement that the brain be organized as a universal machine with a finite memory if psychology is to be independent of neuroscience is recognized by Johnson-Laird only with the curiously oblique statement that the underlying hardware has to offer 'the computational power of recursive functions'. The conditional nature of the hypothesis has disappeared. What one ought to say is something like this: 'IF the brain is organised like a universal computer then there is a sense in which psychology is independent from neuroscience.' Such a conditional statement prompts us to ask whether the brain really is organized in such a way rather than acting on the assumption that it is. Contemporary neuroscientists are wary of claims about likenesses between brains and computers:

> These days the brain is often loosely compared to the CPU of a computer. The brain is a very special type of computer, however. It is a biological computer that has evolved over the course of hundreds of millions of years, and it is critical to appreciate that the brain really has no obvious correspondence at all with the computers you are familiar with on your desktop. (Squire *et al.* 2003, p. 15)

Psychologists have tended to suppose that the task of understanding how the brain works belongs to disciplines other than psychology. That is true in a sense, but psychology is a very wide-ranging discipline and as techniques such as brain scanning have become more widely available, cognitive neuroscience has gained more advocates and it has become important to develop theories that bring together what is known about brain and mind rather than imposing an artificial separation between them on the basis of an analogy between software and hardware in a computer which may be incorrect and misleading.

## Virtual control regimes

The concept of virtual architecture, as mentioned earlier in the chapter has been used not just in the context of a hierarchy of machines but also to handle the design of the control regime that governs how the hardware and software of a computer interact and how the computer interacts with the external environment. Chapter 14 described briefly how the internal organization of a von Neumann computer was designed to minimize the need for contact with the external environment during the execution of a program. The reason for this was the enormous disparity in speed of processing between the fast electronic interior of the computer and the slow mechanisms available for communication with the external environment. Contact with the environment was minimized by storing as much of the necessary data as possible in the high speed memory and by arranging the program so that each step taken was determined by the last. A program was written as a series of steps or instructions, each of which was numbered. A program counter was then used to keep track of the number of the current instruction.

The simplest control regime involves executing instructions in sequence. Instruction 1 is executed first, followed by instruction 2 and so on. This is achieved by adding one to the program counter after the execution of a step. However, an essential part of program execution is the capacity to make the next step conditional on the results of the current step rather than simply having it follow in sequence. This led to the introduction of conditional branching which allowed the value of the program counter to be calculated from intermediate results rather than simply incremented. In this way, complex cycles of processing could be controlled entirely internally with no need for external intervention. This control regime works very well when a task can be mapped out entirely in advance of its execution and all conditional choice points identified, but it is much less satisfactory as the basis for an account of human cognition where ongoing internal activity has to be carried out while monitoring the environment and where the current focus of attention is frequently disrupted by new demands from the environment.

## Production systems

A widely adopted solution to this problem that has been used extensively in cognitive modelling and artificial intelligence has been to implement a virtual control structure called a production system (Newell 1973). Production systems vary substantially, and in psychologically important ways in many of their details, but have a common core. The fundamental idea is that the 'program' of a production system exists in the form of a set of 'productions'. A production is, essentially, an if-then rule or a condition-action pair. A Turing machine instruction is a simple form of production. However, whereas a Turing machine instruction has exactly five terms, a symbol and a state of mind in the condition part and a symbol, a state of mind and a movement in the action part, the productions in a production system can be more complicated. As an example, consider the production **Get-Next** which is from a model of serial recall implemented in the ACT-R architecture, Anderson and Lebiere (1998, p. 204);

> **Get-Next**
> IF    the goal is to retrieve the nth element of the mth group of the list and x is the element at position n in group m in the list
> THEN    set a sub-goal to process x and update the goal to retrieve the n+1st element

There is no limit, in principle, other than the memory space available, on the complexity of a single production or on the number of productions that a given system can contain. Typically, a production system architecture incorporates a distinction between a working memory and a production memory.

The working memory at a given time contains a collection of elements which collectively constitute the current condition of the system, which can be called $COND_{WM}$. $COND_{WM}$, which is analogous to a configuration of a Turing machine, is then matched with the conditions of the productions in the production memory. If no matches are found, the contents of working memory have to be modified, for example by encoding information about the external world. This produces a new $COND_{WM}$ and the attempted pattern matching process can be repeated. If $COND_{WM}$ is matched by the condition part of a single production in the production memory, the action part of the production is carried out which typically leads to modification of the contents of working memory. The cycle is then repeated. If there is more than one production whose condition matches $COND_{WM}$ a common procedure is to choose a single one to execute via a conflict resolution procedure. Thus the activity of a production system architecture can be thought of as a sequence of pattern matching and action execution processes.

## Turing machines and production systems

Given that a Turing machine instruction is a simple form of production, it is valuable to consider in a little more detail the similarities and differences between Turing machines and production systems. Taking the similarities first, the primitive control element in each system is the production. There is no pre-programmed execution sequence in a production system. The sequence is partly determined in a Turing machine: the current configuration determines the next state, but the next configuration also depends on input. The set of productions in the production memory is functionally equivalent to the standard description of a target machine on the tape of a universal machine. The production system and the Turing machine also achieve their focus in broadly the same way. The production system has a working memory in which the elements constituting the current condition, $COND_{WM}$ are found. The Turing machine equivalent of a state of the working memory is the configuration **(q,s)** consisting of the current state of the control and the symbol on the scanned square. It is notable that the conditions of productions in a production system often make reference to goals or subgoals of the system, as well as to specific data elements. This may be thought of as similar to the distinction between the state of mind of the Turing machine (which may encode its goals) and the data element on the tape.

Turning to the differences between production systems and Turing machines, one point that has already been mentioned is that Turing machine instructions always have the same simple form whereas the productions in a production system may be quite complex. This makes it possible for productions to be specified at a scale which is psychologically more realistic than the single square at a time focus of the Turing machine. Consider, for example, a further ACT-R production, this time taken from a set of productions that specify rules for multi-column addition, Anderson and Lebiere (1998, p. 8)

**Last-Column-Carry**
> IF      the goal is add the numbers in a column and an item has been read into the bottom number slot and that item is a + and there is a carry to be passed on
> THEN   note the problem as finished write out the carry and pop the goal

This production encodes a simple situation which notes both that a terminal symbol has been encountered and that there is a carry to propagate. The simultaneous recognition of two facts is something that people do very readily but that cannot easily be reproduced in the Turing machine even though the restrictions on the capabilities of the Turing machine stem from the constraints on human perception and action.

A second difference between production systems and Turing machines is that in a production system there may be multiple matches to the condition in working memory whereas there is only ever one action defined for a given Turing machine configuration. Thus the Turing machine's behaviour is always determined by its configuration whereas in a production system it is typically necessary to decide which of a number of matching productions should be executed. This again has a psychological plausibility which is lacking in the Turing machine. Humans typically find themselves in situations where different possibilities for action are equally plausible and a decision has to be made among them.

A final, important, difference is that the productions in a production system are internal, although their action parts may eventually have external effects, whereas the instructions for a Turing machine, in both the condition and the action parts, include elements referring to the external environment and elements referring to the agent. A configuration for a Turing machine is instantiated when a particular internal state of the control automaton or mini-mind is paired with the symbol on a given square of the tape, whereas the condition for a production is instantiated solely by reference to the contents of working memory. Production systems share with standard computer systems the problem of deciding how information is to be got into the system from the outside world whereas the Turing machine interacts with external information directly. This is a crucial topic which is considered further in Chapter 17. It is also important to be aware that a production system is part of the hierarchy of virtual machines and is typically run on von Neumann hardware. Thus any constraints imposed by that hardware apply as much to production systems as they do to any other type of control regime. If, therefore, the brain is not a von Neumann computer, it cannot implement a production system unless it can be shown how a production system is compatible with a different type of hardware architecture.

## Summary

Virtual architecture is a powerful concept. It stems from the distinction between hardware and software introduced by Turing in terms of standard descriptions but it has ramifications which go beyond his purposes. However, just as a standard description requires a universal mini-mind to interpret it, so also a production system or any other virtual structure requires underlying hardware for its operations. With these points in mind, we turn now to examine the computational theory of mind, and connectionism.

# 16 The Commitments of the Computational Theory of Mind

## Introduction

The fundamental claim made by proponents of the computational theory of mind (CTM), particularly as expressed by the physical symbol systems hypothesis, is that the brain is a universal computer and the mind is its software. This chapter sets out the commitments of the theory and Chapter 17 evaluates it. There is, unfortunately, considerable scope for confusion when studying the existing literature because much of it treats von Neumann architecture and Turing machine architecture as interchangeable whereas, as earlier chapters have shown, they should be kept separate with respect to their implications for psychology. It will help to have a clear picture in mind of the different architectures. Figure 16.1 shows in a very simple way the principal elements **C** and **M** of the von Neumann architecture and the corresponding finite state control and tape of the Turing machine.

The memory **M** of the von Neumann computer is functionally equivalent to the tape of the Turing machine and the control **C** is functionally equivalent to the finite state control of the Turing machine. These simple functional equivalences are adequate for very broad brush theorizing provided one is not concerned with the details. At more detailed levels there are substantial differences between the ways in which the two types of architecture work as Chapters 14 and 15 have shown. The control and memory of the von Neumann machine are wired together to allow the control to have random access to the memory and the machine language is closer to Turing's instruction note model than it is to the Turing machine. However, the high level functional equivalences make it possible to treat models of the mind based on the Turing machine and models based on von Neumann architecture as roughly equivalent. The two models in Figure 16.2 can be thought of as equivalent in this way. The right hand side of Figure 16.2 shows, however, that there is something odd about treating the Turing machine in this way because it amounts to embedding the mind within the mind as one of its parts and including, as another of its parts, a structure that was in the external environment in the original model. The inclusion of the mind as one of

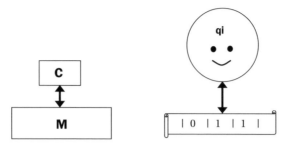

**Figure 16.1**   The fundamental components of von Neumann and Turing machine architecture.

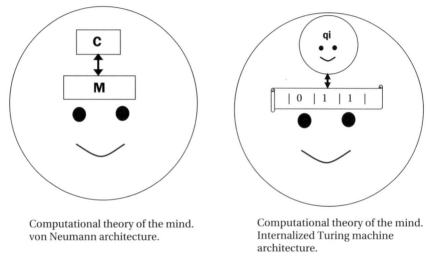

Computational theory of the mind. von Neumann architecture.

Computational theory of the mind. Internalized Turing machine architecture.

**Figure 16.2**   Two proposals for the organization of cognitive architecture.

its parts makes the model homuncular. There is, in this case, nothing theoretically troubling about the homunculus. It does not, for example, lead to an infinite regress of representational systems because it is known to be physically realizable, but it clearly departs from Turing's original thinking. The left hand side of Figure 16.2, by contrast, does not depart from von Neumann's thinking. In the EDVAC draft document as Chapter 14 makes clear, von Neumann described the parts **C** and **M** as corresponding to the associative parts of the brain and elsewhere in the text of his Silliman lectures (von Neumann 1958) he made a number of observations about similarities between the brain and computers although he was also careful to discuss differences as well.

The two parts of Figure 16.2 show that Turing and von Neumann did not hold the same view of the relation between the mind and the computer even though both were computer pioneers and both were interested in broad questions about the nature of intelligence and the possibility of synthesizing it mechanically. The fact that they did not have equivalent views makes it important to separate the computational theory of mind from its connection with Turing machines. It should properly be thought of as associated with von Neumann architecture or with Turing's instruction note model which explicitly removed references to states of mind. It is possible to construct an ecological theory of cognitive computation, using the Turing machine as its foundation, which is very different from the computational theory of mind. Ecological functionalism, outlined in Chapters 19 and 20, is just such a theory. The reason why it is desirable is that the evidence now suggests that the computational theory of mind is unlikely to provide an adequate explanation of human cognitive functioning.

## The CTM and von Neumann architecture

The computational theory of mind has been expounded and defended in various forms by numerous theorists over a period of more than forty years and attacked by others for an almost equally lengthy time. Despite this extensive discussion, there is still some debate about just what the commitments of the theory are. A good place to start, therefore, is with a description of what theorists ought to be committed to if they believe that the mind is the product of a neural system that has the computational power and organization of a von Neumann architecture. The hypothesis that the brain is a von Neumann computer, rigorously followed through, leads to the following assertions.

1. There are control structures realized in neural hardware that function like the central control, **C**, of a von Neumann computer.
2. There are memory structures realized in neural hardware that function like the memory, **M**, of a von Neumann computer.
3. There is an internal language, sometimes called the language of thought, (Fodor 1975) which is the machine language of the neural computer. It corresponds to the order code of a von Neumann computer.
4. Thought processes are serial transformations of symbol structures in the memory **M**, under the control of a program which is also located in **M** and executed by **C**.
5. There are input and output mechanisms, corresponding to **I** and **O** in the von Neumann architecture, that connect the internal computational environment with the external world. The input mechanisms represent the world in a way that makes it 'accessible to thought' Fodor (1983). The output mechanisms enable the results of thought processes to have effects on the world. **I** and **O** are analogous to the perceptual and motor systems of the human organism.

6. There are external resources corresponding to **R** in the von Neumann architecture that provide additional memory for the neural computer.

Several important consequences flow from the hypothesis that the brain has the architecture of a von Neumann computer. One of the most important of these is point 3, the need for a language of thought. If the brain is a von Neumann computer then it must have an internal language in which its programs are expressed. If the brain does not have such a language then it is not a von Neumann computer. The internal language is the source of the potential behavioural flexibility of the computer. It is the equivalent of Turing's standard description language. Flexible behaviour is the result of design which points, as it were, in two directions. A von Neumann machine has a fixed set of primitive operations, varying in number but always small relative to the vast number of programs that can be specified in terms of it. It is only because the set of primitives is fixed and small in number that it is possible to build the machine at all. This fixed set of operations is wired into the machine and is distinguished from programs which specify sets of these operations.

> If the device is to be *elastic*, that is as nearly as possible *all purpose*, then a distinction must be made between the specific instructions given for and defining a particular problem, and the general control organs which see to it that these instructions – no matter what they are – are carried out. (von Neumann 1945, p. 19)

The general control organs are the hardware structures comprising **C**, which carry out the primitive operations, while the instructions defining a particular problem are symbolic representations of these hardware operations. A machine language instruction points two ways, to the program of which it is a part and to the processor which it affects. It has a symbolic representation as a string of binary digits, for example, 01101001, but it also causes the processor to behave in a particular way, by causing a data path to be opened or shut or a specific operation to be carried out on the data currently in the control mechanism. An instruction, in effect, undergoes a transformation in the course of a fetch-execute cycle. When considered as the contents of a memory location, stored somewhere in **M**, an instruction is simply a collection of binary digits. When located in the processor after a 'fetch' operation, the instruction becomes the means whereby the physical operations constituting the operation are carried out in the 'execute' part of the cycle.

It is crucial to understand that a particular instruction like 01101001 may be mapped onto one primitive operation in one computer and a different one in another computer. This shows that machine language programs are not interchangeable. Each processor has its own machine language and programs for that processor must be written in its language. The apparent independence of software from hardware, which makes it possible to run a specific program on different types of hardware, is simply a convenience for the programmer. High level programming languages use constructs which represent desired functions such as addition or multiplication but these programs have to be supported by other programs called compilers or interpreters, which turn the high level functional specification of a task into the low level machine language specification which actually causes the processor to execute a sequence of elementary instructions. High level language programs, by themselves, do not cause processors to do anything. They are virtual machines.

If the brain is a von Neumann computer, then it must have a central processor, distinct from the main memory, to which program instructions and data are routed. It must have a machine language in which instructions to the central processor are encoded and it must have the means to fetch instructions from the memory and to cause the processor to execute them. If this is so, then it should be possible to find the neural location of the processor and to work out its machine language. It is this language that supports the virtual machines which constitute thinking and makes it possible to distinguish thinking from other kinds of neural activity.

If the brain is a von Neumann computer it must also have input and output systems, analogous to I and O. These systems carry out two functions in computers: (i) they translate the physical activity of the user, for example finger movements on a keyboard, into the different physical form that is used for the storage of alphanumeric symbols in the memory of the computer; (ii) they encode the inputs into the machine language of the computer; The central processor of a von Neumann computer cannot interact directly with anything other than a stream of instructions expressed in its machine language. In order, therefore, for a computer to engage in interaction with the outside world, as happens with personal computers whenever they are used for familiar applications like word processing, not only must the external physical medium be transformed into the internal one but a coding process must also be applied to render the input 'visible' to the internal computer. These points apply to the brain if it is a von Neumann machine. The input and output systems provide the means for the cognitive system to perceive and act on the world and they also translate to and from the neural machine language.

## Fudging the issues

The commitments of a theorist who argues that the brain has the architecture of a von Neumann computer can be set out clearly as shown. It is, however, relatively common for the question of physical architectural commitments to be fudged and it is important to understand why this can seem acceptable although it should not. Consider first some examples. In a well-known critique of connectionist theorizing, Fodor and Pylyshyn (1988) defended the computational theory of mind (which they call the 'Classical' theory). They characterized the commitments of the classical theory as follows:

> Classical models of the mind were derived from the structure of Turing and von Neumann machines. They are not, of course, committed to the details of these machines as exemplified in Turing's original formulation or in typical commercial computing; only to the basic idea that the kind of computing that is relevant to understanding cognition involves operations on symbols. (Fodor and Pylyshyn 1988, p. 4)

There are several points to make about this passage. First, it fails to distinguish the fundamentally different views of Turing and von Neumann. Second, it says that symbol processing is the core commitment of the theory. It doesn't actually say that the symbol processing is internal but that is intended. Third, the passage says that classical models are 'of course' not committed to the details of von Neumann computers or Turing machines. It is not said why 'of course' is appropriate but it is possible to infer from other things that Fodor and Pylyshyn say that it is because they think of the mind in terms of virtual architecture and, as we shall see, because they are aware that the relation between mind and brain is actually somewhat looser than that between hardware and software in a computer. However, as Chapters 14 and 15 show, virtual architecture is only possible in a machine which has very specialized hardware. It is a mistake to suppose that you need not be specific about the details of the underlying physical architecture when you are concerned with virtual architecture. In fact, if you are not committed to a von Neumann type of architecture, it is particularly important to state what your understanding of hardware is like because of the rarity of other architectures.

Despite their noncommittal stance on hardware Fodor and Pylyshyn are, nevertheless, prepared to make strong assumptions about the relationship between symbol structures and the brain. They propose that there are two fundamental principles governing classical cognitive architecture. Its mental representations have combinatorial syntax and semantics and the processes that transform representations are sensitive to the structures of the representations. Fodor and Pylyshyn (1988, p. 13) describe these principles as

> the claims that define Classical models, and we take these claims quite literally; they constrain the physical realizations of symbol structures. In particular, the symbol structures in a Classical model are assumed to correspond to real physical structures in the brain and the *combinatorial structure* of a representation is supposed to have a counterpart in structural relations among physical properties of the brain.

Further on in the paper, however, they again excoriate what they call 'the absurd assumption that the mind has *exactly* the architecture of some contemporary (von Neumann) computer', because it is clear that 'the behavior of an organism, is determined not just by the logical machine that the mind instantiates, but also by the protoplasmic machine in which the logic is realized' (Fodor and Pylyshyn 1988, p. 59). Given this joint determination of behaviour, one might think that a concern with the 'protoplasmic' machine would be central, but they also suggest that 'our knowledge of how cognitive processes might be mapped onto brain tissue remains very nearly nonexistent' (Fodor and Pylyshyn 1988, p. 57). When one summarizes the commitments that Fodor and Pylyshyn recognize, they amount to the following:

- Neural computing involves operations on symbolic mental representations;
- Symbolic mental representations have combinatorial syntax and semantics;
- Cognitive processes are sensitive to the structures of mental representations;
- Combinatorial syntax and semantics, and structure sensitivity constrain the physical realization of symbol structures;
- Physical as well as logical structure is relevant to the determination of behaviour.

The final point is the one I want to focus on here. Fodor and Pylyshyn argue that it is absurd to think of the mind as having exactly the architecture of a von Neumann machine because physical as well as logical properties affect behaviour. This point suggests, quite correctly, that the linkage between cognitive and physical descriptions of the human system is less tight than the linkage between software and hardware descriptions of a computer. The possibility of high level software descriptions in the computer case, however, depends absolutely and fundamentally on the reliability of the underlying hardware. If high level descriptions cannot be mapped onto the physical primitives of a computer reliably it does not work. An error in a single bit can and does result in total program failure. One of the triumphs of computer engineering has been to produce hardware with almost unbelievably high reliability which does allow users to deal confidently and exclusively with virtual software machines.

Fodor and Pylyshyn accept that the physical structure of the brain interferes, as it were, with the logical structure of the cognitive system but they do not consider this as imperilling the whole idea that the mind is a computer. Yet they ought to be concerned unless they have some good *a priori* reason for confidence in the brain as a computer. As soon as one moves from the logical realm, in which perfectly reliable machinery with infinite memory capacity can be defined and explored, to the physical realm in which theories have to deal with less than perfect machinery of finite capacity, the physical and biological plausibility of the constraints a logical proposal imposes on a physical substrate should be of paramount importance.

By and large, such constraints have not been treated as fundamentally important in cognitive science. Fodor and Pylyshyn are by no means alone in arguing strongly for the idea that the mind is a computer without feeling the need to give an equally strong characterization of the underlying hardware. The proximal cause of the willingness to treat physical and logical requirements as separable stems from the fact that the description of what a universal machine is doing is best given in terms of the program it is executing rather than in terms of its hardware configurations. The sequence that a universal Turing machine outputs is the sequence computed by the target machine whose standard description it is executing. The mapping from the key presses I am making to write this text to the appearance of letters on the screen of my computer is under the control of layers of software and is not directly a function of the hardware.

Psychology, we are often told, is the study of programs, not the study of hardware. However, it is glaringly obvious that the equation of mental operations with software and neural operations with hardware is defensible only if it turns out that the brain is indeed a computer of the right sort. Computational psychology of the kind advocated by enthusiasts for the computational theory of mind is viable only if the brain really is a computer. This is an empirical issue which requires empirical investigation but many cognitive scientists treat it as an issue which can be resolved positively *a priori*. There seem to be two basic reasons for this. Oversimplifying, one is the idea that you can make a computer out of anything and the other is the idea that everything is a computer. If you can make a computer out of anything you can certainly make it out of neural tissue and if everything is a computer then the brain is a computer.

## Can you make a computer out of anything?

Turing may be said to have caused the trouble by giving a purely functional specification of a universal computing machine divorced from a commitment to any particular physical realization. Early experience then showed that it is possible to make computer memories out of many different substrates including shock waves in liquid, ferro-magnetic cores, semi-conductors and so on. It is also possible to make control circuitry out of a wide range of materials. Philosophers have added to the range of possibilities by considering various schemes such as armies of people organized to execute the sequence of moves made by a universal Turing machine. What these practical successes and innovative thought experiments show is that practical computation should not be associated exclusively with any particular medium.

What is important is not the medium *per se* but whether it can be organized appropriately, and it appears that some initially unpromising media can be so organized. The idea of using shock waves in liquid as a memory is initially unpromising but as delay line technology, the memory medium for some of the earliest computers, showed it turned out to be possible although technically difficult.

These considerations do not, however, license the conclusion that a computer can be made out of anything. You cannot make a computer out of shock waves in liquid alone. If the computer is to be usable, the shock waves have to be carefully controlled as the designers of the Pilot ACE mentioned in Chapter 2 found out and that involves all sorts of other media equally carefully arranged. A practical computer has to have a power supply and generates heat which has to be dissipated. Size and speed are also of paramount practical importance. It may be possible, in theory, to use an army of people to simulate a universal computer, but theoretical possibility is of no significance if, in practice, the space available is a desk-top or if results are required in micro-seconds rather than weeks. The fate of the machines designed by Charles Babbage, a century before Turing, offers a cautionary tale. Babbage designed computing machines to be made out of cogs and levers. His designs were practicable although they stretched the available manufacturing techniques to the limit by demanding unprecedented precision, but they foundered because the expense involved in building them was not sufficiently offset by the advantages of having them. They were not fast enough to justify their costs. Similarly, although electronic technology is not theoretically essential for computing, it is most unlikely that practical computers would have become such prominent parts of contemporary life had they not operated as quickly as they do. In practical contexts therefore, it is essential to understand the nature of the substrate in which computation is supposed to be realized and the constraints under which the computer is to function. This applies as much to the brain as it does to any other medium.


## Is everything a computer?

Two broad kinds of argument have been used to suggest that everything is a computer. Again, the trouble may be said to stem from Turing's purely functional specification of mechanical computation. The first kind of argument uses the detachment of functional from physical specification in the following way. What is important in a practical computation is not states of matter *per se* but the functional relationships among them. Suppose, then, we have a Turing machine which has a transition defined from state **q1** to **q2** given a particular input. Let us take a particular physical object, say a stretch of wall. The wall appears to be in a constant state, but we know that it really consists of atoms in constant motion. So, at a detailed level of description, the wall is constantly changing state. Suppose, then, we interpret the micro-physical state of the wall at a given time as implementing state **q1** of the putative machine, and the different micro-physical state at a convenient later time as representing state **q2**. Under this interpretation the wall can be said to be implementing the state transition from **q1** to **q2**. The principle can be extended from single state transitions to sequences of state transitions. If other states of the wall are interpreted as inputs and outputs, the micro-states of the wall provide everything needed to specify a Turing machine. It follows that there is a mapping from the functional definition of the Turing machine onto the micro-states of the wall which is such that the wall can be said to be computing the function computed by the Turing machine. If this is true of a wall it is true of any other physical object. Everything, therefore, can be said to be a computer given a suitable interpretation. Arguments of this kind have been used by opponents of the computational theory of mind to suggest that the thesis that the mind is a computer is trivially true and therefore uninformative.

Suppose, for the sake of the argument, that it is true that the micro-states of a wall could be identified and measured accurately enough to enable the putative mapping to the states of a Turing machine. Had this been a useful thing to do, we might have expected computer designers to specify such mappings rather than spend time designing the machines we now use. The reason why this route was not taken is that the wall cannot be used for practical computation. Practical computation requires a physical system which can be placed in a given starting state with a particular program and relevant data, which will then run automatically through a sequence of states terminating in an identifiable state which provides the user with information they did not previously have such as the value of a given function for a specific argument. The wall does not and cannot do this. The user has to specify the mapping from functional to physical state for each step and must know the outcome of the computation in advance in order to specify the full sequence of states of the wall that is functionally equivalent to the desired computation. The appropriate response, therefore, to the idea that the successive micro-states of any physical object can be interpreted as a computation is 'So what?' The matter has no bearing at all on whether or not useful, controllable computers can be built. It is certainly not the case that everything is a useful, controllable computer. If someone were to show how to harness the states of a wall for practical computation that would, of course, be a different and altogether more impressive achievement.

There is another, more plausible, suggestion associated with the idea that everything is a computer. It derives from a particular way of understanding what Turing and other logicians in the 1930s and since have achieved. Turing and others, particularly Alonzo Church, were grappling with the question of how to formalize the notion of an 'effective procedure'. In everyday terms, an effective procedure is one that reliably achieves a result. In the sphere of calculation, an effective procedure is generated by breaking a problem down into a series of sub-problems each of which is easier to solve than the problem as a whole. This process is iterated until there is no question about the effectiveness of the basic steps. When each basic step is guaranteed and the sequence of steps defining a higher level procedure has been properly determined the procedure as a whole is guaranteed to be effective. Such a procedure is described as an algorithm. Church was able, using a method of this kind, to identify the effectively calculable functions with recursive functions and Turing was able to identify them with Turing computable functions. It was then shown that each recursive function was Turing computable and vice versa. This showed that the two, superficially very different, formal schemes were equivalent in scope. Since the pioneering efforts of Church and Turing, other schemes to define algorithms have been proposed and, thus far, each has turned out to encompass exactly the same set of functions. The identification of effective procedures with Turing machines or recursive functions or whatever does not constitute a proof that effective procedures are recursive functions or Turing machines because the notion of effective procedure is informal. It remains possible, therefore, that some day, someone will find an intuitively satisfying definition of effective procedures that is not formally equivalent to any of the other existing definitions.

Powerful though the formal results are, they do not appear to justify the conclusion that everything is a computer although they have been used in this way. It is apparent when one looks carefully at what Turing did, for example, that his formalization concerned specifically the effective procedures that could be carried out by a human computant calculating with paper and pencil. Turing's results appear, therefore, to be narrower than what is required to support the thesis that everything is a computer. Not all effective procedures are calculations and not all effective procedures are carried out by humans. The key idea that underpins the idea that everything is a computer depends on the representational capacities of universal machines. It turns out, as we now understand, that the functioning of any machine whose elementary operations are clearly understood can be described in terms of a program and simulated on a universal computer. The way that aircraft wings function can be studied in this way as, indeed, can the wings of birds and the functions of the brain. If, as seems plausible, every machine can be simulated by a computer program, there is a sense in which that machine can be treated as a computer since a computer program is itself the description of a computer that could be built. Programs then, in a sense, enumerate computers.

Does this license the conclusion that the brain is a universal machine and that psychology can be studied independently of hardware considerations? It does not, because the argument does not show that the brain is a universal computer. There is a hierarchy of types of computer with different capacities. The argument may be strong enough to show that the brain is a computer of some kind but it does not show that it is a universal machine rather than a finite automaton or a fixed function Turing machine. If the brain is a finite automaton there is no distinction between hardware and software to be made. If the brain is a mono-functional Turing machine the contents of its memory are data not programs and the general account of cognition is different from that which would be appropriate if the machine were universal. It is therefore legitimate to insist that proponents of the computational theory of mind demonstrate the feasibility of treating the brain as a universal machine even if its architecture is not exactly that of a von Neumann machine. That is the least that is required to support arguments proposing a radical separation of psychology from neuroscience or thinking from other mental functions. The issue is particularly important because the evidence that the brain is a universal machine is not strong.

## The attractions of the computational theory of mind

If the computational theory of mind were true it would, as briefly discussed in Chapter 15, solve a number of long standing problems about the nature of mind and mental processing. It would show how it is possible for mental states both to have causal powers and to be about things other than themselves. It would also provide an explanation for the flexibility and adaptability of human mental processes and, perhaps, for the capacity for innovation that is such a marked feature of the human species.

### Rationality and causal powers

One of the major proponents of the idea that the computational theory of mind accounts for the rationality and intentionality of thought has been the philosopher Jerry Fodor. He has vigorously promoted the theory in a series of important books and papers spanning more than thirty years. Fodor has argued trenchantly that the computational theory is the only plausible account of how the mind works that is able to explain both how states of mind can have causal powers, that is make things happen, and can be semantically evaluable that is, be about things and hence either true or false. A short statement of his general approach (Fodor 1994, p. 299) is the following:

> Folk psychology supposes that we act out of our beliefs and our desires; it is both relentlessly causal and relentlessly intentional. The analogy between thoughts and symbols – discovered, I suppose, by Plato, and refined by the likes of Descartes, Hume, Mill and Freud – helps us to see how thoughts could have both sorts of properties: we have only to assume that there are *mental* symbols. Turing's idea that mental processes are

computational helps us see how thinking could take one from truths to truths: we have only to assume that mental processes are driven by the intrinsic properties of mental symbols. Put the two ideas together and one begins to have a glimmer how something that is merely material can nonetheless be rational.

According to this view, reasoning is a form of naturalized proof theory. The premises of an argument are encoded as symbol structures which are then transformed according to mental axioms and previously derived theorems to produce a conclusion that follows from the premises. Fodor is not alone in characterizing reasoning in proof theoretic terms. The originator of proof theory, the famous German mathematician David Hilbert, appears to have taken a similar view. In a paper on the foundations of mathematics, Hilbert said that 'The fundamental idea of my proof theory is none other than to describe the activity of our understanding, to make a protocol of the rules according to which our thinking actually proceeds' (Hilbert 1927, p. 475). Fodor has suggested in various places that unless one postulates processes of this kind one is forced to conclude that the capacity for rational thought is miraculous. However strong the case is, though, if the brain does not support explicit symbol processing of the requisite kind then the explanation cannot be right. It is also not Turing's theory and it is unfortunate that Fodor has attributed it to Turing in several of his books. Hilbert's comment is revisited in Chapter 20. One difficulty with the general approach which has been acknowledged in a more recent work (Fodor 2000) is that although proof theory works well for deductive inferences it is much less easy to see how to apply it to abductive or global inferences.

*Mental flexibility*

The explanation of mental flexibility is a key achievement of the computational theory of mind, if it is true. Humans have an enormous behavioural repertoire and seem able to expand it constantly. Humans are, nevertheless, biological machines and machines are typically rather limited in their behaviour. A question thus arises about the sources of human behavioural flexibility. This problem is solved, in principle, if behaviour is produced by a universal computer. The hypothesis that the brain is a universal computer explains how it is possible for someone to react differently to the same input on different occasions and to develop new ways to behave. The explanation is based on the idea that the input is processed by different programs on different occasions. In the heyday of behaviourism it was argued that stimuli were associated one to one with responses. The argument is implausible for the simple reason that the organism is capable of responding to the same stimulus in different ways on different occasions. To explain this, simple S-R theories were augmented by a contribution from the organism and S-O-R theories were developed. The physical symbol systems hypothesis (Newell and Simon 1976) proposes specifically, as indicated in Chapter 2, that the organism contributes the resources of a practical universal computer. It is thus possible, in principle, to link stimuli to responses in indefinitely many different ways. If the mind does provide the resources of a practical universal machine, there must be mental symbols. Allen Newell contrasted the representational possibilities offered by mental symbols with the restricted possibilities of what he called 'analogical' representations. An analogical representation is one which maps the characteristics of what is to be represented onto the intrinsic properties of the representing medium. The traditional hour-glass, for example, represents the passage of time by the flow of sand through the narrow neck of the instrument. The quantity and granularity of the sand, and the size of the aperture control the flow rate in such a way that the sand is transferred from the top of the glass to the bottom in a fixed period. The hour-glass has some important advantages. It is cheap and relatively simple to make, very easy to operate, reliable, moderately robust and has no running costs apart from the tiny energetic cost of turning it. Its disadvantage, if such it can be called, is that it has just one function, indicating the passage of a given period of time. The time period cannot be changed and the device cannot easily be incorporated into something more sophisticated, for example a timer that will give an audible signal when the period it measures has elapsed. It is also a poor instrument for assessing with any precision what fraction of the period it measures has passed.

It is characteristic of analogical representations that they depend on the intrinsic qualities of the representing medium. Sand works well for hour-glasses but water would work less well. Water, by contrast, can be used to represent the flow of current in electrical circuits but sand is less suitable. A system that can support multiple analogical representations typically requires multiple media or a medium with appropriately rich dynamics. The alternative is what Newell (1990, p. 61) called the 'Great Move'.

> Instead of moving toward more and more specialized materials with specialized dynamics to support an increasingly great variety and intricacy of representational demands, an entirely different turn is possible. This is the move to using a neutral, stable medium that is capable of registering variety and then *composing* whatever transformations are needed to satisfy the requisite representational laws. Far from representational constriction, this path opens up the whole world of indefinitely rich representations.

The stable, neutral medium to which Newell refers is realized in Turing machines with the tape whose squares hold tokens of the symbol alphabet of the machine, in computers with memory whose basic units are bi-stable circuits and, by hypothesis, in humans with neural circuitry.

The arguments of Fodor and Newell, taken together, suggest that the postulation of mental symbols is essential for the joint causal/representational capacities of thought and for the wide, possibly unlimited, range of behaviours that humans can display. Both theories propose that humans have, in their heads, the functional equivalent of the tape of a practical universal machine or the primary memory of a computer. The material of earlier chapters makes it completely clear that this was not Turing's theory, but it might be true. However, if it is true, it makes severe demands on the brain. If the brain instantiates a universal machine which manipulates internal symbol structures then, in addition to a memory capable of holding those symbol structures, it has to have control circuitry to fetch and execute instructions and data and it has to have a machine language in which its computations are carried out. These are essential aspects of a universal machine.

Newell, while recognizing that 'neural technology' is the technology of human cognitive architecture wants to use the idea that the mind is a symbol system as a guide to its internal structure. 'My objective is to ground the assertion that the human is a symbol system on external behavioural aspects, so that it can serve as a design constraint for considering the nature of the internal structure' (Newell 1990, p. 116). Roughly speaking, the argument that Newell deploys is this. If you look at the variety of behavioural patterns ('response functions' as he calls them) that the human system can produce you are led to conclude that it must be a universal machine because only a universal machine could be that flexible. But how is it possible to be sure? Any claim that mental phenomena are the products of a universal neural computer is vulnerable to an argument of the following kind:

1. If the mind/brain relation is the same as the software/hardware relation in a universal computer then the brain must support the basic operations of a universal computer.
2. The brain does not support the basic operations of a universal computer.
3. The mind/brain relation is not the same as the software/hardware relation in a universal computer.

This is a valid argument whose logical form is *modus tollens*. It shows that the computational theory of mind needs empirical verification at the hardware level before it is taken too seriously as a fundamental account of how thinking works. If support is lacking, the theory cannot be correct no matter how appealing it might be. Chapter 17 makes a critical evaluation of the computational theory of mind.

# 17 Evaluating the Computational Theory of Mind

## Introduction

The starting point for an evaluation of the computational theory of mind is the fundamental notion that the mind stores and processes discrete symbols in essentially the way that computers do. To evaluate this claim one needs to have a clear understanding of what it is for something to be a discrete symbol. In computer terms, the core requirement is abstractly described as type identifiability. Each symbol token is a representative of a particular type and type identifiability is the requirement that the type of a symbol token should be unmistakeable and reliably recognizable. 0 and 0 are tokens of the same type, whereas 0 and 1 are tokens of different types.

   Handwriting is a good practical example that shows the importance of type identifiability. Handwriting that is easy to read contains symbol tokens that are easily type identifiable whereas handwriting that is hard to read contains symbol tokens that are ambiguous and hard to identify. The differences between tokens of different types can be instantiated in many ways. 0 and 1 differ in shape on the printed page, but the zero and one states in computers are usually represented by a difference in current flow. The details of the instantiation can differ provided that tokens are reliably recognizable as instances of their type. If the brain is a computer with anything like the von Neumann architecture its hardware must be capable of symbol operations of the kind found in computers. It must be capable of storing symbol tokens indefinitely, and they must be of a kind that can be transferred from one part of the system to another. In a computer, the basic storage unit is a bi-stable device called a flip-flop. Flip-flops have been built to various design specifications but they all have in common two fundamental capacities; they can reliably be set into one of two states and once set they will reliably retain the state setting until it is changed. A single flip-flop stores a single bit of data, namely a token of 0 or a token of 1. It is not essential to use flip-flops for main memory. The Pilot ACE and the EDVAC used acoustic delay lines, and other technologies are possible such as the paper tape and pencil marks of the Turing machine, but flip-flops are the basis for computer memories now and have always been used in the control circuitry. A fundamental question, therefore is, does the brain use flip-flops for memory and control purposes?

## Does the brain contain flip-flops?

A definitive answer to this question is surprisingly hard to come by. The influential work of McCulloch and Pitts (1943), introduced in Chapter 2, which was based on the assumption that the crucial property of neurons was the 'all or none' nature of the neural action potential and its stereotyped character, suggests a positive answer to the question and proposes that the basic symbolic code of the brain is binary. McCulloch and Pitts argued that this made it possible to treat 'the response of any neuron as factually equivalent to a proposition which proposed its adequate stimulus' (1943, p. 352). McCulloch and Pitts acknowledged that there were properties of neurons such as facilitation, extinction and learning which could change the response functions of neurons but they argued that 'the alterations actually underlying facilitation, extinction and learning in no way affect the conclusions which follow from the formal treatment of the activity of nervous nets, and the relations of the corresponding propositions remain those of the logic of propositions' (1943, p. 352). This can be viewed, I think, in one of the two ways. It can be read as arguing that the logical character of nervous system activity is primary, or it can be read as arguing that the logical analysis covers that part of nervous system activity which consists of signalling but does not cover the activities involved in facilitation, extinction and learning. In either case, it is assumed that the information stored and transmitted by neurons is fundamentally binary and that neural organization is fundamentally hierarchical.

It is less plausible now than it seemed in 1943 to claim that information transmission in the nervous system is fundamentally binary. There is no doubt that the occurrence of an action potential is type identifiable and distinct from the absence of an action potential. But it is far from clear that single neurons act as flip-flops or that collections of neurons do. The individual neuron is certainly not a bi-stable device. It is not a switch which is set to ON or OFF and reliably signals either state. It is much better thought of as a monitoring device which integrates a large number of inputs and reports activation when a sufficiently highly aroused state has been reached. A neuron typically has thousands or tens of thousands of inputs, some excitatory, some inhibitory, and the position of the synaptic junction between the axon of the pre-synaptic cell and the cell body of the post-synaptic cell is significant. Electrical signals are rapidly attenuated because of the high resistivity and poor insulation properties of neural membranes. Input via a synapse which is positioned on a dendritic spine far from the cell body may well have less impact on the state of a neuron than a similar input arriving near the axon hillock. These factors suggest that the output condition of a neuron is better thought of in probabilistic terms rather than as a specific logical function of its inputs. Even if the latter is appropriate, the function may best be described as a disjunction of conjunctions such that the output may be triggered by any one of a number of possible combinations of inputs. Furthermore, it is the rate of firing which is primary rather than the presence or absence of an action potential. The general rule is that the higher the rate of firing the greater the intensity of input. If single neurons cannot be characterized as bi-stable devices, it is unlikely that connected groups of neurons will function that way either. The differences between computer and nervous system circuits led Kohonen (1988, p. 12) to suggest that

> The principles of computer memories can hardly be realized in biological organisms for the following reasons: i) All signals in computers are binary whereas the neural signals are usually trains of pulses with variable frequency. ii) Ideal bistable circuits which could act as reliable binary memory elements have not been found in the nervous systems.

If the brain does not contain bi-stable circuits as its basic information storage elements the fundamental idea that the brain is a universal computer becomes implausible. The primary reason for this is that if type identifiable symbols do not exist in the brain, it lacks an independent code in which the equivalent of its standard descriptions can be expressed. If neurons cannot be set to particular values in the way that flip-flops can then they cannot be used to store and transmit sequences of symbols. The fundamental point about the software in a computer is that the encoded symbol structures are distinct from and independent of the underlying hardware which provides only the means for storage and transmission. Compare the output from a neuron with the output from a single location in a computer's memory. The output from a neuron contains the information 'this much activity from this source now' whereas the output from a memory location contains the information 'this particular string of bits representing such and such', where 'such and such' may be an instruction or a piece of data.

## Positional specification of meaning in the brain

It appears, in fact, that computers and brains use fundamentally different methods to convey meaning. In a computer with random access memory, individual locations are not meaningful but their contents are. In a brain, the meaning of a train of impulses depends crucially on location. A train of pulses in the optic nerve, for example, means that visual input has occurred whereas a train of pulses in the auditory nerve means that auditory input has occurred. The wiring of both brains and computers is highly specific but for fundamentally different reasons. The wiring of a computer is arranged in such a way that the contents of any memory location can be transferred to the central processor, operated upon in some way and then transferred back to any other location in the memory. The wiring of the brain is arranged in such a way that an impulse from a particular source has a particular destination or set of destinations. The organization is highly specific. There is no random access in the brain because there is no central processor that can select an arbitrary memory location and receive input from that location. Signals specify their sources, not hardware neutral codes.

## Hierarchical encoding

McCulloch and Pitts' idea that a neuron 'proposes its adequate stimulus' gains some of its power from the fact that, if it is correct, it shows how hierarchical arrangements might exist in the brain. If the outputs of two conjunctive cells provide the inputs for a third conjunctive cell, the output of that third cell will constitute a second order conjunction. Second order cells can then function as inputs to third order propositions and so forth. In this way it is possible, in principle, to build up propositions or symbol structures of unlimited complexity.

There is some support for this idea in the famous work of Hubel and Wiesel on receptive fields in the visual cortex of the cat. Building on foundational work by Kuffler and by Barlow, Hubel and Wiesel proposed a hierarchy of cell types starting with simple cells which respond to the presence of stimulation in a particular part of their receptive field. For an introduction to this work, see Squire *et al.* (2003, chapter 27). The outputs of simple cells form the inputs to complex cells which respond to features of objects in the environment such as stopped oriented edges. The hierarchy continues with 'hypercomplex' cells which respond to more complex, higher order properties and terminates with what are called 'cardinal' cells. In 1972 Horace Barlow synthesized this approach and presented what has become known as the 'neuron doctrine'. An important part of Barlow's concern was to account for how it is that we recognize not just the form, motion and positions of objects in the visual field but are also able to identify them as particular objects.

> Solving this key problem was central to Barlow's development of the neuron doctrine. He proposed that the primary visual cortex dealt only with the elemental building blocks of perception, the detection of orientated line segments, or the local motion of these segments, for example. In order to build these into neurons that were selective for a cat, chair, or grandmother, he proposed a hierarchical sequence of processing within single cortical areas and through the many visual areas ... . The neurons at each stage of the hierarchy would become progressively more selective to

the attributes of the stimulus, so that while the neurons in the primary visual cortex would respond to many different objects, neurons at the highest level of the hierarchy of processing would respond only to particular objects. Barlow (1972) suggested that the activity of about 1000 of these high-level 'cardinal' neurons would be sufficient to represent a single visual scene. (Douglas and Martin 1990, pp. 431–2)

In McCulloch and Pitts' terminology, one would think of an object like a cat, chair or grandmother as the 'adequate stimulus' for a cardinal cell. Attempts to find cardinal cells have had only limited success. Neurons with the appropriate high order properties have been found, but only in limited areas of the neo-cortex and they do not behave entirely as one would expect a cardinal cell to behave. The general conclusion from a number of studies is that 'Single cortical neurons appear unable to signal unambiguously the presence of a particular stimulus or "feature" and therefore cannot act as cardinal cells.' Douglas and Martin (1990, p. 433).

## Constituency and neural constraints

In the light of these considerations about neural organization and functioning, it is instructive to consider the proposals of theorists like Fodor and Newell who seek to derive constraints on neural organization from the idea that the mind processes symbols in the same fundamental way that computers do.

The computational theory of mind entails strong constraints on the underlying medium. The most powerful of these comes from the notion of constituency. The logical expression (A & B) is a conjunction of two constituents 'A' and 'B' linked by the structural relation '&'. The individual identity of the terms is important because (A & B) is not the same as (A & C) and the nature of the structural relation is important. (A & B) is not the same as (A v B). Moreover, in some structural relations position within an expression matters and in others it does not. (A & B) has the same meaning as (B & A) but (A implies B) does not have the same meaning as (B implies A). If the mind processes symbol tokens via their syntax, then the syntactic differences between expressions arising from differences both in the terms and the nature of the structural relationships must be reflected in the encoding. As Fodor and Pylyshyn said in their critique of connectionism

> [I]t is not enough merely to specify a physical encoding for each symbol; in order for the *structures* of expressions to have causal roles, structural relations must be encoded by physical properties of brain states (or by sets of functionally equivalent physical properties of brain state). (Fodor and Pylyshyn 1988, p. 14 fn.9)

It is known that complex mappings of this kind can be sustained in computers because their memories are appropriately structured at the lowest level. The physical structure of a computer *enables* its symbol processing functions. The computer can store and process symbolic expressions because it has the kind of physical structure that it has. In the computational theory of mind, however, the idea of symbol processing is taken to *constrain* the organization of the underlying neural hardware. The brain stores and processes symbolic expressions, it is asserted, therefore it must have physical structure of a certain kind. The evidence suggests that the brain does not have physical structure of the relevant kind and thus calls into question the basic hypothesis that it processes symbols in the way that computers do. In computers, it is a fundamental principle that structure and function are separate. Function is determined by instructions and data not by the organization of the hardware. In brains by contrast, it appears that structure and function are tightly interwoven. 'History has shown that structure and function are simply two sides of the same coin, inexorably intertwined – both necessary and both dependent on the other' (Swanson 2003, p. vii).

### Encoding and decoding: the transduction problem

Suppose, for the sake of the argument, that the hardware of the brain does provide the structures needed for a practical universal machine of roughly the von Neumann design. It has, that is, a memory in which programs and data can be stored and it has control processes to execute its programs. It is then necessary to ask how it is provided with data. The question arises because if the brain is a universal machine everything it processes must be translated into its internal machine language. This can be called the 'encoding requirement'. The relevant parts of the von Neumann architecture are the input and output systems I and O and the question that has to be addressed is how I and O are realized in the human case if, like a computer, the mind processes only symbolic representations.

   Human life is characterized by the scope and immediacy of its contact with the external world. The senses or *perceptual systems* as they were called by Gibson (1966) are primarily directed outwards and are remarkable for their sensitivity to a wide variety of stimuli and for the ways in which they can focus attention on specific aspects of the total sensory flux. If the human nervous system has input and output systems that are functionally equivalent to I and O it ought to be possible to discover how they work and thus to equip computers with the same ability to act on the environment as people have.

   It is notorious, however, that it has thus far proven extremely difficult to equip von Neumann architecture computers with the means to perceive the external environment and to move about in it securely and purposefully in the way that humans, and other animals, do. This may be because we do not understand sufficiently well how our perceptual systems work to be able to reproduce their performance or it may be that we do not apprehend the world through symbolic representations encoded in a language of thought. The 'or' is inclusive: it may be that both these points are true.

Humans are surrounded by their environments and remain responsive to some inputs even when asleep. Our perceptual systems constantly monitor both internal and external conditions. These systems are exquisitely sensitive and serve both to inform and orient the organism. The eyes, ears, nose and mouth have their specific functions and the whole skin is equipped with pressure and pain sensors. In addition, muscles are equipped with sensory nerves that provide positional and kinetic information. If the whole system has the architecture of a von Neumann computer, none of these perceptual systems has direct contact with the machinery responsible for thinking because thinking, by hypothesis, consists of the manipulation and transformation of symbolic representations of the world encoded in the machine language of the internal computer. It must, therefore, be the case that the eyes, ears, and other organs are delivering selections from the raw sensory flux to systems which then somehow encode them into a form suitable for thinking. Proponents of the computational theory of mind are divided about how serious a challenge it is to give an adequate account of these processes. Allen Newell (1990), for example, considers the issues to be essentially matters of detail whereas Jerry Fodor has long pondered what appear to be fundamental questions about how the syntactic structures in the internal symbolic milieu can retain appropriate semantic relations to the world which they represent.

One specific difficulty is the way in which the encoding requirement places a burden on the input mechanisms that they are not well equipped to deal with. This is the burden of deciding which aspects of the sensory flux currently impinging on the organism should be encoded for cognitive mechanisms to think about. Pylyshyn (1984) is clear about the issues which he discusses in terms of what he calls the 'transducer function'.

> Neither the specification of a transducer's input nor of its output is unproblematic. … Because the output is to serve as the basis for the only contact the cognitive system ever has with the environment, it should provide all (and only) cognitively effective information. It should not provide information that could never serve as the basis for a cognitive distinction. … On the other hand, the output must provide the basis for all potential distinctions that could show up in cognitive phenomena – for example, in any perceptual effect, whether conscious or not. Consequently, the output of the set of transducers available to an organism *must preserve all distinctions present in the environmental stimulation that are also relevant to the explanation of some behavioral regularity.* (Pylyshyn 1984, p. 158)

One key point to note, as attempts to program von Neumann computers have shown, is that von Neumann architecture does not, in itself, make the external world meaningful to its possessor. That is to be expected, because the whole point of the von Neumann architecture is that it can be programmed to respond arbitrarily to its inputs, which is the basis for behavioural flexibility. There is no predisposition in the architecture to respond in one way rather than another to a given input. But a tendency or disposition to respond in specific ways to particular classes of input is part of what makes environments meaningful. The pair of symbols 'ee' at the start of the tape of Turing's universal machine, for example, is meaningful to it because it has a particular pattern of response built in. The von Neumann architecture does not have that sort of capacity. The architecture relies on its current program to make it respond to particular inputs in particular ways. It is, therefore, programs that make particular encoded inputs *relevant* to the internal machine and it is programs that are used to explain how behavioural flexibility works on the hypothesis that the mind is a von Neumann computer. But if one asks how the input is classified in the first place, how sense is made of what is there to be perceived, in order for distinctions that are behaviourally relevant to be registered, the internal architecture is helpless. Programs are on the wrong side of the input mechanisms. They deal solely with the outputs of those mechanisms and cannot determine how inputs are selected. Thus the burden, as Pylyshyn rightly points out, is thrown back on the input mechanisms themselves. They have to decide what is, or is not, relevant to the processing of the cognitive system. The only way that a mechanical system can do this is by functional specialization. An input is *relevant* to a mechanism if it causes that mechanism to respond and is not relevant if it does not. Relevance is, therefore, a matter of special purpose functionality. If this is how the cognitive system works it seems very curious. The internal universal computer, that which by hypothesis makes us intelligent, is at the mercy of input systems which are much less intelligent but which decide what the internal computer is going to compute with. It is rather like having a general decide what his army is going to do on the basis of information provided by raw recruits. One might have thought that one primary purpose of thought should be to determine which parts of the environment to pay attention to and another to monitor the choices made. Having dumb gatekeepers interposed between thought processes and that which they are primarily about seems unlikely to be true but it is a consequence of the computational theory of mind. Bickhard and Terveen (1995) offer an extensive critique of the assumptions underlying the computational theory of mind and pay particular attention to the difficulties of what they call 'encodingism'. The transduction problem is an instance of this problem.

## Could the brain have evolved as a universal computer?

The argument that the brain does not store and process symbols like a computer and the argument that the brain does not have input and output mechanisms like a computer are broadly based on empirical considerations. A rather general argument, with a more *a priori* character, suggesting that the brain is not a universal machine because it could not have evolved to be programmable in the requisite way, was developed by Michael Conrad (1974, 1985, 1988) a computer scientist with a particular interest in biological computation. Conrad approached biological computation from a standpoint in computer science rather than in psychology and his arguments provide a different perspective on the issues. Conrad proposed that two fundamental characteristics of computing systems, programmability and efficiency are linked to evolvability by a trade-off principle which says that

> *A system cannot at the same time be effectively programmable, amenable to evolution by variation and selection, and computationally efficient.* The von Neumann computer opts for programmability. The trade-off theorem suggests that an alternative domain of computing is in principle possible, where programmability is exchanged for efficiency and adaptability. Biological systems, as the products of evolution, must operate in this alternative domain. (Conrad 1985, pp. 464–5)

To understand the arguments for the trade-off principle it is crucial to understand the physical basis of the analysis. Information processing systems are 'systems which dissipate energy in certain interesting (or highly selective) ways' (Conrad 1974, p. 83), and Conrad maintained that programmable systems are essentially much less efficient than non-programmable systems, because of the way they use their physical resources. The basic idea is quite simple but depends on a broad interpretation of the sorts of processes that can be called computational. Some cognitive scientists claim that for a process to count as a computation it must be a rule-governed process of the kind executed by a universal Turing machine. Conrad argued that this view is unjustifiably restrictive.

> Turing machines ... are particular models of computation. They are particularly useful as reference points for evaluating the amount of computational work performed by arbitrary dynamical systems, not as delimiting the class of behaviors admitted to be forms of computing. (Conrad 1988, p. 287)

He suggested, on the basis of a strong interpretation of the Church–Turing thesis, that any physical process can properly be treated as a computational process.

> [A]ll physically realizable dynamics *are equivalent to computation* in that they can be simulated by a von Neumann computer under the idealization that space and time bounds can be ignored. (Conrad 1985, p. 468)

The difference between a universal Turing machine and an arbitrary physical system, said Conrad, is not that the one computes and the other doesn't but that the former has a potentially universal simulation capability because it is programmable, whereas the latter will usually have a very restricted simulation capability because it is not programmable. Notice the contrast with the argument about whether everything is a computer discussed in Chapter 16. Conrad argues that there is a sense in which everything is a computer but only when it is understood that computers come in very different guises. Thus a wall may be thought of as a computer but only if one accepts that its 'restricted simulation capability' prevents it from usefully simulating anything except itself. Conrad's argument is used in order to distinguish different types of computation not to argue that every type of computation is the same, which would render the concept trivial.

The trade-off principle shows that programmability is purchased at the cost of efficiency. The fundamental reason for this cost is that programmability implies controllability, and exercising control is an energy intensive business. The engine of a car, for example, converts only a fraction of the energy it consumes into motion of the wheels. This is due, in part, to the large amount of energy absorbed in controlling the sequence of combustions which delivers power to the wheels. Computation is also a physical process and Conrad's argument shows that controlling computational processes necessarily decreases the energy available for the task just as control of any other physical process decreases the available task energy. This aspect of the trade-off principle explains the very notable differences in efficiency between universal machines and the machines they simulate. The standard description of a target machine on a universal machine's tape is a control process which constrains the subsequent behaviour of the universal interpreter. The large number of moves that the universal machine has to make to simulate a single move of a target machine is indicative of the costs of programmability.

Perhaps more surprising is the aspect of the trade-off principle which shows that programmability and evolutionary adaptability are incompatible. One might be inclined, intuitively, to suppose that the behavioural flexibility which is conferred by programmability would be consistent with evolutionary adaptability. Conrad developed an argument which shows this to be an unreliable intuition. He starts by arguing that for a system to be evolvable it must be capable of 'accepting' at least one structural change. 'A system accepts a structural change if its performance improves or if it is capable of lasting long enough to accept another change, eventually leading to an improvement' (Conrad 1988, p. 294). The argument for this threshold condition rests on probabilistic analyses relating the time scale of evolutionary processes to the likelihood of multiple, simultaneous, structural changes. Conrad then argues, using a proof similar to Turing's proof of the unsolvability of the halting problem, that the problem of ascertaining whether a programmable system meets this condition, is, in general, unsolvable, even when the criterion for an 'acceptable' structural change is very weak. By contrast, there are structural changes which non-programmable systems can be shown to 'accept' in the required sense. Thus, at a minimum, 'programmable systems are not as effectively structured for evolution as nonprogrammable systems' (Conrad 1988, p. 293).

Conrad's arguments lead to the conclusion that the brain is not organized like a digital computer or a universal Turing machine because it is the result of an evolutionary process. This view is reinforced by the aspect of the trade-off principle which shows that a system will be more efficient if it is non-programmable. There is no reason, however, why the brain should not have evolved so as to include among its huge number of internal states, some which implement the finite state control of a universal machine, whose programs are to be found in the environment. This yields a system which is both efficient and responsive to its environment. Conrad draws a conclusion which is compatible with Turing's analysis of human computation and the ecological proposal advanced in the final two chapters of this book.

> [I]t would be possible to build a structurally nonprogrammable computer that is nevertheless effectively programmable at an interpretive level. There is a model for such a machine: People can read and follow rules despite the fact that the human brain, as a product of evolution, must be structurally nonprogrammable. (Conrad 1985, p. 475)

Conrad does not say that this is essentially the model on which Turing's analysis of computation was originally based but it clearly is so.

### Summary

The difficulties for the computational theory of mind which have been discussed in this chapter are consequences of the supposition that the brain is a Turing machine rather than the control automaton of a Turing machine whose tape is in the environment. In Chapters 19 and 20 a sketch of what such a theory might look like is presented. Before this, Chapter 18 discusses connectionist models of the mind which have been proposed as alternatives to the approach based on von Neumann architecture.

# 18 Connectionism

## Introduction

Since the mid-1980s there has been a resurgence of interest in classes of computational models based on networks of simple processors and the connections among them. Such models are variously described by the terms 'parallel distributed processing', 'neural networks' and 'connectionism'. It seems to be the case that physicists tend to talk about neural nets whereas psychologists tend to talk about connectionist models. For present purposes the differences are unimportant and I shall treat the different names as synonymous. The focus is on how network models relate to the computational theory of mind and to Turing machines.

## McCulloch–Pitts networks

Network models of computation have a history which is almost co-extensive with the history of symbolic models. One of the important founding documents is the paper by McCulloch and Pitts (1943) which established the link between computation in networks of idealized neurons and computation in Turing machines. Their networks were of two kinds, those with recurrent loops which they called 'nets with circles' and those without such loops. The neurons in a McCulloch–Pitts network are linear threshold devices. Their outputs are additive functions of their inputs, which may be positive or negative, and the output is a fixed value which is transmitted if the input exceeds a specified threshold. McCulloch and Pitts stated, although they did not prove, that nets with circles are computationally equivalent to the finite control automata of Turing machines and that such nets, if equipped with scanners and a tape like a Turing machine are computationally equivalent to Turing machines. To say that nets with circles are equivalent to the control automata of Turing machines means that for any given control automaton a functionally equivalent network can be constructed, and vice versa. The issues are discussed in detail in Minsky (1967).

## Learning in single-layer networks

McCulloch–Pitts networks do not learn. Each network has a fixed architecture which is specified by the designer. An important step towards understanding the possibilities of learning in networks was made by Hebb (1949) whose work was introduced in Chapter 2. Hebb formulated the principle that learning may be implemented by increasing the strength of the connection between a pair of neurons whose firing to a particular input is positively correlated. A formal model of learning in simple networks called perceptrons was developed by Rosenblatt (1962). Rosenblatt studied what are called 'single-layer' perceptrons. These have input and output nodes and a single layer of connections between them. Rosenblatt was able to prove the perceptron convergence theorem which showed that a single-layer perceptron would succeed in a learning task if a solution to the task existed. The importance of this result lay in the fact that learning could start from different places and with different examples. The convergence theorem proved that the different starting points did not affect whether or not the perceptron would succeed in its learning task. Minsky and Papert (1969) dealt a serious blow to the hope that single-layer perceptrons might provide a foundation for the study of a wide range of learning phenomena by showing that there were some simple problems for which they could be proven to fail.

## Multi-layer networks

The current enthusiasm for connectionist models is based on networks with more than two layers of nodes and more than one layer of connections. In addition to input and output layers there are also layers called 'hidden' layers interposed between them. There are, therefore, multiple layers of connections, from the input nodes to the hidden nodes and from the hidden nodes to the output nodes, and it is demonstrable that networks with hidden layers can solve some of the learning problems that are unsolvable by single-layer perceptrons. Learning is harder to achieve in multi-layer perceptrons than in single-layer ones because of the more complex network topology, but a type of supervised learning, informally known as 'back propagation' has been intensively studied and is the basis for much of the current psychological interest in connectionist nets.

## Symbol systems versus connectionism

There has been a fierce debate between cognitive scientists who argue that the mind is best thought of as a symbol system and those who argue that it is best thought of as a connectionist network. The paper, already discussed, by Fodor and Pylyshyn (1988) promotes the computational theory of mind and criticises connectionism. The paper by Smolensky (1988) is a response on the side of connectionism. The debate has not been resolved conclusively in favour of either side although each continues to have its partisans. Textbook writers, for example Dawson (1998), Harnish (2002) tend to consider both in a 'compare and contrast' fashion. The conclusion I have come to is that connectionists, like symbol systems theorists, are still labouring in the shadow of the von Neumann architecture although they explicitly reject it. The shadow is still there because connectionists, like symbolists, see themselves as needing to give an account in which the relation between the mind and the external environment is purely representational. In other words, although they reject ideas based on discrete state computation and thus specifically reject the Turing machine model, they still take the view that the mind has the power of a Turing machine and thus suppose that that power needs to be represented in networks.

## Styles of connectionist modelling

One common way in which a connectionist project is conducted is to identify a cognitive capacity, such as the capacity to form the past tenses of verbs or a phenomenon such as the functional asymmetry of the Stroop colour word naming task (Stroop 1935) as a target. A network with a given basic architecture is then trained using a suitable corpus of examples until a predetermined criterion of performance is reached. During the training phase, the strengths of the connections between nodes in the network are modifiable. When criterial performance has been achieved, connection strength modification is discontinued and the structure can be considered fixed. During the operational phase, the network's capacity to produce the desired associations is assessed. In some cases, such as the modelling of past-tense acquisition, the training phase is of primary psychological interest as a model of part of the process of language acquisition. In such a case the performance of the network in the operational phase is significant only in so far as it provides a measure of the extent to which performance criteria have been met. In other cases, for example the Stroop task or models of concept acquisition, the operational phase is of more psychological interest and the training phase is used solely to induce the connectivity needed to establish the set of input–output paired associations which constitutes the basic performance of the system. What is generally then of most interest is the study of the extent to which performance generalizes to unfamiliar inputs, and the exploration of the internal structures of connectivity which support such performance. These have been investigated using statistical techniques such as cluster analysis and principal components analysis. Internal patterns of connectivity are explored for the insights they might provide into the way conceptual information is stored. Another technique which has been used is to alter the connectivity so as to simulate the effect of a brain lesion, for example, and to note whether observed changes in performance bear some measurable similarity to the pathology of actual cases of brain damage.

## Networks and finite automata

An important question is how a network might best be characterized when it is considered as a fixed entity, that is after its training has been completed or when a snapshot is taken of its structures at some moment during the training regime. A fixed connectionist network, that is one which is not learning, is accurately construed as a finite state machine. The argument for this view is based on considering the sets of inputs and outputs which such a network can handle, and the character of its internal activation states when it is in operation. In the light of the characterization of fixed nets as finite automata, the learning process can be thought of as transforming an initial finite automaton which may not compute a recognizable function, but none the less computes some function, into one which computes, to a more or less accurate degree, the associative function specified by the set of input–output pairs which forms the corpus of training examples. The corpus of training examples, as well as providing data for the machine, also provides the means to specify the error feedback which the machine receives at each training step.

## Supervised learning

It will be helpful to consider in a little more detail, the processes by which a typical connectionist network is trained using error backpropagation. I shall consider the case of a network with an input layer, an output layer and one layer of hidden nodes. Figure 18.1 shows a simple example.

I do not propose to give a fully detailed account of the equations that govern the behaviour of the network, but mainly to make points of comparison with finite automata. There are numerous good technical accounts of network computations available. The two volumes of *Parallel Distributed Processing*, Rumelhart and McClelland (1986); McClelland and Rumelhart (1986) are still useful; Simpson (1990) has details of a wide range of network models, architectures and algorithms; and Dawson (2004) sets connectionist methods in a broad discussion of psychological modelling.

The network of Figure 18.1 has four input nodes, three hidden nodes and four output nodes. In many connectionist models, as in the example shown, there are fewer nodes in the hidden layer than in either the input or output

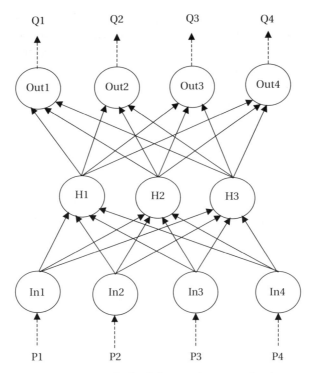

**Figure 18.1**   An example feed-forward connectionist network.

layers, a property which encourages the formation of encodings which will generalize to novel inputs. The solid arrows represent internal network connections. The example shown is fully connected, that is, each input node is connected to all the hidden nodes, and each hidden node is connected to all the output nodes. Other patterns of connectivity are possible but full connectivity is common, probably the norm. The dashed arrows represent connections with the external environment. Input is received from the environment and output is sent to it. Each input node receives a distinct element of the input pattern and each output node produces a distinct element of the output pattern. In Figure 18.1 the input pattern P = (P1, P2, P3, P4) and the output pattern Q = (Q1, Q2, Q3, Q4). The number of different possible patterns depends on the number of elements in a pattern and the possible values of each element. Suppose, for example, that each element in P and Q could be either 0 or 1. Then there would be sixteen input patterns and sixteen output patterns. If, instead, the elements of a pattern could be lower-case letters of the English alphabet there would be $26^4 = 456976$ input and output patterns. Adding more input and output nodes increases the number of possible patterns as does increasing the range of values for elements of a pattern. In all cases, however, the number of input patterns that a particular network can receive is finite. This is so, even if one allows the values of elements to range over an interval of real numbers, for example from $-1$ to $+1$. Although such an interval contains an infinite number of real numbers, in practice only a finite number of them can be represented because a real network can compute with only finite precision. Thus the input and output pattern sets of a network are finite, just as the input and output alphabets of a Turing machine are.

As mentioned earlier, two types of task are commonly studied with feed-forward networks. The first is the task of reproducing an arbitrary mapping from input to output. Typically, the researcher chooses a set of input–output mappings which has an appropriate interpretation in a specific domain, for example the mapping between present and past tense forms of verbs. The task for the network is to learn the mapping, such that when it is presented with an input pattern P it produces as output the matching pattern Q. In some cases final success is the only issue of interest but in other cases such as the learning of past tense verb forms, where there are developmental phenomena such as over-regularization to account for, the learning trajectory as well as the final performance is of interest. The second type of task is classification or categorization, in which the input patterns are treated as members of categories. In a typical case a subset of the patterns constitutes the training set and the remainder the test set. The task of the network is to induce the 'rules' for category membership from the training set alone so as to exhibit generalization by classifying the members of the test set correctly without explicit training on them. In both types of task, a specific input pattern P is associated with a specific output pattern Q. What differs is the interpretation of the relation between them.

Now we consider the internal workings of the network and the way in which the desired association between P and Q is achieved using the backpropagation algorithm. Typically, networks are simulated on computers, but it is reasonable to think of them as physical systems. The nodes, for example, might be thought of as clusters of neurons, or regions of the cerebral cortex and the connections between nodes as bundles of nerve fibres. Typically, a network is fully connected physically, but this does not mean that all connections are of equal value. Some may be positive and others negative; some may be strong and others weak. To represent this, each connection in a network is assigned a value known as its connection strength. Typically, connection strengths are real values between $-1$ and $+1$. In the network of Figure 18.1 there are two sets of connections to consider. Those between the input nodes and hidden nodes, and those between the hidden nodes and output nodes. If we represent a connection by an ordered pair, for example (In1, H1), we can represent its connection strength by assigning the ordered pair a value, for example (In1, H1) = 0.5. It is clear from Figure 18.1 that there are twelve input-layer to hidden-layer connections to assign and also twelve hidden-layer to output-layer connections. Thus the network as a whole has 24 different connection strengths.

It is typically also the case that the hidden nodes and the output nodes of a network are assigned values known as 'thresholds'. These are often positive real numbers, usually within a specified range. We can represent a threshold by assigning a value to a node name, for example, H1 = 1.2. The threshold of a node represents the independent contribution that the node makes to the activity of the network. In the network of Figure 18.1 seven threshold assignments would be needed. Input nodes typically are not assigned thresholds but transmit, unchanged, the values of the input elements they receive.

To get a network started, assignments of connection strengths and thresholds are typically made randomly within the constraints of the bounds on the possible values. This means that the behaviour of the network will, initially, also be random and it will have to be trained to produce the desired output. We now consider how this is done.

The first step is to understand how an input pattern produces an output pattern. There are two stages in this process: (1) The elements of the input pattern P are combined with the connection strengths between the input nodes and hidden nodes, and the thresholds of the hidden nodes to produce activation values for the hidden nodes. (2) The computed activation values of the hidden nodes are combined with the connection strengths between the hidden nodes and the output nodes, to produce activation values for the output nodes. These activation values constitute the current output pattern Q.

The combination processes that generate the activation values are reasonably straightforward. Let's consider the case of H1 in Figure 18.1. What we'll call its raw activation value $RAW_{H1}$ can be described by an equation as follows:

$$RAW_{H1} = H1 + P1(In1,H1) + P2(In2,H1) + P3(In3,H1) + P4(In4,H1)$$

The equation says that the raw activation value for H1 is the sum of its threshold plus the values of all the elements of the input pattern modulated by the strengths of the connections they have with H1. The final activation value $ACT_{H1}$ is produced by computing the value of a function $f$ which takes $RAW_{H1}$ as its argument. Thus

$$ACT_{H1} = f(RAW_{H1})$$

The function $f$ is typically something called a sigmoid threshold function, otherwise known as a 'squashing' function because it maps the raw activation values into the range of values between 0 and 1. The reason for doing this is to stabilize the network's performance by preventing inputs which produce high activation levels from dominating the representations formed. We don't need to worry about the details here. The important point is that the activation value $ACT_{H1}$ is made up of contributions from all the elements of the input pattern and the current threshold of H1. The activation values for H2 and H3 are computed in the same way.

The activation values for the output nodes are calculated in a similar fashion. Let's take Out2 as an example.

$$\text{RAW}_{\text{Out2}} = \text{Out2} + \text{ACT}_{\text{H1}}(\text{H1,Out2}) + \text{ACT}_{\text{H2}}(\text{H2,Out2}) + \text{ACT}_{\text{H3}}$$
$$(\text{H3,Out2})$$
$$\text{ACT}_{\text{Out2}} = f(\text{RAW}_{\text{Out2}})$$

Again, it's clear from the equations that the activation value $\text{ACT}_{\text{Out2}}$ is composed of contributions from each of the hidden nodes, modulated by the relevant connection strengths. Notice that the contribution of each of the hidden nodes is its current activation value which is, itself, derived from the input pattern elements and the input to hidden-layer connection strengths. Thus each of the input pattern elements has an indirect effect on each of the output pattern elements.

Let's suppose, for the sake of the argument, that the input patterns are binary, that the desired output patterns are also binary, that the inputs and outputs represent numbers and that the desired association is $Q = P+1$. Thus the task of the network is to add one to its input. If $P = 0000$, $Q = 0001$ and so on. We'll stipulate that if $P = 1111$, $Q = 0000$. Thus the desired relationship is addition modulo 16.

When an input pattern is first presented to the network, the output activation values are most unlikely to produce the desired output pattern because the initial values of the connection strengths and node thresholds have been set randomly. We'll call the actual output pattern $Q_{\text{ACT}}$ and the desired output pattern $Q_{\text{DES}}$. Thus, if the input pattern was $P = (0,0,0,0)$, $Q_{\text{DES}}$ would be $(0,0,0,1)$ but we might have $Q_{\text{ACT}} = (0.1, 0.5, 0.1, 0.7)$. The other input patterns would also most probably produce incorrect outputs.

It's clear that we can easily calculate the discrepancy between $Q_{\text{DES}}$ and $Q_{\text{ACT}}$ by subtracting the actual value of the output element from the desired value. For the example given the discrepancies are $(-0.1, -0.5, -0.1, 0.3)$. The discrepancies are used to adjust the node thresholds and the connection strengths of the network in such a way that when the pattern is next presented $Q_{\text{ACT}}$ will tend to be closer to $Q_{\text{DES}}$. To understand how this is done we need to think about the sizes of the discrepancies, the contributions of nodes and the role of connection strengths. We also need to bear in mind that adjustments which are favourable for one pattern may be unfavourable for another; as a result it is generally better to make small changes rather than large ones.

Let's start by continuing with the example above. The discrepancy between $Q1_{\text{ACT}}$ and $Q1_{\text{DES}}$ is quite small $-0.1$. If we ask which parts of the network are responsible for the value of $Q1_{\text{ACT}}$ and hence for the discrepancy, it quickly becomes apparent that almost the whole network is involved. In fact it's everything which is connected either directly or indirectly to Out1 and the threshold of Out1 itself. Figure 18.2 shows the culprits.

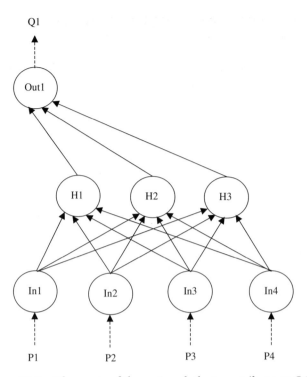

**Figure 18.2**   The parts of the network that contribute to $Q1_{ACT}$.

If we count them up we find that there are 23 components; four input pattern elements, four node thresholds and fifteen connections. The input pattern elements can't be changed so there are 19 modifiable components that produce $Q1_{ACT}$ when pattern (0,0,0,0) is presented to the network. Unfortunately we can't just divide the discrepancy by 19 and subtract a bit from each component. There are at least two good reasons why this won't work. First, the contributions of the components are not all equal and second, most of the components also contribute to all the other discrepancies and reducing one discrepancy in this way may increase another. Fortunately, we can approach the problem systematically.

First we observe that the smaller the discrepancy between $Q_{ACT}$ and $Q_{DES}$ the smaller the changes need to be. So we use as the basis for changes, not the actual discrepancy but, a proportion we can call the working discrepancy which decreases as the discrepancy becomes smaller. I won't go into the details here but for each element of the output pattern we can calculate a working discrepancy. We will call these $Q1_{WD}$, $Q2_{WD}$ and so on.

We now use the working discrepancies to calculate an error term for each of the hidden nodes. The error term is based on a proportion of the activation value of the hidden node and a proportion of the working discrepancy for each element of the output pattern. Let's take H1 as an example. The error for H1 is calculated as

$$ERR_{H1} = (ACT_{H1})_{WD}((H1,Out1)Q1_{WD} + (H1,Out2)Q2_{WD} + (H1,Out3)$$
$$Q3_{WD} + (H1,Out4)Q4_{WD})$$

This is simpler than it appears at first sight. It is the product of two terms, $(ACT_{H1})_{WD}$ and $(H1,Out1)Q1_{WD} + (H1,Out2)Q2_{WD} + (H1,Out3)Q3_{WD} + (H1,Out4)Q4_{WD}$. The first term is a proportion of $ACT_{H1}$ produced in the same way as the working discrepancies are produced from the actual discrepancies, hence we call it $(ACT_{H1})_{WD}$. The second term is a sum of the working discrepancies of the output pattern elements, each multiplied by the strength of its connection to H1. Thus the error $ERR_{H1}$ is a reflection of the contributions of H1 to all the discrepancies in the output pattern. Similar calculations are made for H2 and H3.

Once the error terms for the hidden units have been calculated, modifications to the network can be made. We can start with the output node thresholds and work back. Taking Out1 as an example,

$$Change(Out1) = \alpha(Q1_{WD})$$

where $\alpha$ is a positive constant controlling the learning rate, and $Q1_{WD}$ is the working discrepancy for Q1. $\alpha$ is normally small relative to the activation values of the output-layer nodes. The other output-node thresholds are modified in a similar manner. Next we modify the connections between the hidden-node layer and the output-node layer. Taking (H1,Out1) as an example,

$$Change(H1,Out1) = \alpha(ACT_{H1})(Q1_{WD})$$

where $\alpha$ is the learning rate constant, $ACT_{H1}$ is the current activation value of H1 and $Q1_{WD}$ is the working discrepancy of element Q1 of the output pattern Q. The other hidden-layer to output-layer connections are modified using the appropriate terms. Notice that the change made to (H1,Out1) is a function of the current activation value of H1, not the computed error of H1. The computed error of H1 is used to modify the input-layer to hidden-layer connections. Next we modify the hidden-layer node thresholds. Taking H1 as an example,

$$Change(H1) = \beta(ERR_{H1})$$

where $\beta$ is a constant controlling the learning rate and $ERR_{H1}$ is the computed error term for H1. $\beta$ may, but need not, have the same value as $\alpha$. It's clear from this equation that the computed error terms for the hidden-layer nodes are analogous to the working discrepancies computed for the output-layer nodes. Finally, the input-layer to hidden-layer connections are modified. Taking (In1,H1) as an example,

$$\text{Change}(\text{In1},\text{H1}) = \beta(\text{P1})(\text{ERR}_{\text{H1}})$$

where $\beta$ controls the learning rate, P1 is the first element of the input pattern P and $\text{ERR}_{\text{H1}}$ is the computed error of hidden-layer node H1. The remaining input-layer to hidden-layer connections are modified using the appropriate terms.

The process just explored describes the presentation of a single training pattern from the input set and a single cycle of error correction. The performance of the network as a whole is achieved by statistical juggling of the node threshold values and the connection strengths between nodes. It requires repeated presentations of the complete set of training patterns. It's clear that the error calculation for a particular hidden-layer node involves all of the output-layer working discrepancies and all of the connections from that hidden-layer node to the output layer. Clearly some of these contributions will be in conflict with each other. Similar comments apply to the relations between the input nodes and the hidden nodes. What happens is that in most cases the network eventually minimizes the overall error by finding similarities in the (P, Q) pattern pairs, such that the conflicting requirements on hidden-layer nodes can be reduced.

## Performance and limitations of trained feed-forward networks

The important questions for present purposes are how to characterize, in general terms, the functionality of feed-forward networks of the kind described and what their performance limitations are. The first point is the question of capacity. Assuming that the input and output layers of the network have the same number of nodes, and assuming that both input and output vectors are binary, both of which are common assumptions, then there are $2^N$ input patterns and $2^N$ output patterns definable over layers with N nodes. Thus the input and output vectors constitute a finite alphabet of patterns. The question of the maximum number of input–output mappings which a network can store with respect to a given performance criterion is more difficult to determine because multi-layer feed-forward networks are resistant to analysis in this respect (Amit 1989, p. 271). However, although the connection strengths between nodes which serve as the system's memory for patterns are continuous, and although the storage of patterns is distributed over the nodes and connections among them, there is every reason to suppose that network capacity is finite. For simpler but similar, fully connected network topologies using distributed storage, provable capacity limitations are known (Amit 1989, chapter 6) which show that the number of patterns which can be stored and successfully retrieved is proportional to the number of nodes in the network. There is no doubt that some similar limitation applies to feed-forward nets.

The second question is what sorts of functions a given feed-forward network can learn to compute with this finite capacity. Despite the impressive and thought-provoking performances of a variety of feed-forward network applications, the class of functions which simple feed-forward networks can learn to compute is a subset of the class of functions computable by finite state machines. Once one ceases to be bewitched by the fascinating learning process, it is clear that a feed-forward network learns to approximate a function which is defined by a look-up table consisting of the set of patterns (P, Q).

> Simple function approximation is one level above a look-up table in computational complexity; functions can at least attempt to interpolate between examples, and generalize to examples that are not in the learning data set. Learning is still *fairly* simple, although already the subtleties of probability and statistics begin to complicate the matter. However, simple function approximation has less computational capability than a finite state machine. At present, there are no good learning algorithms for finite state machines. Without counting, conditional looping, etc., many problems will simply remain insoluble. (Farmer 1990, p. 183)

Informally, the explanation for the limitations on the performance of a feed-forward net can be couched in terms of its possible responses to its inputs. Consider first a feed-forward net without error correction by backpropagation. The net has some fixed set of connection strengths and some fixed set of node thresholds chosen at random. When the net is given an input, its response is produced by calculating activation values for the hidden layer nodes and using these, in their turn, to calculate activation values for the output layer nodes which produce the elements Q1, Q2,..., Qn of the output pattern. Because the activation equations are fixed, the response of the network for any particular input is also fixed. The crucial point to note is that although the activation, and hence the response, of the network varies from one input pattern to another, for a given pattern the response of the network at different times will be the same. The network's state is not altered by the processing of inputs. For this reason, it is appropriate to describe the network as computing a function from input to output which can be computed by a one-state finite automaton defined for the purpose, and that the network constitutes an implementation of the machine table for that function.

Now consider a network which, having learned to compute a given function from a set of training examples using backpropagation, is being tested on a set of test inputs. By definition the network is no longer learning, that is, backpropagation has been turned off. For the reasons outlined in the preceding paragraph, it is clear that this network will also produce a single fixed output for each of its inputs. The only difference between this case and the case without learning is that the function computed is one chosen by the experimenter and taught to the machine rather than one arrived at by chance as a result of the random assignment of connection strengths and node thresholds. Thus, a fully trained, correctly functioning feed-forward net, is also appropriately described as an implementation of a single state finite automaton. What the training has done is to make systematic, structural modifications to the network to change the function it computes, that is it has changed it from a network which computes an arbitrary function $\phi(P)$ to a network which computes a desired function $\psi(P)$. This is not a trivial achievement but no purpose is served by overestimating what such networks are capable of. The reason, therefore, why simple function approximation by feed-forward nets using backpropagation has 'less computational capability than a finite state machine' is that such nets can approximate only those functions which can be computed by single-state finite automata. In the terminology used earlier in this book, these are one state mini-minds.

If that were the end of the story, it would eventually spell the demise of interest in feed-forward connectionist networks for much the same reasons as interest in single-layer perceptrons declined after the critique of Minsky and Papert (1969). However, the situation is more promising than that. One of the major problems with simple feed-forward nets has been finding ways of making them sensitive to temporal sequences. It is easy to see, in the light of the discussion above, why there should be difficulties of this sort. In order for the temporality of a sequence to be discriminated it is essential that a given input occurring at one point in the sequence be discriminable from the same input appearing at another point. In other words, it is essential for more than one response to be associable with a given input. This requires multiple states and that is precisely what is lacking in a simple feedforward network. One solution has been to simulate temporal sequence with spatial position in the input. In this way, a vector of n bits can be treated as a 'window' on the state of a single bit at n successive moments of time. The most obvious limitation on this technique is that the size of window is limited by the size of the vector onto which it is mapped.

## Networks with recurrent structure

A much more promising technique is the adoption of a network topology which includes recurrence. It has been known since the work of McCulloch and Pitts (1943) that nets with recurrent loops are computationally more powerful than those without because the former, but not the latter, can 'make reference to past events of an indefinite degree of remoteness'. A distinction of this kind exists between simple feed-forward networks, and networks with recurrent connections such as those used in the widely cited paper by Elman (1990).

Work reported by Servan-Schreiber, Cleeremans and McClelland (1989) and Cleeremans (1993) using Elman's network architecture has made a significant advance in understanding the processing of temporal sequences. In addition to input, output and hidden unit layers, Elman's recurrent network has a layer of context units which take their input from the hidden unit layer and feed their output back to it. The input to the context units is a copy of the activation vector of the hidden units at each time step $t$. The context units store but do not alter this vector which is fed back unchanged to the hidden units as part of their input at time $t+1$. This means that at all times other than $t_0$, the hidden unit layer input consists of an input feature vector plus a copy of its own activation pattern from the previous time step. Cleeremans (1993) has demonstrated how this recurrent context layer input to the hidden units can be made functionally equivalent to a modification of the base state of the network, thus allowing it to learn to behave as a multi-state finite automaton, and become sensitive to long distance dependencies in its input sequences.

This is an important result for a number of reasons. First it suggests that connectionist networks with recurrence are sufficient to implement the finite state control structures which Turing's analysis suggests are what is required of the neural part of the cognitive system. Second it shows that this functionality can be learned given appropriate starting structures and adequately distinct input sequences, although Cleeremans reported some difficulties with the backpropagation algorithm. Third, Cleeremans reported that the representations developed over the hidden units, given sufficient numbers of those units, showed sensitivity to sequences of inputs, provided they were of fixed length, as well as achieving the functionality of a finite state machine. This increased functionality led Cleeremans and his colleagues to describe suitably trained recurrent networks as 'graded state' machines. In so far as people often remember something of how they arrived at their current cognitive state as well as what their current options are this is a promising characteristic for a network to possess. It is interesting that such a marked increase in functionality should come about as a consequence of a simple loop which copies activation in a set of units at a given time out to a simple store and then back to those units at a later time.

## Problems and a proposed solution

Although the use of recurrent networks is promising, it has become clear that connectionist networks suffer from problems other than grasping temporal sequence. Connectionist modellers tend to think in terms of single tasks and the most common forms of network are not good at handling multiple tasks which interact. Networks exhibit cross-talk and other phenomena that degrade performance when they are trained on independent tasks (Marcus 2001). It is not surprising that this should be so. It arises from the distributed representations that networks use and these are responsible for many of the features of performance that are seen as advantageous such as generalization to novel stimuli.

The solution, I think, is to recognize that connectionist networks are finite automata and to use Turing's analysis to understand the role they should play in a theory of the mind. That role is, essentially, analogous to the role of a mini-mind in a Turing machine. That being so, it will not, in the long run, be helpful for connectionists to try to find ingenious ways to demonstrate how symbol structures can be encoded in the states of the nodes of a network and the connections between them. To do that is to accept the premises on which the symbol systems approach is based. What connectionists should, but perhaps do not, do often enough is to think about the structure of the environments within which networks are embedded and work out how to share the representational burden between the states of the network and the states of the environment in the way that a Turing machine shares the representational burden of a computation between the mini-mind and symbol structures on its tape. Independent environmental structure is an irreducible part of cognitive architecture. This idea is explored in Chapters 19 and 20.

# 19 Ecological Functionalism: Computation

## Introduction

The difficulties ascribed to the computational theory of mind and connectionism, in Chapters 17 and 18, can be characterized in terms of their relations to Turing's machine model of computation. The computational theory of mind puts an insupportable burden on the internal representational capacities of the organism and requires implausible input mechanisms because it treats the mind as functionally equivalent to a universal Turing machine. Connectionism, by contrast, treats the mind as a finite automaton but does not adequately characterize its relation to the environment or fully recognize the importance of structure in the environment.

Throughout the book it has been emphasized that a Turing machine is a model of a mind interacting with symbol structures in its external environment. At the start of Chapter 14, the point was made that Turing's model led naturally to an ecological perspective on psychology but that this had not been developed because computational psychology had taken its inspiration from von Neumann computers rather than from Turing machines.

## Neural and environmental structure

In this chapter and the next, an outline of ecological functionalism is presented. Ecological functionalism is proposed as a new framework for psychological research based on the ecological understanding of Turing's analysis of computation. The most distinctive characteristic of the approach is the fundamental claim that structure in the brain of the thinker and structure in the environment are of equal importance for cognitive processes. The mind is a finite system of functional states and the environment is the locus of significant structure, including but not restricted to symbol structures, with which the mind interacts. The primary relation between the mind and the world is interaction not representation. The insupportable representational burden of the computational theory of mind is avoided because, to a large extent, the mind interacts directly with the environment rather than with representations of it. At the same time, the existence of autonomous internal structure in the form of relations among functional states, which are not formed solely by the learning of associations between input and output pairs, enables the approach to escape the weaknesses of current connectionist theorizing. Computational universality, the central tenet of the physical symbol systems hypothesis, is understood in a completely different way in ecological functionalism. It is not used to explain the representational capacity of the brain but to underpin an account of the roles of external symbol systems in cognitive processes. These symbol systems are not restricted to the notations used for literature, mathematics, music and other overtly symbolic activities but include social and cultural institutions as well.

## The need for a more expressive formal system

Ecological functionalism is grounded in reflection on Turing's analysis of computation but is not tied to the details of Turing's notation or machine model. In fact, as soon as one starts to think seriously about how to develop the approach it becomes apparent that a more expressive formal system is needed. The point at issue is not how powerful the system is but how easily and naturally it can be used to express the concepts needed for the development of psychological theories.

The Turing machine is an ideal vehicle for expressing ideas about how humans compute numbers using paper and pencil but is far from ideal for expressing ideas about the wide range of other topics with which psychological theories are concerned, such as how social interaction works, how thoughts are affected by current emotions or how to prepare an athlete to reach peak performance on the day of an important competition. The most important limitation of Turing's system, from the standpoint of psychology, is its restriction to the analysis of single, sequential processes. There is no way to describe concurrent processes in Turing's notation. This limitation is shared by the vast majority of formal systems which have been used in psychology. Even connectionist systems, as mentioned at the end of Chapter 18, are typically dedicated to the analysis of single tasks. This has been recognized explicitly by the authors of an influential volume on connectionist studies of development:

> [M]ost current models are in fact highly task-specific and single-purpose …
> in order to study the development of complex behaviors, it will be crucial
> to have models which have greater developmental and ecological plausi-
> bility. These must be models which are capable of carrying out multiple
> behaviors (in computer jargon, multi-tasking) in complex environments
> which require behaviors which are coordinated and integrated. (Elman *et al.*
> 1996, pp. 392–3)

It is conceivable that existing connectionist models may be refined to over-come the current difficulties they have in multi-tasking, but the fully con-nected network topology that is commonly used is not promising because, as the discussion of Chapter 18 showed, the distributed nature of the network processes makes all the activities of the network interdependent. It is hard, therefore, to see how one might model concurrent tasks which have various degrees of interconnectedness and autonomy. Ecological functionalism takes a different approach and proposes to use a formal system specifically developed for the study of concurrency, in which issues about interaction and autonomy are central. There are both psychological and formal facets of ecological functionalism. They are not easy to separate but this chapter is devoted mainly to a description of the formal system and Chapter 20 to the distinctively psychological considerations.

## Studying concurrency: the $\pi$-calculus

The formal system that I believe may provide a valuable tool for psychological research, although it was not designed specifically to meet the needs of psychologists, is called the $\pi$-calculus. The first paper describing the $\pi$-calculus was published some fifteen years ago (Milner *et al.* 1989) and the first textbook ten years later (Milner 1999). It is too early to say for sure that the $\pi$-calculus will turn out to be as important for computational psy-chology as Turing's work has been, but it provides a variety of ways of rea-soning rigorously about systems of processes which communicate with each other and can change their connectivity.

A short, non-technical, introduction is given here, to illustrate how $\pi$-calculus might take us forward from the bases of ecological functionalism established by Turing. In the first text on the $\pi$-calculus, Robin Milner noted that the science of communicating systems is not yet well established. We do not have, he said, 'an agreed repertoire of constructions for building and expressing interactive systems' (Milner 1999, p. 3). He pointed out, however, that most computing nowadays involves interaction and that it was neces-sary to define an underlying model with a small number of basic concepts 'in terms of which *interactional* behaviour can be rigorously described' (p. 3). He proposed 'a model whose basic action is to communicate across an inter-face with a *handshake*, which means that the two participants synchronize this action' (Milner 1999, p. 3).

Milner gave a number of examples of systems that communicate via hand-shakes of the kind he had in mind, including not just computers but systems like vending machines and their users. He pointed out that although some communicating systems have fixed links, others have links that change. Computers accessing Internet sites and mobile phones are common con-temporary examples. Systems with transient, changing links are described as having *mobile* connectivity. The range of systems that might profitably be brought under the umbrella of a general theory of computation based on interaction is very wide.

> We do not normally think of vending machines or mobile phones as doing computation, but they share the notion of interaction with modern distributed computing systems. This common notion underlies a theory of a huge range of modern informatic systems, whether computational or not. (Milner 1999, p. 4)

Minds, brains and people can be added to the list of 'informatic systems' which might be understood in terms of a general theory of interaction. The components of the brain function concurrently and interact to produce mind. Minds function concurrently and interact in social groups.

*Processes and names*

The basic entities of the $\pi$-calculus are processes and names. Processes describe the behaviour of things like vending machines or mobile phones, or people for that matter. Processes can have components which are themselves processes. This point is of fundamental importance for psychological applications because it provides exactly what is needed to take Turing's analysis forward. In Turing's model, the mind is described as a sequential process which cycles through its finite set of functional states. The underlying, physical system which is being modelled is complex and its states have concurrently active components, but the only description of the process available in the model is a list of successive state names because succession is the only relation defined between functional states which are taken to be elementary and indivisible. In the $\pi$-calculus a more realistic model can be constructed without sacrificing the distinction between mini-mind and tape on which Turing's analysis of computation was based. The mind can be described as a concurrent bundle of sequential processes which can communicate among themselves. The states of the bundle, taken as a whole, may be used to represent the states of a mini-mind but, because the composite has components, it is also possible to take a view of it as a system containing structured interactions among those components. This possibility means, for example, that one could put back into a formal account of paper and pencil calculation, component processes describing the attentional and emotional states of the computant and the perceptual and motor processes with which symbols are scanned and printed and the pencil is moved from place to place. The $\pi$-calculus thus offers the possibility of functional accounts at various levels with decomposition into concurrent as well as sequential components.

The modelling of environments is also significantly enhanced by characterizing environments in terms of processes for essentially the same reason. An environment can be described as a process which may have component processes. C.A.R. Hoare, the developer of CSP, another calculus for studying concurrent processes, has said

> [T]he environment of a process itself may be described as a process, with its behaviour defined by familiar notations. This permits investigation of the behaviour of a complete system composed from the process together with its environment, acting and interacting with each other as they evolve concurrently. The complete system should also be regarded as a process, whose range of behaviour is definable in terms of the behaviour of its component processes; and the system may in turn be placed within a yet wider environment. In fact, it is best to forget the distinction between processes, environments, and systems; they are all of them just processes whose behaviour may be prescribed, described, recorded and analysed in a simple and homogeneous fashion. (Hoare 1985, p. 65)

The tape of a Turing machine and its symbolic contents can be described as a composition of processes and a whole Turing machine can be described as a composition of a mini-mind process and an environment process interacting in ways defined by configurations. In addition, the composite $\pi$-calculus process expressing the behaviour of a Turing machine can be embedded in a larger environment without losing its functionality. That environment may perfectly well include other composite Turing machine processes. Given that a Turing machine is a formalized model of a human computant, and that it is clearly possible to offer formal process descriptions of humans engaged in other activities, it becomes possible to envisage a powerful, computational approach to social as well as individual processes. Moreover, psychology is redolent with process descriptions at all levels of analysis from the neural to the social. The $\pi$-calculus offers the means to start building an integrative theory that spans a range of these levels.

Names are the means whereby processes communicate. They constitute links between processes, but the calculus is not prescriptive about exactly what links are and allows for a range of interpretations.

> For example, names can be thought of as channels that processes use to communicate ... names can be used to represent names of processes or names of objects ... . Further, although the $\pi$-calculus does not mention locations explicitly, often when describing systems in $\pi$-calculus, some names are naturally thought of as locations. (Sangiorgi and Walker 2001, p. 3)

This semantic flexibility is valuable for psychological applications because it supports models at different levels of analysis. In a social psychological application, for example, names might be interpreted as the names of people, whereas in a neuropsychological application names might be interpreted as names for regions of the brain, following, for example, something like Brodmann's classification.

## Behavioural equivalence

The processes described by $\pi$-calculus terms are generally non-deterministic because it is usually the case that more than one interaction is available to a process at a given time. As a result it is generally more difficult to decide when concurrent processes exhibit equivalent behaviour than it is to decide when serial processes do. It is, nevertheless, essential to have some means for comparison. Milner expresses the point in a way which will strike a chord with many psychologists.

> Until we know what constitutes similarity or difference of behaviour, we cannot claim to know what 'behaviour' *means* – and if that is the case then we have no precise way of explaining what our systems do! (Milner 1999, p. 4)

The $\pi$-calculus was designed with the study of behavioural equivalence as a central focus. One technique is to define equivalence in terms of contexts and to say that two different processes have equivalent behaviour if one can be substituted for the other in a given context without changing the behaviour of the larger system. My computer, for example, has a Pentium 4 processor at its heart. It would, I hope, continue to run exactly as it does now, if the existing processor were taken out and replaced by another Pentium 4. The larger system constitutes the context in which Pentium 4 processors can be described as behaviourally equivalent.

Behavioural equivalence need not entail identity. Companies who hire employees to fill particular job specifications may consider two different people as behaviourally equivalent provided that both can carry out all the tasks required. The principle of job sharing is founded on the idea that two different people can count as behaviourally equivalent in this way. Performance with respect to the job specification is the context in which equivalence is assessed.

Assessment of behavioural equivalence based on contexts becomes more stringent as the range of contexts is increased. A newly qualified surgeon may be behaviourally equivalent to a consultant with many years experience in the context of stitching an incision, but not in the context of open heart surgery. One school teacher may be behaviourally equivalent to another in the context of a well-behaved class but not in a badly behaved one.

The most stringent criterion possible is behavioural equivalence across arbitrary contexts. This is not normally a criterion we apply to the study of human occupations, but it may be applicable to the way in which we make moral judgements. When we think of someone as a 'good' person, the implication tends to be that their behaviour will exhibit certain characteristics regardless of context. We also use comparative contexts as a way of making judgements about people. There might be friends to whom one would happily lend money knowing them to be scrupulous about repayment, but to whom one would be cautious about lending books. The notion of equivalence 'up to' a certain criterion is extensively developed in the $\pi$-calculus.

Another way to think about behavioural equivalence is in terms of two different categories of actions that a process may engage in. There are *internal* actions which are typically the results of interactions between the components of a process. They are not visible to an observer. An individual's thoughts may be construed as internal actions of this sort. The second category comprises the *visible* actions of a process. These describe the potential a process has for interacting with its environment. The distinction is not absolute and, for analytical purposes, can be drawn in different places on different occasions. It is sometimes a matter of focus or perspective whether an action is to count as internal or visible. The interactions between neurons, for example, would be visible interactions in the context of a study of neural circuits but would be internal in the context of an account of the social interactions between people.

The $\pi$-calculus has two types of equivalence, one that takes account of internal actions and one that does not. *Weak* equivalence, roughly speaking, discounts internal actions and two processes are weakly equivalent if they are equivalent with respect to their visible actions. *Strong* equivalence takes internal actions into account as well and processes are strongly equivalent only if they are equivalent with respect to both visible and internal actions.

In general, the focus of interest is on finding weak equivalences and defining and studying these is a major focus of the $\pi$-calculus. This is also an appropriate focus for psychological applications. Many, perhaps most, psychological investigations can be characterized as focusing on weak behavioural equivalences. An example is the classic paper by Miller (1956) which showed that the capacity of human short term memory (STM) is seven chunks plus or minus two. The finding can be described as a behavioural equivalence because it proposes that two humans will perform in essentially the same way in arbitrary contexts with respect to STM capacity, and it is a weak equivalence because it abstracts from the specific details of how or where the chunks are stored.

Another example drawn from social psychology concerns group membership and nepotistic behaviour. It has long been clear that humans selectively favour members of particular groups, kin being a prime example. The remarkable strength of this proclivity was demonstrated by Tajfel *et al.* (1971) who showed, using what is known as the 'minimal group' paradigm, that people will selectively favour others even when all that is known is that they share membership in a group defined by a preference, say for one artist rather than another. The finding is striking because the notion of group involved is extremely weak. The abstraction from everything except membership implies that selective favouritism will be found or can be predicted to occur in almost any context where two or more groups are formed regardless of other group characteristics.

Taking just one more example, the very general idea that psychology can be studied independently from neuroscience rests on the assumption that there is a level of analysis at which humans are weakly equivalent which abstracts from the details of neural system functioning. The assumption implies that differences in neural system functioning will not generally be explanatory at the psychological level.

## Types and patterns of behaviour

The concept of behavioural equivalence implies the utility of different levels of analysis. Systems which differ in detail may be equivalent at more abstract levels. An important feature of the $\pi$-calculus, which aids the construction of multi-level models, is that it allows the definition of types. In familiar programming languages, types are used to define high level structures. It is possible to define structures such as arrays and stacks and to use these to build more complex structures. It is also possible to define types with particular values. A common type which is built into many languages is the 'boolean' type which has only two possible values 'true' or 'false'. Types in $\pi$-calculus define and classify patterns of behaviour, rather than structures and specific values, and promote reasoning about them. One might think of such definitions as doing for concurrent processes what Turing's $m$-functions did for serial processes.

Type definitions and equivalences are potentially valuable tools for the study of topics such as modularity. Among the characteristics of modular processes as they were described by Fodor (1983) were informational encapsulation and limited central access to the internal computations of modules. Informational encapsulation implies that a module carries out its processing without access to everything that the system of which it is a part knows about. It is sometimes said that a module has a proprietary database of information on which it can draw. It is, therefore, as though the module is enclosed within a membrane which is impervious to information transfer from the outside. Limited central access implies that the membrane is also impervious from the other side and that the larger system is unable to inspect the internal processes by which a module reaches its conclusions. Neither informational encapsulation nor limitation on central access was hypothesized by Fodor to be absolute. Types may be used to define the extent to which processes forming the context of a specific process can have access to its internal operations and thus regulate the degree to which central access is allowed. Fodor noted that it appears to be the case that there is a gradient of accessibility such that computations near the sensory periphery are less accessible to central cognition than those nearer the centre. A formal system like $\pi$-calculus will enable such suggestions to be more precisely characterized and analysed. The equivalence concepts may also be of interest here. In a completely open system, in which all the components of a process were accessible to the context it might be that only substitution by strongly equivalent processes would be possible, whereas at the other end of the spectrum in the case where no central access was possible, substitution by weakly equivalent processes might be possible.

## Changing connectivity

A further, highly valuable, feature of the $\pi$-calculus is the way that it enables the user to model changing patterns of connectivity between processes. Human social structures are very obviously characterized by such changes and it is likely that transient linkages between different parts of the brain are also made as the demands of task environments change. The treatment of connectivity is a feature which makes the $\pi$-calculus a better choice for psychological investigations than earlier systems for studying concurrency which were not able to deal with systems whose patterns of connectivity change dynamically.

Changing connectivity is discussed in terms of 'mobility'. There are various kinds of mobility including physical movement from one place to another and changing patterns of linkage among physically static processes. Sangiorgi and Walker (2001, p. 1) distinguish '*links* that move in an abstract space of *linked processes*' from '*processes* that move in an abstract space of linked processes'. The basic $\pi$-calculus treats the mobility of links but it can also be used to model the mobility of processes, and higher order calculi have been developed to tackle process mobility directly. Consider the concept of friendship which can be thought of as a kind of linkage between individuals. Patterns of friendship can and often do remain invariant across changes of physical location, although psychologists are aware of the importance of physical propinquity to the likelihood of friendships being formed in the first place.

Connectionist networks illustrate the potential utility of a focus on linkages for psychological investigation. The learning behaviour of connectionist networks is a function of changing connection strengths or linkages between nodes. However, the changes in linkages between nodes in a connectionist network are, in the most common model, a function of the accuracy of the network's representation of an association between input and output feature vectors. Changing connectivity is thus exogenously driven and it is not easy to see how one might use a connectionist model to study changes in connectivity that have endogenous causes. Moreover, the mechanism for changing linkages in connectionist networks is to change the strengths of connections rather than to make or break links between nodes. The $\pi$-calculus offers much more general tools for modelling changes in connectivity.

One simple example of how these tools might be used can be based on the mini-minds explored in Chapter 4. In the course of that chapter a subset of 36 mini-minds was derived from the larger set definable with four functional states and two inputs. The state diagrams for the subset can be found in Appendix 4.2. The members of the subset were derived by applying constraints of psychological plausibility to the larger set. Each mini-mind has a unique, fixed, pattern of transitions between its states. Behaviour is defined solely in terms of state changes driven by configurations and the patterns of behaviour have distinctive characteristics. Mini-mind 4659 is 'optimistic' because, given a random sequence of inputs, it spends most of its time in the very happy state, whereas mini-mind 13179 is 'pessimistic' because, given the same sequence of inputs, it spends most of its time in the very sad state. If one thinks about the functioning of normal minds it is rarely the case that someone is always optimistic or always pessimistic. More commonly one expects to find minds that are sometimes one way inclined and sometimes the other. There is nothing in Turing's theory which enables such changes to be modelled. The $\pi$-calculus provides the means for exploring changes in connectivity systematically, as a function of either exogenous or endogenous forces. Thus we could model the changes needed to transform the optimistic mini-mind into the pessimistic one and vice-versa. Given that the pattern of transitions in a mini-mind, in conjunction with its inputs, defines the task it computes, a systematic exploration of changes in connectivity offers a way of characterizing switches of attention between tasks and thus offers the foundation for a theory of attention based on the focusing of concurrent processes.

The physical locations and distribution of processes are distinct from the issues with which the $\pi$-calculus deals, although there are calculi, such as the Ambient Calculus (Cardelli and Gordon 1998) which focus on the location and distribution of processes and use some of the same constructions as the $\pi$-calculus. Taking the mobility of links as the means of studying the dynamics of changing connectivity among processes is a strategic choice which may need to be revised as experience grows. It has the great advantage, certainly for non-mathematicians, that the theory is well worked out and relatively easy to understand whereas the theory of process movement is harder and not yet fully understood.

It should be clear that the $\pi$-calculus is very general and abstract. It is not committed to any specific type of computational architecture and, indeed, does not itself include a distinction between agents and environments. Processes are the basic entities. One of the great advantages of the freedom from commitment to any specific architecture is the removal of the danger that one will take as a theoretical essential, something that is simply a contingent feature of that architecture. Instead there is an onus on the modeller to specify the entities and interactions between them that are theoretically significant.

## Turing machines and $\pi$-calculus processes

Turing's insights will not be abandoned by the adoption of the $\pi$-calculus, or a similar system, as the basis for formalizing psychological hypotheses. It is fairly easy to specify a Turing machine in terms of the calculus but that is not the point. The point is to use the calculus to express a theory with the same components as Turing's at the scale with which he was concerned, but also to allow for detailed characterizations at the sub-personal and suprapersonal levels which are equally characteristic of psychological investigation. Investigations at all these levels can be characterized as ecological because they all involve interactions between processes.

The $\pi$-calculus offers ways with which we can begin to reason about systems of interactions that characterize, rather naturally, the sorts of activities that the nervous system is known to engage in, the sorts of activities that individuals engage in and the sorts of activities that are characteristic of groups. Quite where the enterprise to study the activity of the thinking, socializing brain in terms of process calculi will ultimately lead, is not yet clear. It currently exists as a goal and a strategy, as a task to tackle rather than a completed story. At the end of his introductory text on the $\pi$-calculus Robin Milner said:

> At the present time we cannot expect a theoretical model such as that which is provided by this book to be definitive; the new developments are too immature for that. But as we seriously address the problem of modelling mobile communicating systems we get a sense of completing a model which was previously incomplete; for we can now begin to describe what goes on *outside* a computer in the same terms as what goes on *inside* – i.e. in terms of interaction. Turning this observation inside-out, we may say that we inhabit a global computer, an informatic world which demands to be understood just as fundamentally as physicists understand the material world. (Milner 1999, p. 156)

Ecological functionalism might, I hope, help to unify the psychological study of what goes on inside the individual with the study of what goes on between individuals. Turing's analysis of computation has been a spectacular success and the study of serial processes has profoundly influenced the ways in which we think about thinking. It is clear, however, that the serial model does not provide an adequate basis for understanding the behaviour of systems in which parallel processes are fundamental. It will be a fitting tribute to Turing's genius if our understanding of the mind is increased by a theory of parallel computation which was inspired by the success of a technology based on his serial analysis of mental functioning.

# 20 Ecological Functionalism: Psychology

## Introduction

The fundamental claim of ecological functionalism, as proposed in this book, is that structure in the brain of the agent and structure in the environment are of equal importance for cognitive processes. In Turing machine terms, the mind is a finite automaton which interacts directly with its environment rather than with internal symbolic representations of the environment as the computational theory of mind proposes. There is no symbolic language of thought because the brain is not a universal machine. This claim has consequences for the way that ecological functionalism approaches a number of central issues in psychology.

In 1987 Allen Newell delivered the William James lectures with the general title 'Unified Theories of Cognition' and in 1990 the lectures were published as a book with the same title. As the title suggests Newell wished to promote the development of psychological theories which try to integrate the vast number of detailed empirical findings and micro-theories that exist in a somewhat fragmented discipline. He felt that psychologists had a better mastery of the fine details of their discipline than they had of the broad picture. In Chapter 1 of his book, Newell set out a number of constraints that jointly affect and determine the structure of the mind. A unified theory of cognition would ultimately need to show how it satisfied the constraints and, in doing so, would generate the requisite broad picture. The list presented here is adapted from his figure 1.7, Newell (1990, p. 19). The perspective of ecological functionalism can be outlined in terms of how it approaches the constraints.

1. Behave flexibly as a function of the environment.
2. Exhibit adaptive (rational, goal-oriented) behaviour.
3. Operate in real time.
4. Operate in a rich, complex, detailed environment. This involves:
   (a) The perception of an immense amount of changing detail;
   (b) The use of vast amounts of knowledge;
   (c) Controlling a motor system with many degrees of freedom.

 5. Use symbols and abstractions.
 6. Use language, both natural and artificial.
 7. Learn from the environment and from experience.
 8. Acquire capabilities through development.
 9. Operate autonomously, but within a social community.
10. Be self-aware and have a sense of self.
11. Be realizable as a neural system.
12. Be constructable by an embryological growth process.
13. Arise through evolution.

I have much more to say, at present, about some members of the list than about others. In self-defence, though, I should point out that no current framework has the capability to tackle them all. At the time of writing his book, Newell said that Soar, the production system architecture which he proposed as the basis for a unified theory, addressed points 1, 2, 3, 4(b), 5 and 7 in detail, 4(a) and 4(c) in outline only, and the remainder not at all. A more recent review of a range of integrative architectures by Pew and Mavor (1998, chapter 3), which included neural networks, Soar and a number of other production system architectures, concluded that none of them addressed the full range of issues needed for a comprehensive theory of cognition although their collective achievements were impressive and wide ranging.

## Behavioural flexibility

The fundamental premise of the symbol systems hypothesis is that the mind is a universal machine. The hypothesis is conceptually simple, clear and powerful and guarantees behavioural flexibility because any computable function can be interposed between perception and action. This solution to the problem of behavioural flexibility is not adopted by ecological function- alism because, if the arguments presented in Chapter 17 are correct, the mind is not a universal machine but a finite automaton. From the perspec- tive of ecological functionalism there appear to be four possibilities: (a) the mind is organized like the fixed, finite control automaton of a universal machine and behavioural flexibility depends entirely on environmental programs; (b) the mind is a finite automaton which is dynamically reconfig- ured to meet changing environmental demands; (c) the mind is a fixed sys- tem with multiple functions which are triggered by specific environmental inputs; (d) the mind is some combination of (a)–(c). It is highly likely that (d) is the answer. The mind appears to have a range of ways of coping with the need to behave flexibly. Option (a) alone is implausible because the mind is not just a reactive device. Experience with connectionist networks suggests that option (b) alone is implausible because a mind which was constantly being reconfigured by its environment would lack the stability needed for proper functioning. (c) is an option favoured by some evolutionary psychologists. It is sometimes described as the 'massive modularity' hypothesis. It is implausible, by itself, because it is difficult to see how flexible responses to novel situations could be achieved and because it implies that behaviour should be a mosaic of unconnected processes. Option (d) is messy and complicated but seems to be the way things are. Minds certainly can function like the interpreters of universal machines. Symbol systems such as books which people can and do use to program their own behaviour demonstrate this conclusively. Social and cultural institutions can also be thought of as virtual machines with which the interpretive mind interacts. Minds clearly are also dynamically reconfigured, sometimes temporarily, sometimes permanently. There are also innate mental functions which are automatically triggered by specific inputs. A theory of behavioural flexibility will, therefore, need to identify the innate mental functions, understand the extent to which dynamic reconfiguration is possible, and explore the design and effects of cultural and social institutions.

## Rational, adaptive, goal-oriented behaviour

The constraint of rationality can be viewed as the inverse of behavioural flexibility. A universal machine which, by definition, can engage in any mechanical behaviour is capable of behaving randomly, irrationally or maladaptively. Understanding rationality thus amounts to understanding how adaptive, goal-oriented behaviour is controlled. Rational behaviour in computationally universal symbol systems is typically achieved by equipping them with goals in terms of which possible behaviours can be assessed. Complex systems frequently have multiple goals and these are often managed in production system architectures by the use of a goal stack. Goals are task related and tasks are generally chosen for a production system architecture thus leaving open the question of where the goals which control human behaviour have their origins. Ecological functionalism accepts the idea that behavioural control is achieved via goals and proposes to explain human goals in terms of two primary forces, evolution and socialization.

## Real time operation

Real time operation is not a problem for ecological functionalism in quite the same way that it can be for computational architectures which rely on background processing at electronic speeds which are not plausible for real neural systems. It is a problem for ecological functionalism in the sense that it is not currently understood how the brain does what it does in the limited time available. The fact that real time operation does function as a constraint on computer-based architectures stems, I believe, from the strategic decision made when the principles of von Neumann computer architecture were being established in the late 1940s (cf. the discussion in Chapter 14). The decision was to use serial operation and high speed components rather than parallel operation and slower components. As a result, when parallelism and multi-tasking are addressed in contemporary computer-based architectures they are typically achieved by interleaving serial processes. Each serial process may operate much faster than real time while the interleaved system as a whole functions in real time. Conversely, each serial process might be designed to operate in real time while the system as a whole is slower. In either circumstance it can be difficult to judge the plausibility of a model because it may not be known how, in a real neural architecture, the interleaved processes might interact and whether the timing assumptions made are correct. Ecological functionalism, which takes genuine multi-tasking as a basic feature of cognitive architecture, has the problem of identifying the multiple tasks and how they interact but doing this correctly will result in a system which functions in real time. Thus the real time constraint for ecological functionalism will be tackled by studying the interactions of concurrent processes directly.

### Environmental embedding

The nature of the relationship between the agent and the environment is a central concern of ecological functionalism. The symbol systems approach to cognitive computation assumes that the fundamental explanatory concept for this relationship is representation. Ecological functionalism accepts the need for representation as part of the relationship but argues that interaction is the fundamental concept. The environment does not, in general, have to be represented for agents to act successfully. It has to be interacted with.

The form in which Newell presented the fourth constraint on his list is significant. The division into three parts, perception, application of knowledge and control of motor processes reflects what Pew and Mavor (1998) describe as a modified stage model of human information processing. Information flows into the system via perceptual processes which construct representations; these are operated on by central processes using stored knowledge and outputs are produced to control the motor system. There is a theoretical separation of the 'lower-level perceptual and motor activities' from cognitive processes which are characterised as 'higher'. This is an understanding which is widely shared. Anderson and Lebiere (1998, p. 143) say, for example,

> Theories of higher-level cognition typically ignore lower-level processes such as visual attention and perception. They simply assume that lower-level processes deliver some relatively abstract description of the stimulus situation on which the higher-level processes operate.

Newell makes some interesting comments about this kind of situation. He explicitly recognizes that the lack of attention paid to perceptual and motor processes is a serious omission but argues that it results from a strategic decision.

> The reason cognitive psychology does not pay attention to these mechanisms is neither lack of awareness nor lack of desire. We all understand, especially when we take an evolutionary perspective, how intimate is the relation of perception, cognition, and motor behavior. Cognition no doubt grew out of systems largely devoted to perceptual-motor activity ... . The difficulty is that the total system is too complex to handle all at once, and the sorts of considerations that go into perception and motor action seem too disparate to integrate. So the strategy is divide and conquer. (Newell 1990, p. 160)

One immediate point to make is that perceptual and motor processes are bound to seem disparate and hard to integrate with cognitive processes from a standpoint that assumes cognition to involve internal symbol processing while perception and action provide the input and output mechanisms. Newell's strategic division is based on deep theoretical assumptions for which there is very little independent support. It is also convenient that the strategy coincides so well with the practical division of the parts of a computer. If, instead, one thinks of computation in Turing machine terms as structured sequences of interaction between a mind and its environment there is no principled division between perception and action on the one hand and cognition on the other. There is a division between structure in the mind and structure in the environment but both are involved in perception, in action and in cognition and it is wrong to assume that the primary relation between these sources of structure is representational. By bracketing off the difficulties involved in understanding the rich and complex detail of the environment, and by assuming that perceptual systems will always be able to translate into internal symbolic form what the 'central' systems need to transact their business, symbol systems theorists give a theoretical hostage to fortune.

The standpoint which ecological functionalism takes with respect to environmental embedding draws on the ecological psychology of J.J. Gibson (1966, 1979) but suggests that the Gibsonian view of interaction underestimates the role of the agent and leads to an unbalanced view of the relation between the agent and the environment. One of Gibson's fundamental contributions to psychology was to insist on the complex, highly informative, invariant structure that exists in real environments. Some invariant structure is statically specified but a great deal, Gibson argued, is specified dynamically as the agent moves around and the point of observation changes, as illumination changes, as the gaze of an observer sweeps over the environment and as local disturbances in the field of view occur, such as water rippling as the wind blows over it. Gibson argued that invariant structure provided information for the observer and that this information was perceived directly. By this he meant that

> it is not mediated by *retinal* pictures, *neural* pictures, or *mental* pictures. *Direct perception* is the activity of getting information from the ambient array of light. I call this a process of *information pickup* that involves the exploratory activity of looking around, getting around, and looking at things. (Gibson 1979, p. 147)

The concept of direct perception has been controversial (See Ullman 1980; Fodor and Pylyshyn 1981; Turvey *et al.* 1981). Some theorists, on both sides of the argument, have characterized the theory of direct perception as implying that a complete account of perception can be given without involving the internal states of the perceiver. Gibson, himself, did not say this but nor did he attempt to give a full account of how the internal states of the perceiver might function in perceptual processes. It is noteworthy, however, that the quote above specifically rejects only the idea that information is mediated by a relationship of picturing. It leaves open the possibility that direct perception can be understood in terms of interactions between structure in the environment and in the agent and Gibson used the term 'resonance' in his book on perceptual systems, (1966), to describe the relationship between the nervous system and environmental information.

Ecological functionalism proposes to marry a Gibsonian perspective on the environment with a computational account of the internal, functional states of perceivers. The interactions between these sources of structure can be understood as configurations in Turing's sense of the term. Preliminary theoretical work in this direction has been done. There are, for example, striking functional similarities between Gibson's concept of 'affordance', which he used to characterize the interactions of agents and environments, and the configurations of Turing machines (see Wells 2002).

## Use of symbols and abstractions

Symbol systems theorists postulate internal symbol structures to explain how thought works. Ecological functionalism rejects this view and argues that thought is to be explained in terms of interactions among the multiple, functional processes of the brain in interaction with external symbol systems.

Once the idea that the mind is a symbol system is set aside, it becomes possible to appreciate and explore the remarkable capacities that external symbolic notations provide for us. This is where the true significance of Turing's universal machine becomes evident. The control of the universal machine is a fixed finite automaton. What makes it special is that it uses an external system of symbols, in which standard descriptions are encoded, to extend its power. A non-universal Turing machine computes a sequence representing a single computable number. A universal machine can, with the appropriate input, compute any one of an infinite number of sequences. The use of a symbol system extends its powers indefinitely. That is the true lesson for humans. The use of external symbol systems extends our cognitive powers indefinitely. They enable us, among other things, to capture and study the ways that we think. Consider, by way of an analogy, the use of high speed motion picture technology to study the properties of movement. The gaits of horses, the flight of humming birds and insects and the impact of bullets on various materials have all been studied by capturing them on film and examining the film at slow speeds or frame by frame. In a similar way the development of formal methods for writing down chains of reasoning has allowed us to explore processes that, prior to the development of writing, were available only fleetingly in transient form. This, I believe, is the true significance of David Hilbert's remarks about proof theory.

> The formula game that Brouwer so deprecates has, besides its mathematical value, an important general philosophical significance. For this formula game is carried out according to certain definite rules, in which the *technique of our thinking* is expressed. These rules form a closed system that can be discovered and definitively stated. The fundamental idea of my proof theory is none other than to describe the activity of our understanding, to make a protocol of the rules according to which our thinking actually proceeds. (Hilbert 1927, p. 475)

I think, perhaps, that Hilbert may even have underestimated the significance of symbolic notations because they enhance as well as describe the activity of our understanding. The remarkable results of Gödel and Turing, for example, may have been unthinkable had it not been for the existence of formal systems of notation and the accumulated mathematical tradition. James Gleick's biography of the physicist Richard Feynman contains a revealing snippet of a conversation between Feynman and the historian Charles Weiner about the significance of writing:

> He [Feynman] began dating his scientific notes as he worked, something he had never done before. Weiner once remarked casually that his new parton notes represented 'a record of the day-to-day work', and Feynman reacted sharply.
> 'I actually did the work on the paper', he said.
> 'Well', Weiner said, 'the work was done in your head, but the record of it is still here'.
> 'No, it's not a *record*, not really. It's *working*. You have to work on paper, and this is the paper. Okay?' (Gleick 1992, p. 409)

Feynman and Weiner were both correct, and we do not have to do logic or physics to see this. Writing an essay, a paper or a book is an interaction between mind and medium which is both work and record. It is rarely the case, in my experience that my thoughts obediently line up as words in a mental space which I can then write down. Much more commonly, the writing of a sentence is a process of successive approximation to a somewhat opaque idea of what is adequate, which involves modifications, false starts, hesitations, and so forth. One writes and one revises. This is the *working* aspect. That which eventually passes muster is the *record*, but it is always possible to re-read a sentence and ask 'Is that really what I think? Is that what I want to say?'

Liberation from the doctrine of an internal, language like, symbolic notation as the basis for thinking throws into sharper relief the distinctive roles that symbol systems actually do play in supporting and extending the cultural horizons of our species. Notations are ways of crystallizing aspects of experience and understanding which can then be shared rather than remaining the inchoate property of individuals. The human agent stands in relation to external, culturally mediated symbolic resources as the control automaton of a universal machine stands to the standard descriptions of the target machines whose behaviour it simulates.

Humans have developed a wide range of symbol systems for different purposes. It is worth noting that different systems serve best for different things. Alphabetic systems work best for the representation of natural language. Numerical systems work best for the representation of logical and quantitative relations. The notation developed for representing Western tonal music takes pitch and duration as its fundamental elements, and works best for music based on the tempered scale. When a human learns to use a new symbol system, this is functionally equivalent to building a new universal machine interpreter. Notations provide new ways to think. Turing's notation for $m$-functions freed him to think about higher level organization than would have been possible had he been obliged to write out each $m$-function in full. The symbol for equality, the use of placeholders, the notations for zero, for negative integers, for rational numbers and for complex numbers all served to liberate the mathematical imagination.

Musical notation makes it possible to demonstrate the similarities among melodic and harmonic ideas at different pitches and time scales. The enormous symphonic works of the late-nineteenth and early-twentieth centuries by composers as different in personality and temperament as Anton Bruckner and Gustav Mahler would have been impossible without this notation. Mahler is reputed to have said that blindness would have had a more damaging effect on his musical life than deafness because it would have prevented him from reading and writing scores.

Representational line drawing has played a crucial role in both artistic and scientific development. The great Spanish neuroscientist Santiago

Ramon y Cajal owes a part of his fame to his meticulous drawings which continue, over a century later, to set a challenging standard for accuracy and structural insight.

Each notational system is a structured source of interaction between the internal states of the agent and an external medium. Perhaps the apparent naturalness of the idea that the mind processes symbols internally becomes less compelling when we think about the plethora of such systems. Is there any value in the idea that musical skill depends on the presence of musical symbol structures in the mind? Are there internal staves with notes written on them? It seems unlikely. Perhaps the naturalness of language makes it easier for us to entertain the idea that there are tokens of linguistic symbols or concepts existing as distinct physical entities in the mind and less easy to suppose that this may be an illusion of our experience.

## Use of language, both natural and artificial

Ecological functionalism has not been motivated by particular concern for the phenomena of language despite their obvious importance and there is little to say at this stage except to note that the primary emphasis on interaction seems apt for the understanding of some linguistic phenomena. Ordinary language learning, for example, depends on the child being exposed to an appropriate linguistic environment. Without such exposure at sensitive stages of development, normal language learning is impaired. It is also worth making the general point that if linguistic phenomena can be explained adequately within the symbol systems framework they can also be explained within the framework of ecological functionalism provided one accepts that parts of the relevant structures are to be found in the external environment.

## Learning from the environment and from experience

One of the primary motivations for the resurgence of interest in connectionist models in the 1980s was the belief that they offered a more natural account of learning than models based on internal symbol processing. Learning in connectionist models consists, primarily, in changing connection strengths between nodes and is derived from Hebb's principle that correlated activity between neurons tends to lead to strengthening of the connections between them. Symbol systems models, by contrast, characterize learning in terms of the acquisition of new, internal, symbol structures. These may be data structures or productions. Each type of account has specific kinds of problems related to generalization. The learning in connectionist networks can disrupt existing associations. This may be thought of as a kind of over-generalization. The learning of new symbol structures can, by contrast, under-generalize because it is hard to represent explicitly the consequences of learning a new fact or inference. Ecological functionalism understands learning primarily in terms of the kinds of changes that occur in connectionist nets, but because these changes will be modelled in terms of changing connectivity among concurrent $\pi$-calculus processes, the architectural possibilities are more wide ranging.

## Acquisition of capabilities through development

Ecological functionalism as presented here has not been motivated by a specific concern for development but the fundamental emphasis on interaction as the primitive formal concept suggests that the approach, although based on a discrete state formalism, may be found to have commonalities with both dynamical systems and connectionist perspectives on development.

Dynamical systems theorists typically reject computational methods. Thelen and Smith (1994), for example 'categorically reject machine analogies of cognition and development' (p. xix). Behaviour and development, they argue, are dynamically highly complex.

> There is a multiple, parallel, and continuously dynamic interplay of perception and action, and a system that, by its thermodynamic nature, seeks certain stable solutions. These solutions emerge from relations, not from design. When the elements of such systems cooperate, they give rise to behavior with a unitary character, and thus to the illusion of structure. But the order is always executory, rather than rule driven, allowing for the enormous sensitivity and flexibility of behavior to organize and regroup around task and context. (Thelen and Smith 1994, p. xix)

Apart from the reference to thermodynamic equilibria all the concepts used in this quotation could have come from earlier parts of this book. The emphasis on parallelism, the continuous interplay of perception and action, the achievement of unitary behaviour by a system with multiple elementary components. A similar correspondence can be found with the concerns of connectionist theorists and this suggests that, although ecological functionalism is a computational framework because its formalism is a general model of computation as well as a system for the study of concurrency and communication, it is well suited to tackle the issues addressed by leading developmental theorists.

## Autonomous operation within a social community

One of the most promising aspects of the pairing of ecological functionalism with the techniques of the $\pi$-calculus is the scope it offers for exploring the social domain. It is striking that social psychologists have made much less use of computational techniques than cognitive psychologists although the potential benefits of computational studies of social processes are substantial. Ostrom (1988) argued that there were several types of complexity in social psychological theorizing that would benefit from computational methods including the interfacing of multiple systems and the modelling of response systems. Garson (1994) reviewed the history, nature and future of computer simulation in social science generally and suggested that although it had had relatively little impact, new ground could be broken as graphical user interfaces were developed and as interest in distributed systems increased. Hastie and Stasser (2000) contributed a chapter on computer simulation to a handbook on research methods in personality and social psychology. They cited Ostrom's paper and argued for the potential importance of computational methods but recognized that they were still used in only a small minority of social psychological studies.

It is perhaps not surprising that this should be so when the underlying model of computation is serial and more obviously suited to studies of individuals. The use of a formal system such as $\pi$-calculus which takes interaction as primitive and is specifically designed for the study of concurrency should make the application of computational methods in social science both more natural and more fruitful.

## Self-awareness and sense of self

Ecological functionalism has rather little to offer with regard to self-awareness at this early stage of its development. A tradition of research has become established which explores self-perception and self-knowledge from a broadly ecological perspective and it may be that ecological functionalism can contribute to this tradition. Neisser (1993) provides an introduction. The interactive perspective of ecological functionalism might also rather naturally be aligned with the approach of George Herbert Mead (1934) who argued that mind and self are products of social interaction.

## Neural realization

The dominant assumption in contemporary psychology is that the mind is dependent on the brain. In general, damage to the brain tends to impair mental functioning and, as cognitive neuroscience convincingly demonstrates, specific functional impairments are associated with damage to specific regions of the brain. Thus there is widespread general recognition that computational theories of mental architecture and mental processing must be compatible with what is known about the functioning of the brain, although there is still debate about the precise nature of the relationship between mind and brain. In practice most psychological theorizing and experimentation is carried out independently of neural system considerations. In order to study reaction times, for example, it is not necessary to have a model of their neural implementation. If, however, one has an interest in synthesizing theory across the range of domains tackled by psychology, questions about the relationship between neural level and cognitive level phenomena come to the fore.

Ecological functionalism places fewer constraints on the nature of that relationship than the physical symbol systems hypothesis. The characterization of the mind as the functional states of a finite control automaton is compatible with more schemes for their realization than is the hypothesis that the mind requires the resources of a universal computer with a finite memory.

One area where the $\pi$-calculus may be of significant value is in building models of brain connectivity on the basis of data derived from fMRI and other scanning methods. At present, the most common approaches use static techniques such as structural equation modelling although the combination of structural equation models with variable parameter regression allows coefficients to vary smoothly over time and thus provides a dynamic model (Büchel and Friston 2001). $\pi$-calculus may provide a viable alternative for the creation of dynamic models of brain connectivity. Since the calculus is not tied to ecological functionalism, such models would be independent of claims about the centrality of agent–environment interactions but their development might be taken as pointing towards the suitability of the calculus for the project of unifying neural level models with models of psychological processes at other levels.

## Construction by an embryological growth process

Newell had nothing to say about how a symbol system might be constructed by an embryological growth process and ecological functionalism, at this early stage, is equally mute on the subject. As with neural system level considerations, however, the $\pi$-calculus, with its focus on interaction and emphases on concurrency and changing connectivity, may well prove a more natural system for modelling embryological growth than computational models which focus on symbol processing.

## Evolutionary history

The evolutionary constraint is an important source of motivation for ecological functionalism. Wells (1998) combined this constraint with the first on

Newell's list, the requirement for behavioural flexibility, and this book builds on the ideas discussed there. Steven Pinker has proposed that a combination of computational theory and the theory of evolution provides the foundation on which a general understanding of the mind can be built. The mind, he suggests, 'is a system of organs of computation designed by natural selection to solve the problems faced by our evolutionary ancestors in their foraging way of life' (Pinker 1997, p. x). Pinker's book builds on ideas developed by Leda Cosmides and John Tooby. A detailed account of their perspective can be found in Tooby and Cosmides (1992). They, and Pinker, try to combine evolutionary thinking with the symbol systems approach to cognitive computation. If the arguments of Chapter 17 are correct, this combination of theories is untenable.

Ecological functionalism incorporates evolutionary arguments as an essential part of its explanatory framework. The reason for this becomes clear when one thinks about the control of behaviour. The behaviour of a Turing machine is controlled by its configurations. Ecological functionalism adopts this perspective on control even though configurations are characterized as entities with complex components whose relations to behaviour are non-deterministic. The configurations of a Turing machine are designed to carry out a particular task and the mesh between structure in the mini-mind and structure on the tape is specified by the designer of the machine. Both sources of structure have to be considered in order for their interactions to work correctly.

Humans interact with their environments in complex ways. Many of these interactions have been constructed by human endeavour and ingenuity but many have not. There is a large and growing body of evidence that humans come into the world pre-equipped to deal with some of the fundamental regularities of terrestrial existence. Foster and Kreitzman (2004), for example, provide a fascinating insight into the biological clocks that regulate the lives of living creatures in fundamental ways including the moderation of emotional arousal and other psychological states. In the absence of a designer, evolution by natural selection is the only plausible explanation for the pre-determined structural interactions between humans and their environments which determine classes of behaviour.

One of the key concepts in evolutionary theory is adaptation. Humans are capable of complex, structured sequences of interaction with their environments because they are adapted to those environments in a variety of ways and at a variety of levels. Turing's analysis of computation characterizes functional states as states of the whole mind and ecological functionalism proposes that interactions at the level of the whole organism have been shaped by natural selection. Evolutionary analysis at the level of the whole organism is, therefore, one of the key tools to use in understanding classes of behaviour systematically. Tooby and Cosmides provide an impressive list of tasks that would have been important over time scales long enough for evolutionary adaptation to occur. They can be thought of as an elaboration of some of Newell's constraints on mind.

> Over the course of their evolution, humans regularly needed to recognize objects, avoid predators, avoid incest, avoid teratogens when pregnant, repair nutritional deficiencies by dietary modification, judge distance, indentify plant foods, capture animals, acquire grammar, attend to alarm cries, detect when their children needed assistance, be motivated to make that assistance, avoid contagious disease, acquire a lexicon, be motivated to nurse, select conspecifics as mates, select mates of the opposite sex, select mates of high reproductive value, induce potential mates to choose them, choose productive activities, balance when walking, avoid being bitten by venomous snakes, understand and make tools, avoid needlessly enraging others, interpret social situations correctly, help relatives, decide which foraging efforts have repaid the energy expenditure, perform antici-patory motion computation, inhibit one's mate from conceiving children by another, deter aggression, maintain friendships, navigate, recognize faces, recognize emotions, cooperate, and make effective trade-offs among many of these activities, along with a host of other tasks. (Tooby and Cosmides 1992, p. 110)

There are 36 specific tasks mentioned in this list quite apart from the catch all reference to 'a host' of other tasks. Some of the tasks are social, some physical, some more clearly related to what we normally think of as cognitive tasks. Almost all involve interactions between the agent and the environment. However, although the broad significance of evolutionary thinking for ecological functionalism is clear, it is much less clear whether evolutionary theory provides reliable clues about the relationships between functions and mechanisms. There is a tendency in evolutionary psychology for theorists to fail to make the important distinction between function and mechanism when discussing adaptation.

Ecological functionalism has, as one of its goals, the clarification of the relationship between function and mechanism. Arguments in evolutionary psychology with premises based on analyses of function tend to move to conclusions about mechanisms and fail to see that functional and mecha-nistic descriptions are not equivalent. It is largely because of this failure, I believe, that enthusiasm for 'massive modularity' has become so common. The idea, roughly speaking, is that every distinct adaptive problem, func-tionally defined, will create a selection pressure for a modular mechanism to solve it. Since there is a massive number of adaptive problems which have been solved successfully, there must be a massive number of modular mechanisms. Thus, for example, picking at random from the list of adaptive problems given by Tooby and Cosmides, one postulates mate selection mechanisms, venomous snake avoidance mechanisms, navigation mecha-nisms and so forth. Tooby and Cosmides are among the theorists who fail to make the distinction between function and mechanism. They say, for example, 'Different adaptive problems are often incommensurate. They cannot, in principle, be solved by the same mechanism' Tooby and Cosmides (1992, p. 111).

Turing's analysis of computation suggests that this argument is not well founded. The mini-mind of a universal machine is a single mechanism. Provided there is sufficient structure in its environment to specify a function to be computed, the universal machine can compute that function. By analogy one can argue that if there is enough information in the environment to specify an adaptive problem, and if the human mind is organized like the mini-mind of a universal machine, then the single mechanism of the mind can solve the adaptive problem. This may not actually be how the mind works, but the argument does show that functional specialization need not, in principle, require modular machinery. Steven Mithen (1996) has argued on rather different grounds that different aspects of human cognition are far too interconnected for massive modularity to be plausible.

## Conclusion

Ecological functionalism appears as capable, in principle, of tackling the constraints that a theory of mind has to meet as any other approach but why should it be preferred to existing approaches? These, while less than perfect, have made substantial contributions to our understanding of the human mind and deploy methods that are familiar and reasonably well understood. What, one might ask, is the unique selling point of ecological functionalism? What does it offer which might persuade psychologists to invest the time and effort needed to acquire a new technical vocabulary and to think about familiar matters in unfamiliar ways. For me, its great attraction is the way in which ecological functionalism suggests the convergence of two, apparently disparate, approaches to psychology. One is the idea that thinking is a kind of computation, the other is the idea that thinking is a product, not of the brain alone but of the situated organism. The principal exponent of ecological psychology in the twentieth century was J.J. Gibson, a theorist of great power and lucidity and an ingenious experimenter. Gibson was sceptical about computational psychology as are most of those who have continued the ecological approach that he pioneered. Proponents of computational psychology have often been equally sceptical about Gibson's ecological approach. Some have suggested that his theories are contradictory and incoherent. Turing's analysis of computation shows where the strengths and weaknesses of both the ecological and computational approaches lie and also shows, in principle, how to construct a rigorous theory which builds on the strengths of both. Thinking, from the standpoint of ecological functionalism, is a form of situated computation. It is the unexpected synthesis of two apparently opposed positions that seems to me to indicate the potential of ecological functionalism. The test of a framework, however, is not what one can say about it in principle but what one can do with it. Ecological functionalism will be valuable for psychology if it proves to be empirically fruitful. That is a matter for future work.

# References

Amit, D.J. (1989). *Modeling Brain Function. The World of Attractor Neural Networks*. Cambridge: Cambridge University Press.

Anderson, J.R. and Lebiere, C. (1998). *The Atomic Components of Thought*. Mahwah, NJ: Lawrence Erlbaum Associates.

Aspray, W. and Burks, A. (1987). *Papers of John von Neumann on Computing and Computer Theory*. Cambridge, MA: MIT Press.

Barlow, H.B. (1972). 'Single Units and Sensation: A Neuron Doctrine for Perceptual Psychology'. *Perception*, 1: 371–94.

Bartlett, F.C. (1932). *Remembering. A Study in Experimental and Social Psychology*. Cambridge: Cambridge University Press.

Bickhard, M.H. and Terveen, L. (1995). *Foundational Issues in Artificial Intelligence and Cognitive Science. Impasse and Solution*. New York, NY: Elsevier Science Publishers.

Büchel, C. and Friston, K. (2001). 'Extracting Brain Connectivity'. In P. Jezzard, P.M. Matthews and S.M. Smith (eds), *Functional MRI. An Introduction to Methods*. Oxford, UK: Oxford University Press.

Burks, A.W. (1966). Editor's Introduction to von Neumann (1966). *Theory of Self-Reproducing Automata*. University of Illinois Press.

Cardelli, L. and Gordon, A. (1998). 'Mobile Ambients: Foundations of System Specification and Computation Structures'. *Lecture Notes in Computer Science*, Vol. 1378, pp. 140–55, Berlin: Springer-Verlag.

Church, A. (1936). 'An Unsolvable Problem of Elementary Number Theory'. *The American Journal of Mathematics*, 58: 345–63. Reprinted in Davis (1965), pp. 89–107.

Cleeremans, A. (1993). *Mechanisms of Implicit Learning. Connectionist Models of Sequence Processing*. Cambridge, MA: MIT Press.

Conrad, M. (1974). 'Molecular Information Processing in the Central Nervous System. Part I: Selection circuits in the brain'. In M. Conrad, W. Güttinger, and M. Dal Cin (eds), *Physics and Mathematics of the Nervous System*. Berlin: Springer-Verlag, pp. 82–107.

Conrad, M. (1985). 'On Design Principles for a Molecular Computer'. *Communications of the Association for Computing Machinery*, 28(5): 464–80.

Conrad, M. (1988). 'The Price of Programmability'. In R. Herken (ed.), *The Universal Turing Machine. A Half Century Survey*. Oxford, UK: Oxford University Press, pp. 285–307.

Copeland, B.J. (1994). 'Artificial Intelligence'. In S. Guttenplan (ed.), *A Companion to the Philosophy of Mind*. Oxford, UK: Blackwell Publishers Ltd., pp. 122–31.

Copeland, B.J. (1997). 'The Broad Conception of Computation'. *American Behavioral Scientist*, 40: 690–716.

Copeland, B.J. (2002). 'Narrow Versus Wide Mechanism'. In M. Scheutz (ed.), *Computationalism. New Directions*. Cambridge, MA: MIT Press, pp. 59–86.

Copeland, B.J. (ed.) (2004). *The Essential Turing*. Oxford, UK: Oxford University Press.

Craik, K.J.W. (1943). *The Nature of Explanation*. Cambridge: Cambridge University Press.

Davis, M. (1965). *The Undecidable. Basic Papers on Undecidable Propositions, Unsolvable Problems and Computable Functions*. New York, NY: Raven Press Books Ltd.

Dawson, M.R.W. (1998). *Understanding Cognitive Science*. Oxford, UK: Blackwell Publishers Ltd.

Dawson, M.R.W. (2004). *Minds and Machines. Connectionism and Psychological Modeling*. Oxford, UK: Blackwell Publishing.

Dennett, D.C. (1991) *Consciousness Explained*. Boston, MA: Little, Brown & Company.

Douglas, R.J. and Martin, K.A.C. (1990). 'Neocortex'. In G.M. Shepherd (ed.), *The Synaptic Organization of the Brain*. Third Edition. Oxford, UK: Oxford University Press, pp. 389–438.

Elman, J.L. (1990). 'Finding Structure in Time'. *Cognitive Science*, 14(2): 179–211.

Elman, J.L., Bates, E., Johnson, M.H., Karmiloff-Smith, A., Parisi, D. and Plunkett, K. (1996). *Rethinking Innateness. A Connectionist Perspective on Development*. Cambridge, MA: MIT Press.

Farmer, J.D. (1990). 'A Rosetta Stone for Connectionism'. *Physica D*, 42: 153–87.

Feferman, S. (2001). 'Preface to Turing (1939)'. In R.O. Gandy and C.E.M. Yates (eds), *Collected Works of A.M. Turing. Mathematical Logic*. Amsterdam, The Netherlands: Elsevier Science B.V., pp. 71–9.

Feynman, R.P. (1996). *Feynman Lectures on Computation*. Edited by Tony Hey and Robin W. Allen. Boulder, Colorado: Westview Press.

Fodor, J.A. (1975). *The Language of Thought*. Hassocks, Sussex, UK: The Harvester Press.

Fodor, J.A. (1983). *The Modularity of Mind. An Essay on Faculty Psychology*. Cambridge, MA: MIT Press. A Bradford Book.

Fodor, J.A. (1994). 'Fodor, Jerry A.'. In S. Guttenplan (ed.), *A Companion to the Philosophy of Mind*. Oxford, UK: Blackwell Publishers Ltd.

Fodor, J.A. (1995). 'The Folly of Simulation'. In P. Baumgartner and S. Payr (eds), *Speaking Minds. Interviews with Twenty Eminent Cognitive Scientists*. Princeton, NJ: Princeton University Press.

Fodor, J.A. (2000). *The Mind Doesn't Work That Way. The Scope and Limits of Computational Psychology.* Cambridge, MA: MIT Press.

Fodor, J.A. and Pylyshyn, Z.W. (1981). 'How Direct is Visual Perception? Some Reflections on Gibson's "Ecological Approach" ', *Cognition*, 9: 139–96.

Fodor, J.A. and Pylyshyn, Z.W. (1988). 'Connectionism and Cognitive Architecture: A Critical Analysis'. *Cognition*, 28: 3–71.

Foster, R. and Kreitzman, L. (2004). *Rhythms of Life. The Biological Clocks that Control the Daily Lives of Every Living Thing.* London, UK: Profile Books Ltd.

Franklin, S. (1995). *Artificial Minds.* Cambridge, MA: MIT Press.

Gandy, R. (1980). 'Church's Thesis and Principles for Mechanisms'. In J. Barwise, H.J. Keisler and K. Kunen (eds), *The Kleene Symposium.* Amsterdam: North-Holland Publishing Company, pp. 123–48.

Gandy, R. (1988). 'The Confluence of Ideas in 1936'. In Herken (1988). *The Universal Turing Machine: A Half Century Survey.* Oxford, UK: Oxford University Press, pp. 55–111.

Garson, G.D. (1994). 'Social Science Computer Simulation: Its History, Design and Future'. *Social Science Computer Review*, 12(1): 55–82.

Gibson, J.J. (1966). *The Senses Considered as Perceptual Systems.* Boston: Houghton Mifflin.

Gibson, J.J. (1979). *The Ecological Approach to Visual Perception.* Boston: Houghton Mifflin.

Gleick, J. (1992). *Genius. Richard Feynman and Modern Physics.* London, UK: Abacus Books.

Gödel, K. (1931). 'On Formally Undecidable Propositions of *Principia Mathematica* and Related Systems I'. *Monatshefte für Mathematik und Physik*, 38, pp. 173–98. Reprinted in J. van Heijenoort (ed.), *From Frege to Gödel. A Source Book in Mathematical Logic, 1879–1931.* Cambridge, MA: Harvard University Press, pp. 596–616.

Goldstine, H.H. (1972). *The Computer from Pascal to von Neumann.* Princeton, NJ: Princeton University Press.

Guttenplan, S. (ed.) (1994). *A Companion to the Philosophy of Mind.* Oxford, UK: Blackwell Publishers Ltd.

Harnish, R.M. (2002). *Minds, Brains, Computers. An Historical Introduction to the Foundations of Cognitive Science.* Oxford, UK: Blackwell Publishers Ltd.

Hastie, R. and Stasser, G. (2000). 'Computer Simulation Methods for Social Psychology'. In C.M. Judd (ed.), *Handbook of Research Methods in Social and Personality Psychology.* Cambridge, UK: Cambridge University Press, pp. 85–114.

Haugeland, J. (ed.) (1981). *Mind Design. Philosophy, Psychology, Artificial Intelligence.* Cambridge, MA: MIT Press.

Hebb, D.O. (1949). *The Organization of Behavior.* New York, NY: Wiley.

Hilbert, D. (1927). 'The Foundations of Mathematics'. *Abhandlungen aus dem mathematischen Seminar der Hamburgischen Universität*, 6: 65–85.

Reprinted in J. van Heijenoort (ed.), *From Frege to Gödel. A Source Book in Mathematical Logic, 1879–1931*. Cambridge, MA: Harvard University Press, pp. 464–79.

Hoare, C.A.R. (1985). *Communicating Sequential Processes*. London, UK: Prentice-Hall International, UK, Ltd.

Hockney, R.W. and Jesshope, C.R. (1988). *Parallel Computers 2. Architecture, Programming and Algorithms*. Bristol, UK: Adam Hilger.

Hodges, A. (1983). *Alan Turing: The Enigma*. London, UK: Vintage Books.

Hodges, A. (1997). *Turing. A Natural Philosopher*. London, UK: Phoenix.

Hodges, A. (2001). 'The Nature of Turing and the Physical World'. In R.O. Gandy and C.E.M. Yates (eds), *Collected Works of A.M. Turing. Mathematical Logic*. Amsterdam, The Netherlands: Elsevier Science B.V., pp. 259–64.

James, W. (1890). *The Principles of Psychology*, Vol. 1. Henry Holt and Co. Unabridged version republished by Dover Publications Inc. 1950.

Johnson-Laird, P.N. (1983). *Mental Models. Towards a Cognitive Science of Language, Inference, and Consciousness*. Cambridge, UK: Cambridge University Press.

Kim, J. (1993). *Supervenience and Mind. Selected Philosophical Essays*. Cambridge, UK: Cambridge University Press.

Kleene, S.C. (1936). 'General Recursive Functions of Natural Numbers'. *Mathematische Annalen*, 112(5): 727–42.

Kohonen, T. (1988). *Self-Organization and Associative Memory*. Second Edition. Berlin: Springer-Verlag.

Lee, C.Y. (1963). 'A Turing Machine which Prints its Own Code Script'. *Proceedings of the Symposium on Mathematical Theory of Automata*. Brooklyn, NY: Polytechnic Press of the Polytechnic Institute of Brooklyn, pp.155–64.

Lucas, J.R. (1961). 'Minds, Machines and Gödel'. *Philosophy*, 36: 120–4.

Maloney, J.C. (1999). 'Functionalism'. In R.A. Wilson and F.C. Keil (eds), *The MIT Encyclopedia of the Cognitive Sciences*. Cambridge, MA: MIT Press, pp. 332–5.

Marcus, G.F. (2001). *The Algebraic Mind. Integrating Connectionism and Cognitive Science*. Cambridge, MA: MIT Press.

McClelland, J.L., Rumelhart, D.E. and the PDP Research Group (1986). *Parallel Distributed Processing. Explorations in the Microstructure of Cognition. Volume 2. Psychological and Biological Models*. Cambridge, MA: MIT Press.

McCulloch, W.S. and Pitts, W.H. (1943). 'A Logical Calculus of the Ideas Immanent in Nervous Activity'. *Bulletin of Mathematical Biophysics*, 5: 115–33.

Mead, G.H. (1934). *Mind, Self and Society: From the Standpoint of a Social Behaviorist*. Edited by C.W. Morris. Chicago, IL: University of Chicago Press.

Miller, G.A. (1956). 'The Magical Number Seven Plus or Minus Two: Some Limits in Our Capacity for Processing Information'. *Psychological Review*, 63: 81–97.

Miller, G.A., Galanter, E. and Pribram, K.H. (1960). *Plans and the Structure of Behavior*. Austin, Texas: Holt, Rinehart and Winston, Inc.

Milner, R. (1999). *Communicating and Mobile Systems: The π-calculus*. Cambridge, UK: Cambridge University Press.

Milner, R., Parrow, J. and Walker, D. (1989). 'A Calculus of Mobile Processes, Parts I and II'. Technical Report ECS-LFCS-89-85 and -86. University of Edinburgh.

Minsky, M.L. (1967). *Computation: Finite and Infinite Machines*. Englewood Cliffs, NJ: Prentice-Hall Inc.

Minsky, M.L. and Papert, S.A. (1969,1988). *Perceptrons. An Introduction to Computational Geometry*. First Edition 1969, Expanded Edition 1988. Cambridge, MA: MIT Press.

Mithen, S. (1996). *The Prehistory of the Mind. A Search for the Origins of Art, Religion and Science*. London: Thames and Hudson.

Neisser, U. (ed.) (1993). *The Perceived Self. Ecological and Interpersonal Sources of Self-Knowledge*. Cambridge, UK: Cambridge University Press.

Newell, A. (1973). 'Production Systems: Models of Control Structures'. In W.C. Chase (ed.), *Visual Information Processing*. New York: Academic Press.

Newell, A. (1990). *Unified Theories of Cognition*. Cambridge, MA: Harvard University Press.

Newell, A. and Simon, H.A. (1976). 'Computer Science as Empirical Inquiry: Symbols and Search'. *Communications of the Association for Computing Machinery*, 19: 113–26. Reprinted in Haugeland (1981), pp. 35–66.

Ostrom, T.M. (1988). 'Computer Simulation: The Third Symbol System'. *Journal of Experimental Social Psychology*, 24: 381–92.

Palmer, S.E. (1999). *Vision Science. Photons to Phenomenology*. Cambridge, MA: MIT Press.

Penrose, R. (1989). *The Emperor's New Mind. Concerning Computers, Minds, and the Laws of Physics*. Oxford, UK: Oxford University Press.

Penrose, R. (1994). *Shadows of the Mind. A Search for the Missing Science of Consciousness*. Oxford, UK: Oxford University Press.

Penrose, R. (1997). *The Large, the Small, and the Human Mind*. Cambridge, UK: Cambridge University Press.

Pew, R.W. and Mavor, A.S. (eds) (1998). *Modeling Human and Organizational Behavior. Applications to Military Simulations*. Washington, DC: National Academy Press.

Pinker, S. (1994). *The Language Instinct. The New Science of Language and Mind*. London: Allen Lane, The Penguin Press.

Pinker, S. (1997). *How the Mind Works*. London, UK: Allen Lane, The Penguin Press.

Post, E. (1947). 'Recursive Unsolvability of a Problem of Thue'. *Journal of Symbolic Logic*, 12: 1–11. Reprinted in Davis (1965), pp. 293–303.

Pylyshyn, Z.W. (1984). *Computation and Cognition: Toward a Foundation for Cognitive Science.* Cambridge, MA: MIT Press.

Rosen, S. (1969). 'Electronic Computers: A Historical Survey'. *Computing Surveys,* 1(1): 7–36.

Rosenblatt, F. (1962). *Principles of Neurodynamics.* Washington: Spartan Books.

Rumelhart, D.E., McClelland, J.L. and the PDP Research Group (1986). *Parallel Distributed Processing. Explorations in the Microstructure of Cognition. Volume 1: Foundations.* Cambridge, MA: MIT Press.

Sangiorgi, D. and Walker, D. (2001). *The π-calculus. A Theory of Mobile Processes.* Cambridge, UK: Cambridge University Press.

Scheutz, M. (ed.) (2002). *Computationalism. New Directions.* Cambridge, MA: MIT Press.

Servan-Schreiber, D., Cleeremans, A. and McClelland, J.L. (1989). 'Learning Sequential Structure in Simple Recurrent Networks'. In D.S. Touretzky (ed.), *Advances in Neural Information Processing Systems 1.* San Mateo, CA: Morgan Kaufman, pp. 643–52.

Shannon, C.E. (1956). 'A Universal Turing Machine With Two Internal States'. In C.E. Shannon and J. McCarthy (eds), *Automata Studies 34.* Princeton, NJ: Princeton University Press, pp. 157–65.

Sieg, W. (1994). 'Mechanical Procedures and Mathematical Experience'. In A. George (ed.), *Mathematics and Mind.* Oxford, UK: Oxford University Press, pp. 71–117.

Sieg, W. (1999). 'Church–Turing Thesis'. In R.A. Wilson and F.C. Keil (eds), *The MIT Encyclopedia of the Cognitive Sciences.* Cambridge, MA: MIT Press, pp. 116–18.

Siegelmann, H.T. (1999). *Neural Networks and Analog Computation. Beyond the Turing Limit.* Boston, MA: Birkhäuser.

Simpson, P.K. (1990). *Artificial Neural Systems. Foundations, Paradigms, Applications, and Implementations.* New York: Pergamon Press.

Skinner, B.F. (1974). *About Behaviourism.* London: Jonathan Cape Ltd.

Sloman, A. (2002). 'The Irrelevance of Turing machines to Artificial Intelligence'. In M. Scheutz (ed.), *Computationalism. New Directions.* Cambridge, MA: MIT Press, pp. 87–127.

Smolensky, P. (1988). 'On the Proper Treatment of Connectionism'. *The Behavioral and Brain Sciences,* 11: 1–74.

Squire, L.R., Bloom, F.E., McConnell, S.K., Roberts, J.L., Spitzer, N.C. and Zigmond, M.J. (2003). *Fundamental Neuroscience.* Second Edition. London, UK: Academic Press.

Stroop, J.R. (1935). 'Studies of Interference in Serial Verbal Reactions'. *Journal of Experimental Psychology,* 18: 643–62.

Swanson, L.W. (2003). *Brain Architecture. Understanding the Basic Plan.* Oxford, UK: Oxford University Press.

Tajfel, H., Flament, C., Billig, M.G. and Bundy, R.F. (1971). 'Social Categorization and Intergroup Behaviour'. *European Journal of Social Psychology*, 1: 149–78.

Teuscher, C. (ed.) (2004). *Alan Turing: Life and Legacy of a Great Thinker*. Berlin: Springer-Verlag.

Thatcher, J.W. (1963). 'The Construction of a Self-Describing Turing Machine'. *Proceedings of the Symposium on Mathematical Theory of Automata*. Brooklyn, NY: Polytechnic Press of the Polytechnic Institute of Brooklyn, 165–71.

Thelen, E. and Smith, L.B. (1994). *A Dynamic Systems Approach to the Development of Cognition and Action*. Cambridge, MA: MIT Press.

Tooby, J. and Cosmides, L. (1992). 'The Psychological Foundations of Culture'. In J.H. Barkow, L.Cosmides and J. Tooby (eds), *The Adapted Mind. Evolutionary Psychology and the Generation of Culture*. Oxford, UK: Oxford University Press.

Turing, A.M. (1936). 'On Computable Numbers, with an Application to the Entscheidungsproblem'. *Proceedings of the London Mathematical Society*, ser. 2, 42: 230–65. Reprinted in Davis (1965). Reprinted in Gandy and Yates (2001). Reprinted in Copeland (2004).

Turing, A.M. (1939). 'Systems of Logic Based on Ordinals'. *Proceedings of the London Mathematical Society*, ser. 2, 45: 161–228. Reprinted in Davis (1965), pp. 155–222. Reprinted in Gandy and Yates (2001). Reprinted in Copeland (2004).

Turing, A.M. (1946). 'Proposal for Development in the Mathematics Division of an Automatic Computing Engine (ACE)'. Reprinted in Carpenter and Doran (eds) (1986), pp. 20–105. Reprinted in Ince (1992).

Turing, A.M. (1947). Lecture to the London Mathematical Society on 20 February 1947. Reprinted in Carpenter and Doran (eds) (1986), pp. 106–24. Reprinted in Ince (1992). Reprinted in Copeland (2004).

Turing, A.M. (1948). 'Intelligent Machinery'. *National Physical Laboratory Report*. London: HMSO. Reprinted in Copeland (2004).

Turing, A.M. (1950). 'Computing Machinery and Intelligence'. *Mind*, 59: 433–60. Reprinted in Ince (1992). Reprinted in Copeland (2004).

Turvey, M.T., Shaw, R.E., Reed, E.S. and Mace, W.M. (1981). 'Ecological Laws of Perceiving and Acting: In Reply to Fodor and Pylyshyn (1981)'. *Cognition*, 9: 237–304.

Ullman, S. (1980). 'Against Direct Perception'. *The Behavioral and Brain Sciences*, 3: 373–415.

van Heijenoort, J. (ed.) (1967). *From Frege to Gödel. A Source Book in Mathematical Logic, 1879–1931*. Cambridge, MA: Harvard University Press.

von Neumann, J. (1945). 'First Draft of a Report on the EDVAC'. Reprinted in Aspray and Burks (1987).

von Neumann, J. (1948). 'The General and Logical Theory of Automata'. In Aspray and Burks (1987), pp. 391–431.

von Neumann, J. (1958). *The Computer and the Brain*. New Haven, CT: Yale University Press.

Wang, H. (1974). *From Mathematics to Philosophy*. London, UK: Routledge & Kegan Paul.

Watson, J.B. (1913). 'Psychology as the Behaviorist Views It'. *Psychological Review*, 20: 158–77.

Wells, A.J. (1998). 'Evolutionary Psychology and Theories of Cognitive Architecture'. In C. Crawford and D.L. Krebs (eds), *Handbook of Evolutionary Psychology. Ideas, Issues, and Applications*. Mahwah, NJ: Lawrence Erlbaum Associates.

Wells, A.J. (2002). 'Gibson's Affordances and Turing's Theory of Computation'. *Ecological Psychology*, 14(3): 141–80.

Wilkes, M.V. (1987). 'Computers Then and Now'. In *ACM Turing Award Lectures. The First Twenty Years: 1966–1985*. New York, NY: ACM Press, Addison-Wesley Publishing Company, pp. 197–205.

# Index